2017

THE BEST TEN-MINUTE PLAYS

2

2017
THE BEST TEN-MINUTE PLAYS

Edited and with a foreword
By Lawrence Harbison

SMITH AND KRAUS PUBLISHERS   2017

A Smith and Kraus Book
177 Lyme Road, Hanover, NH 03755
editorial 603.643.6431 To Order 1.877.668.8680
www.smithandkraus.com

2017 The Best Ten-Minute Plays
Copyright © 2017 by Smith and Kraus, Inc
All rights reserved.

Manufactured in the United States of America

ISBN: 978-1-57525-915-4
Library of Congress Control Number: 2329-2709

Typesetting and layout by Elizabeth E. Monteleone
Cover by Olivia Monteleone

For information about custom editions, special sales, education
and corporate purchases, please contact Smith and Kraus at
editor@smithandkraus.com or 603.643.6431

TABLE OF CONTENTS

FOREWORD

In this volume, you will find fifty terrific new ten-minute plays, culled from the several hundred I read last year, all originally produced during the 2016-2017 theatrical season. They are written in a variety of styles. Some are realistic plays; some are not. Some are comic (laughs); some are dramatic (no laughs). The ten-minute play form lends itself well to experimentation in style. A playwright can have fun with a device which couldn't be sustained as well in a longer play. Several of these plays employ such a device.

In years past, playwrights who were just starting out wrote one-act plays of thirty to forty minutes in duration. One thinks of writers such as A. R. Gurney, Lanford Wilson, John Guare and several others. Now, new playwrights tend to work in the ten-minute play genre, largely because there are so many production opportunities. Twenty-five or so years ago, there were none. I was Senior Editor for Samuel French at that time, and it occurred to me that there might be a market for these very short plays, which Actors Theatre of Louisville had been commissioning for several years, for use by their Apprentice Company. I made a deal with Jon Jory and Michael Bigelow Dixon of ATL, who assisted me in compiling an anthology of these plays, which sold so well that Samuel French went on to publish several more anthologies of ten-minute plays from Actors Theatre. For the first time, ten-minute plays were now published and widely available, and they started getting produced. There are now many ten-minute play festivals every year, not only in the U.S. but all over the world.

What makes a good ten-minute play? Well, first and foremost I have to like it. Isn't that what we mean when we call a play, a film, a novel "good?" We mean that it effectively portrays the world *as I see it*, written in a style which interests *me.* Beyond this, a good ten-minute play has to have the same elements that *any* good play must have: a strong conflict, interesting, well-drawn characters and compelling subject matter. It also has to have a clear beginning, middle and end. In other words, it's a full length play which runs about ten minutes. Many of the plays which are submitted to me each year are scenes, not complete plays; well-written scenes in many case, but scenes nonetheless. They left me wanting more. I chose plays which are complete in and of themselves, which I believe will excite those of you who produce ten-minute plays; because if a play isn't produced, it's the proverbial sound of a tree falling in the forest far away. In the Rights & Permissions section at the back of this book you will find information on whom to contact when you decide which plays you want to produce, in order to acquire performance rights.

This year, most of the plays in this book are by playwrights who may not be as familiar to you as those in volumes past, though there are new plays by masters of the 10-minute play form whose work has appeared in previous volumes in this series, such as C.S. Hanson, Don Nigro, Glenn Alterman, Mark Harvey Levine and C.J. Ehrlich. Many of the playwrights are just starting out; others have something of a track record – just not in New York.

I have also included a comprehensive list of theatres which do ten-minute plays, which I hope playwrights will find useful.

I hope you enjoy these plays. I sure did!

Lawrence Harbison

2 Actors

ALEXANDER AND THE YELLOW ROTARY PHONE

Deanna Alisa Ableser

ALEXANDER AND THE YELLOW ROTARY PHONE was first produced by the FUSION Theatre Company (FUSIONnm.org) as an award-winning entry in their annual original short works festival, THE SEVEN, June 9th-12th, 2016 at The Cell Theatre and KiMo Theatre in Albuquerque, New Mexico.

Festival Producer: Dennis Gromelski.
Festival Curator: Jen Grigg.
Directed by Jen Grigg.
Lighting and Scenic Design by Richard K. Hogle.
Sound Design by Brent Stevens.
Properties Design by Robyn Phillips.
Production Stage Manager: Maria Lee Schmidt.

The cast was as follows:
MAN: Bruce Holmes
WOMAN: Jacqueline Reid

CHARACTERS

MAN: Male. Anywhere from late 20's- early 60's. Race does not mat-
    ter. Should be nicely dressed and taken care of, but does not have
    to fit any specific style or 'look'.
WOMAN: Female. Anywhere from late 20's- early 60's. Race does
    not matter. Nicely dressed but a bit more disheveled than MAN.
    Also, does not have to fit any specific style or 'look'.

SET: A desk, a chair, and a yellow old-fashioned rotary
phone.

A WOMAN comes on stage and sits down at a desk center stage. There is a yellow unplugged rotary dial phone on the desk. WOMAN looks at it, picks it up and starts dialing a few numbers. SHE hangs it up each time.

A MAN comes on with a cell phone in his hand. HE walks past WOMAN, does a double take and comes back to her.

MAN: Do you need some help?

WOMAN: I'm okay.

MAN: Do you need to call someone? You can borrow my cell, if you need.

WOMAN: I need to call someone on this phone. It's very important.

MAN is looking around at the rotary phone and trying to see if it is plugged in anywhere.

MAN: You do realize it's not plugged it anywhere.

WOMAN: *(looking around)* Dangnabbit!

MAN: Did you just say dangnabbit?

WOMAN: I'm trying not to cuss so much anymore. It's kinda a New Year's resolution.

MAN: I see.

WOMAN: I'm really fine. Look, you seriously don't need to stay and talk to me or anything. I can see you're a busy guy who's probably got an awful lot to do with his life. I mean, I'm extremely grateful you stopped in the first place. That's very kind and thoughtful of you. Thank you.

MAN: Wow. That was a long thank you.

WOMAN: Sorry. I have a tendency to be inappropriately verbose.

MAN: I see.

There is a short pause.

WOMAN: You can leave if you have to. I mean, there's no reason you need to stay. I'll figure out somewhere to plug in this phone. Somehow.

MAN and WOMAN are both looking around.

MAN: I'm not seeing any type of connection.

WOMAN: I'm sure something will show up. Outlets can be kinda magical like that. I've heard that they appear when you need them. I mean, sometimes. Sorta.

MAN: I really could lend you my cell phone. I've got unlimited texts and messages. Really.

WOMAN continues to look around.

WOMAN: The outlet's gotta be here. I was told I needed to use this phone. Specifically. I have the instructions somewhere in my pocket.

WOMAN starts pulling various scraps of paper out of her pocket. SHE crumbles up one by one.

WOMAN: Dangnabbit again. Double.

WOMAN starts more aggressively going through pockets.

WOMAN: I could have sworn I put the instructions in my pocket.

MAN: People don't use rotary phones anymore. Maybe you misunderstood something.

WOMAN: *(getting a bit more frantic)* I didn't misunderstand anything. I need to use this phone. I need to be able to make this call. If I could just get out of this chair, I could search easier. There wouldn't be as much of an issue.

MAN: I don't understand.

WOMAN: I can't get out of the chair once I have sat down. That part I definitely remember from the directions. That part was very clear.

MAN: Look, I really don't know you and I know it's not of my business, but I think maybe someone's playing a prank on you. *(Pause)* Maybe you'd like a cup of coffee. Why don't we get a cup of coffee? Get you out of there. *(Putting hand out)* My name's Alex. Short for Alexander. Like the hero.

WOMAN: I'm sure you've got much better things to do with your life, Alexander the Hero, than sit around and talk to a person who's a bit more than off most likely. Or definitely.

MAN: What type of hero would I be if I left a damsel in distress just sitting there, struggling.

WOMAN: You're not really a hero.

MAN: And you're not really a damsel in distress. So that makes us equal. Nonetheless, at this point, I'm staying for the entertainment value. I'd like to see what's going to happen with this phone. That's unplugged. With no visible outlet or connection. Anywhere.

WOMAN: It's a very important phone call.

MAN: Oh. I get that. Totally. *(Pause)* So, who is it you're supposed to be calling?

WOMAN: I'm not quite sure.

MAN: You're not quite sure who you're supposed to be calling? And you've lost the directions?

WOMAN: It's been a challenging year for me. To say the least. Dang...

MAN: *(interrupting)* Maybe you could go back to where you got the instructions. I'm more than certain they have another copy.

WOMAN: I was told not to leave the chair.

MAN: I could go back and get you the directions. Call it my first step in my transition to hero. I've got GPS on my phone.

There is a short pause.

WOMAN: You don't even know me.

MAN: I told you. I more than intrigued at this point. Sometimes a guy's just gotta go with the game. You seem harmless enough. Sitting there at a desk with an unplugged rotary phone. Yellow. It's not like you're going to pull out a big machete or anything. I've decided that this is the day I'm going to be a hero. Or something like that.

WOMAN: You're extremely weird.

MAN: And you're sitting at a desk with an unplugged rotary phone. Who's calling who a spade?

WOMAN: You've got a point.

MAN: So, we're a team now? Right? It's like an adventure type thing.

WOMAN: You're getting unusually excited over this.

MAN: My life's pretty boring. I'm thinking it's like a fate thing that brought us together.

WOMAN: *(looking around for outlet)* I don't understand why the outlet hasn't appeared by now.

MAN: Who gave you the directions?

There is no response.

MAN: You don't remember, do you?

WOMAN: I'm having a tough time remembering anything. I don't understand. I'm getting so frustrated.

MAN: I'm sure it will come back to you. It always does.

WOMAN: Not always. It doesn't always.

WOMAN picks up phone again and starts dialing a few numbers again and hangs up.

WOMAN: I was told it was a good time to call in my life. I was told it was going to help.

There is the sound of a phone ringing. WOMAN looks at

rotary phone in confusion. SHE looks at MAN who pulls out cell phone. It is not ringing.

WOMAN: Is that your phone ringing?

MAN looks at phone confused.

MAN: I don't understand.

WOMAN: There's no way my phone's ringing. It's not even plugged in.

MAN: You sure you don't remember where you got the instructions.

WOMAN: I'm not remembering very much anymore. It's very frustrating.

MAN: I guess it's not easy being a damsel in distress. Especially if that wasn't your choice.

WOMAN: Not so much.

MAN: You sure you can't leave the chair? You remember that clearly?

WOMAN: I think.

MAN: Maybe you should try. Maybe if someone helps you.

WOMAN: I think I remember clearly. I think.

MAN: I don't want to put you in danger. That's not something a hero should do. *(Pause)* I could just sit here and wait with you. There's nothing wrong with that right. It's almost like we're becoming friends.

There is a short pause.

MAN: I'm sorry things haven't been going so well for you lately.

WOMAN: It's been a challenging year, to say the least.

MAN: I'm sorry.

There is a short pause.

MAN: There's nothing preventing me from looking for the outlet, is there? It's not like you're the only one who can see it, can you? You don't recall anything about that, do you?

There is no answer.

MAN: I'll go look for the outlet. You said they're magical like that. Maybe they just need a little 'hero' power or something. *(Looking at cell phone)* Maybe the fact that I've spent four minutes and thirty seconds with you has imbued me with the magical powers I need to find the outlet.

WOMAN: I take back that I said I was quite verbose. You're exceptionally verbose.

MAN: Maybe you're rubbing off on me. Maybe that's a good thing.

WOMAN: You already said you're not a hero.

MAN: But I'm named after a hero. Surely that's gotta mean something.

WOMAN: I guess.

MAN: *(striking a not very manly hero pose)* I shall go search for your outlets now.

WOMAN: *(laughing)* Thanks. I needed a laugh.

MAN: *(interrupting)* It's been a rough year. I know. *(Pause)* Listen, don't worry. We've now known each Other for over six minutes now. I'm making an executive decision to upgrade the status of our relationship to friends.

WOMAN: Who exactly are you again?

MAN: Alexander. I told you. Your personal soon to be hero.

There is the sound of a phone ringing again. WOMAN looks at her phone and MAN pulls out phone again. This time it is MAN's phone ringing. HE looks unsure.

WOMAN: Aren't you going to answer it?

MAN: It seems a bit of a odd thing to do at this point.

WOMAN: Your phone's ringing. What's odd about that?

MAN: I feel a bit weird answering it at this point.

WOMAN: It's going to stop ringing now. You know that's how it happens. *(Phone stops ringing).* See.

MAN: I'm sure it was nobody important. I don't have a lot of friends. Or important people in my life.

WOMAN: I'm sure that's an understatement.

MAN: Perhaps. Then again, I'm not quite sure. Why don't I help you look for the outlet now?

WOMAN: That would be very kind of you.

MAN starts looking around while WOMAN picks up phone and starts dialing again.

MAN: We're not going to go through this again are we?

WOMAN: Things change. People change.

MAN: You think the phone's magically going to work now? There's still no plug. Still no outlet.

WOMAN: But you're my hero. Or you say you're my hero. That changes the game. Like automatically. I think.

MAN: I never said I would find the outlet. I said I'd look. Those are two markedly different things.

WOMAN: *(putting down phone)* But you're trying. That's important. I can't leave the chair. You're helping me. I don't think you realize how important that really is. *(Pause)* It's been a really difficult year. Or, really difficult couple of years.

MAN: *(still looking for outlet)* Who are you supposed to call on the phone?

WOMAN: Someone who was going to help.

MAN: There are a lot of people around who are willing to help. I mean, if you're willing to give it a chance. Like me, for example.

WOMAN: You don't even know me.

MAN: I know you a lot better than I knew you before. I'm willing to help. I've been willing to help for the past eight or so minutes. Even if I find this outlet, I can stay. I can stay while you make the phone call.

WOMAN: You really don't have to do this.

MAN: It's not a matter of have to. I want to. Sometimes people do things because they want to.

WOMAN: Where were you going?

MAN: Excuse me?

WOMAN: You were walking somewhere when you stopped.

MAN: It's been a long eight-ish minutes.

WOMAN: So, you don't remember?

MAN: I was just taking a walk. I didn't have anywhere important to go. I was just walking. And then I stopped. You intrigued me and so I stopped. There's nothing wrong with that.

WOMAN: So it wasn't important where you were walking to. That didn't really matter to you.

MAN: I was just walking. Sometimes you're just walking. Like you're just sitting. Sitting there waiting to make a call on a yellow phone that not plugged in anywhere. With no possible visible outlet.

WOMAN: And a stranger who comes by and helps you look for it. I guess that's not a bad thing.

MAN: It's not. *(Gets down on his knees)* Dangnabbit.

WOMAN: Nothing magically appeared, did it?

MAN: No. It didn't.

WOMAN: But you thought it would, right?

MAN: I did. Somehow.

WOMAN: Me too.

MAN: It still could though. You said outlets are kinda magical that way.

WOMAN: I did.

MAN: You're not going to leave the chair, are you?

WOMAN: It's really important I stay here. At least for now.

MAN: I don't want to just leave you sitting here. I mean, I don't feel right about that. Since we've become friends of a sort...

WOMAN: You don't have to feel guilty. I mean, I'm just a crazy woman sitting here at a table with an unplugged yellow rotary phone. Remember, if you need to call a spade a spade...

MAN: You're not crazy.

WOMAN: A spade's a spade. I'm sitting here...

MAN: I've seen many more crazy things in my life. You don't need to be embarrassed. You don't need to be ashamed. Sometimes people wait around for different types of things. No judgement.

There is a short pause.

MAN: Look, I really don't mind waiting for you...for the outlet, the phone, whatever. Sometimes someone waiting with you is all that matters. Like a hero. Named Alexander.

WOMAN: I don't know how to...

MAN: You don't need to thank me. You don't need to thank anything. Just accept it and let me wait with you. For the magical outlet. Or whatever it is.

WOMAN: You're very kind.

MAN: You're welcome.

MAN continues to walk around while searching for outlet.
WOMAN starts picking up phone to dial, looks at MAN puts
it down, and slowly starts to smile. Lights fade.

END OF PLAY

ANOTHER DAY

Cynthia Arsenault

Originally produced at "Summerplay 2016: A Festival of New Works," by Changing Scene Theatre NorthWest at the Tacoma Musical Playhouse, 7116 Sixth Ave., Tacoma, Washington 98406

Directed by Pavlina Morris, Assistant Director - Jen Aylsworth, with Nastassia Reynolds as Hermione and Dominic Girolami as Bob, August 22-30, 2016

CHARACTERS:

BOB: A cherry

HERMIONE: A cherry

AT RISE:

It's morning in the orchard. Bob and Hermione, attached by adjoining stems, (actors with red faces, their arms held aloft, hands held) are swinging from a cherry tree. They swing for a while, basking in the sun.

BOB: So what's it been?

HERMIONE: What's been what?

BOB: Us.

HERMIONE: Us?

BOB: Us! How long have us — we — been hanging around? Get it?

HERMIONE: *(She rolls her eyes, good naturedly)* Got it, Bob! And an easy one. Forever!

BOB: No wonder life feels so right.

HERMIONE: Ripe?

BOB: No, right!

HERMIONE: Ohhhhh... Ripe.

BOB: *(louder, again correcting her)* Right!

HERMIONE: Of course, I'm right.

BOB: Yes. You are always right, Hermione.

HERMIONE: Glad we established that.

(They swing around awhile, soaking up some rays.)

It sure is a beautiful day. *(PAUSE.)* Did you say "Ripe"?

BOB: I guess so.

HERMIONE: What brought that on?

BOB: I have a bad feeling about today.

HERMIONE: You're such a negative Nellie! The sun is dazzling. The birds are singing in the treetops. The dew is on our leaves. It's a beautiful day, Bob!

BOB: It is. And that's what's bad about it.

HERMIONE: OK. Trying to follow.

BOB: The day has so much potential, and yet — yet, there's a foreboding in the air, and I have a formidable sense of dread.

HERMIONE: Why?

BOB: Because it's not just another day, Hermione. I fear ... I fear our carefree days, you and me just hanging around, are over.

HERMIONE: "Over" is a foreboding word!

BOB: Which would be the "ripe" part.

HERMIONE: And the dread?

BOB: It won't settle down for me, but it's like a cold spot in a haunted house. What happens to us, H, when our youth is truncated? When our blissful bubble is basically burst?

HERMIONE: Oh my God, I'm getting your drift now. Are you saying... you are saying... that... we're about to ... to be... picked?

BOB: Precisely and not in a good way like for "Cherry of the Year." And then ... then it's "Bye-bye," Niteynite," Seeya," and "Sayonara" to our—

HERMIONE: —Us-ness. *(PAUSE.)* But how can that be? Unripe one day. Ripe the next.

BOB: I know. Weird, huh? Life has a way of moving us along its path. It's the journey everyone says we don't have to rush.

HERMIONE: I'm not racing. And what ... or who gets to decide when I'm ... ripe?

BOB: Of course, you're right.

HERMIONE: Ripe?

BOB: Right! And ripe!

HERMIONE: This is a disaster.

BOB: Now you're getting the picture.

HERMIONE: *(Big pout)* Regrettably.

> *PAUSE.*

But... we'll still be swingers, won't we, Bob? Well, not really swinging swingers, but you know what I—

BOB: A - I don't know and B - I know. Change is in the air.

HERMIONE: I don't like change. I want to grow old and go to seed with you.

BOB: And I, you, Hermione.

HERMIONE: We've been together forever, Bob. Survived chilly nights, killing freezes, and crow attacks. We simply can't let this happen.

BOB: I agree. I can't yin without your yang.

HERMIONE: We must fight back!

BOB: But how?

> *(Pause)*

HERMIONE: We'll wrap our arms around each other and never let go!

BOB: We don't have arms.

HERMIONE: Oh... *(Pause)* Well, we can act stupid to look immature. Pick our noses and make fart jokes.

BOB: No arms means no fingers means no nose picking.

HERMIONE: LOL! But at least I 'm brainstorming to fight this insidious ripeness. What are you doing about it?

BOB: Here's my plan: Cherry up! Leave this orchard with our dignity intact. With our stems held high.

HERMIONE: So ...ok... then. So you think we should give up.

BOB: Not give up. Give in... It's inevitable.

HERMIONE: You say "potahto", I say it's "giving up"... So ...

(Pause. Hermione is frustrated.)

What'll it be? Fight or fold?

BOB: I'm deciding.

HERMIONE: I'm waiting.

(Beat)

BOB: Listen, H.. Do you hear it? *(Pause)* Do you hear the picker?

(There is a mechanical whirring noise in the background that gradually gets louder and louder.)

HERMIONE: Oh my god, I think I do! I do hear it. It's faint, but it's approaching!

BOB: It is!

HERMIONE: Decide faster!

BOB: OK. I decided... Get ready.

HERMIONE: Ready. *(Beat)* Ready for what?

BOB: To be picked.

HERMIONE: *(disgusted)* Picked! That's the best you can do? You always were a loser, Bob. *(Muttering)* Yellow belly, chicken-hearted.....

BOB: We're just two little cherries. We can't fight the agricultural industrial machine!

HERMIONE: No? Remember when we supported our fellow fruits in that struggle? We stood our ground! Well, you know what I mean.

BOB: We were young and foolish then. This is too big and out of our control. The best we can do is hunker down together and ....

(The whirring is louder. He strains to listen.)

It's coming closer!

HERMIONE: OhmyGod!

BOB: Stay with me, H! Whatever happens, hang on! I don't think I could go on without your ruby red smile.

HERMIONE: I'm with you, Bob. And I'm not letting go. We're joined for life.

BOB: I've always felt it! We're pit-mates! Day in and day out forever.

HERMIONE: It can't be over! The universe will not let us be undone.

BOB: I love your positive attitude, H. Your yin-ness.

HERMIONE: I think it's my yang-ness, and you're the yin, but don't worry, Bobby. We're strong and we'll never let them tear us ...

BOB: ... Asunder! I will not be asundered from you!

HERMIONE: Nor I!

BOB: But the picker — it's getting closer! Oh, no! Hang on to your stem, H!

(They huddle together, grabbing their stems.)

HERMIONE: Together forever, Bob!

BOB: We will not yield! Our love will endure!

(The whirring noise comes to a crescendo after which there is prolonged screech. The cherries are pulled towards opposite sides of the stage in a valiant struggle against the force. Their stems become untied from each other. Finally, they collapse on the floor. Bob struggles to his knees and Hermione sits up dazed. They look woefully at each other across the expanse of the empty stage. The screeching suddenly stops. They look around, disoriented. It's a new reality.)

HERMIONE: Well, that was weird.

BOB: Everything seems different now.

HERMIONE: Yeah - *so* different.

BOB: *(trying to recall)* Aren't you ...?

HERMIONE: Hermione. And you're ...?

BOB: Bob ... Nice to meet you, Hermione. But ... maybe... have we met? I sense a cosmic connection with you.

HERMIONE *(squinting at him)* Hmmm... yeah, me, too.

BOB: Well, what now?

HERMIONE: Hmm, I might head on over to the Table Talk pie truck.

BOB: Hmm.. An interesting plan. You like pie?

HERMIONE: I never did before, but today I seem to be in touch with my inner pieness.

BOB: Can I come, too?

HERMIONE: Maybe you want to take a different path, Bob. I hear there are openings in Cherry Garcia at Ben and Jerry's.

BOB: I always did well during those sudden freezes.

HERMIONE: I have a vague recollection of that, too.

BOB: Huh ...Life changes on a dime; doesn't it?

HERMIONE: Yesiree, Bob. And now we're here.

BOB: You know, you're right.

HERMIONE: I know. I'm always right.

BOB: We *are* here....and it's a beautiful day.

HERMIONE: It's another day

END OF PLAY

ASKING FOR IT

Rhea MacCallum

Premiered as part of Mindflood produced by Torrent Theatre at Theatre 54 in New York City, April 21-24, 2016. Sheldon Carpenter, Artistic Director and Ilyssa DePonte, Managing Producer. Cast: Officer – Jeffrey Parrillo; Woman – Katie Reynolds. Email: torrenttc@gmail.com Additionally produced as a winning play in ONSTAGE/ Little Black Dress, INK's Curves Ahead by Acadiana Repertory Theatre in Lafayette, LA, July 14-16, 2015 and at the Prescott Center for the Arts in Prescott, AZ, October 6-8th.

CHARACTERS:
    OFFICER – 20s and up
    WOMAN – 20s and up

    TIME: Evening
    SETTING: Street corner

WOMAN: *(Into cell phone.)* I'm okay. More rattled than anything else. Yeah, I'm sure I don't need an ambulance. Oh, looks like the officer has arrived. Okay, thank you.

(Hangs up.)

OFFICER: Were you the one who wanted to report a hit and run accident?

WOMAN: Yes.

OFFICER: And how were you involved in the accident?

WOMAN: I'm the one who was hit by the vehicle.

OFFICER: You look okay to me…

WOMAN: I have a few scrapes but I'll be okay.

OFFICER: You need to sit down? Are you feeling light-headed or dizzy?

WOMAN: No, I just want to report the crime and get on with my night.

OFFICER: Alleged crime.

WOMAN: What?

OFFICER: Just start at the beginning…

WOMAN: Sure, okay, I was in the mini-mart and when I came out I crossed the parking lot to the cross-walk, pressed the button to get the lights and while I was standing at the corner of the sidewalk a black SUV with tinted windows turning right clipped the curb and hit me, knocking me to the ground and then just drove away.

OFFICER: I see, and what did you buy in the mini-mart?

WOMAN: A bag of chips.

OFFICER: Those aren't good for you.

WOMAN: Does that matter?

OFFICER: Only if you care about your health.

WOMAN: No, I mean, what I purchased. Does it really matter what I purchased?

OFFICER: Did you purchase any alcohol with your bag of chips?

WOMAN: No.

OFFICER: I can verify this with the clerk, ya know.

WOMAN: I didn't buy anything to drink. Nothing at all. Not that it should matter.

OFFICER: Just getting the full picture of what transpired, Miss.

WOMAN: I bought a bag of chips, just chips. You can see them, right here, in my hand.

OFFICER: And why did you need to buy these chips so late at night?

WOMAN: It's seven p.m.

OFFICER: Are you addicted to chips?

WOMAN: A little, I guess.

OFFICER: So you admit to having an addictive personality?

WOMAN: No, I was hungry, but not big-hungry just munchies-hungry, so I left my apartment, walked across the street and came to the mini-mart to satisfy my chip craving.

OFFICER: Is there a particular reason why you had the munchies?

WOMAN: I went to the gym today and the salad I had for dinner wasn't very filling.

OFFICER: It isn't because maybe you smoked a little pot?

WOMAN: No.

OFFICER: If we run a hair test it will come back clean?

WOMAN: I'm not a pot smoker and I really don't see how, even if I were, it would relate to my being hit. By. A moving. Vehicle.

OFFICER: Now when you exited the mini-mart did you talk to anyone, did anyone try talking to you?

WOMAN: No.

OFFICER: You weren't distracted by anything?

WOMAN: There wasn't anyone around, no one was with me, no one was talking to me, walking across the parking lot wasn't the problem. The problem is, I was standing, waiting for the cross-walk light to flash WALK when some asshole in a big, huge, gas-guzzling SUV with super dark tinted windows clipped the corner and hit me, knocking me to the ground.

OFFICER: There's no need to use that kind language.

WOMAN: What language?

OFFICER: You know what you said.

WOMAN: ???

OFFICER: … gas-guzzler. Clearly you are predisposed to have an issue with this vehicle that allegedly hit you.

WOMAN: What do you mean 'allegedly' hit me?

OFFICER: We have not yet established that a hit and run took place.

WOMAN: But I was hit, by the SUV, bounced off the vehicle and hit the ground as the driver sped away. I have scratches.

OFFICER: Yes, but… those scratches may be from a previous encounter.

WOMAN: They're fresh. And red. There's even a little blood.

OFFICER: I need to confirm… did you have a cocktail with your salad, or maybe take a pill, or maybe forget to take a pill?

WOMAN: No.

OFFICER: So you're normally this agitated?

WOMAN: No, normally I'm not hit by a vehicle while waiting for the light to change and normally I'm not interrogated for being the victim of an accident. Look, this has been a really long day and I'm kind of regretting calling this incident in but I felt like I should because a crime was committed and there's somebody out there driving recklessly and I'd really like them to be caught before they seriously hurt someone.

OFFICER: So you had a long day?

WOMAN: Yeah…

OFFICER: Is it possible that your mental facilities were impaired at the time of the incident?

WOMAN: No, I am not mentally impaired.

OFFICER: But you are tired, so maybe you were in the cross walk a little and just didn't notice? Maybe you stepped off the curb just a few seconds too soon?

WOMAN: No, I was standing on the slope of the sidewalk where it dips for wheelchairs. I know this because I was using the slope to help stretch out the back of my calves.

OFFICER: Oh, so you weren't even facing the street then?

WOMAN: I was at an angle.

OFFICER: Did you see the driver before they hit you?

WOMAN: The tinted windows were too dark. I couldn't identify the driver at all other than they looked masculine, broad shoulders, short, cropped hair.

OFFICER: I see. At any point did you maybe motion to the driver as they approached?

WOMAN: No.

OFFICER: You didn't maybe wave or flip your hair or flash him a little extra leg or something?

WOMAN: Definitely not.

OFFICER: And what were you wearing at the time of the incident?

WOMAN: This. This is what I was wearing?

OFFICER: Oh, you didn't maybe go home and clean up, change your clothes?

WOMAN: No, this just happened. I was still talking to the 911 dispatcher when you arrived. There hasn't been any time for me to go anywhere, do anything.

OFFICER: Have you ever noticed this vehicle in the neighborhood before?

WOMAN: No.

OFFICER: So you have no previous encounters with this particular vehicle?

WOMAN: Not that I'm aware of.

OFFICER: Because you remember all the vehicles that have hit you in the past?

WOMAN: This is my first hit and run experience.

OFFICER: Really?! And at your age. You know, that's really a little hard to believe. Maybe you wanted this to happen, but now that it did you're having regrets.

WOMAN: The only thing I regret right now is calling 911.

OFFICER: Did you scream or say no or resist being hit or at any point tell the driver of the vehicle to stop?

WOMAN: I sort of yelped as I bounced off the SUV and hit the ground.

OFFICER: So only after the fact.

WOMAN: Well, yeah, before he hit me I didn't exactly know he was going to clip the curb, otherwise I would have moved.

OFFICER: So you agree that there could have been a miscommunication here.

WOMAN: No, I'm not agreeing with that at all.

OFFICER: Did you at any point… enjoy being hit?

WOMAN: What?! No, it was horrible. For a second all I saw was white and I thought for sure I was a dead woman. It wasn't until I heard the squeal of the tires and opened my eyes that I realized that I was still alive.

OFFICER: And now that it's happened you're filled with regret and want people to think you're just a victim in all this.

WOMAN: I am the victim! Why are you having such a hard time understanding this?

OFFICER: You'd be surprised how many times hit and run accidents are reported then a few days pass and so-called victims retract their statements.

WOMAN: When?! When has that ever happened?!

OFFICER: It happens.

WOMAN: Well, I'm not going to.

OFFICER: Yeah. That's what they all say. At first. But then we open an investigation, start calling all of your friends and family, asking questions about your personal habits and-

WOMAN: Whoawhoawhoa, why would you need to call my friends?

OFFICER: To gather background information, make sure you're a... reliable witness.

WOMAN: Shouldn't my word, my testimony, be enough?

OFFICER: You'd think that wouldn't you.

Well, I have enough information to open my investigation on you.

(Handing her a card.)

But here's my card, ya know, just in case you change your mind.

LIGHTS OUT.

BLUE TENT

Gino DiIorio

Blue Tent was produced by Fort Point Theatre Channel at the Calderwood Pavilion as part of the Boston Play Marathon, May 8, 2016. It was directed by Kathryn Howell. The play was produced by Kate Snodgrass. Robert Mighty was the documentary photographer.

The cast was as follows:

EDEN: Robert Pemberton
FRANKIE: Rick Winterson

CHARACTERS
EDEN: a homeless man in his 50's
FRANKIE: his companion, also in his 50's

Time: The Present
Place: An abandoned loading dock, lower east side of Manhattan

Note: "Blue Tent" was originally written for two actors of color but
it can (of course) be performed by actors of any race.

(A run down loading dock on the lower east side. A man sits below the dock in a folding chair. He is surrounded by boxes and milk crates full of junk. He is dressed in a wind breaker and jeans with a stained sweat shirt underneath. His left hand has a huge cast and in it, he holds a few dollar bills. In his other hand, he holds a lit cigarette. He smokes and fingers through the few bills to see what he's got. On the loading platform above him is a blue tarpaulin, hung with some old rope. We can see that a person is lying underneath the tarp. He remains unseen for most of the play. If the actor or director chooses, he can peek out from under the tarp from time time).

(As the lights rise, they are still and there is silence. After a moment, EDEN's voice comes from underneath the tarp)

EDEN: The trick is to mix a little bit of olive oil in with the butter. And then, just as it starts to smoke, you put the slices in. And you can't let them sit in eggs too long either. Unless of course you're using really thick bread. That works okay.

FRANKIE: Uh-huh.

EDEN: Otherwise the whole thing gets too soggy. Just put it in there for a bit. You know what I'm saying?

FRANKIE: I do.

EDEN: You'll know if you did it right the first time you flip em. They should be golden brown underneath, kind of like a pancake.

FRANKIE: Okay.

EDEN: And you only gotta flip em once.

FRANKIE: Of course.

EDEN: No different than what I was telling you about steak. You can't be playing around with your meat. *(Frankie laughs)* You know what I'm saying?

FRANKIE: I do.

EDEN: No playing with the meat.

FRANKIE: No playing with the meat.

EDEN: You can't be playing with the meat.

FRANKIE: And the eggs are room temperature.

EDEN: Eggs are always room temperature.

FRANKIE: And you start off the bacon on very low.

EDEN: Cold pan.

FRANKIE: Cold pan brought to very low.

EDEN: That's right. And no grease.

FRANKIE: Of course not.

EDEN: Flip em just once.

FRANKIE: Got it.

EDEN: There's your breakfast.

FRANKIE: Yeah.

EDEN: You won't forget?

FRANKIE: I won't forget.

(Pause)

EDEN: You think in heaven you get bacon and eggs for breakfast?

FRANKIE: Every day.

EDEN: French toast?

FRANKIE: Whatever you want Edie.

EDEN: That's good.

(Pause)

FRANKIE: I got a granola bar.

EDEN: You should eat it.

FRANKIE: You sure?

(Pause)

EDEN: Where's my All Clad?

FRANKIE: Hang on.

(Frankie starts digging through things)

EDEN: What?

FRANKIE: I said hang on. I'm looking for it.

EDEN: The 12 inch.

FRANKIE: Yeah, I got it.

(Frankie holds the pan in his good hand)

EDEN: Okay. That's yours.

FRANKIE: Come on.

EDEN: I ain't got no use for it.

FRANKIE: It's all rusted.

EDEN: That's okay. Give it a good scrub, season it with olive oil like
    I showed you. Good as new.

FRANKIE: Can't do it Bro.

EDEN: I want you to have it.

FRANKIE: I can't.

EDEN: Shut the fuck up. You leave it behind, somebody asshole use it as a dog dish. You take it.

FRANKIE: Okay.

EDEN: Promise?

FRANKIE: Yeah.

EDEN: Do anything with that pan.

(We hear Eden having a coughing fit. Frankie sits and twirls the pan, as he waits for the coughing fit to subside).

FRANKIE: What can I get you?

EDEN: Nothing, you can get the fuck outta here.

FRANKIE: I ain't leaving.

EDEN: I told you—

FRANKIE: You know what, I'm fucking sick of you telling me. All my motherfucking life, you telling me. Frankie, get me this, Frankie get me that. Frankie go get me eggs, go get me the butter. What am I, a fucking gopher to you? Is that what I am? Some kinda… glorified zoo chef?

EDEN: What?

FRANKIE: Zoo chef.

EDEN: Sous Chef. Sous! Don't you know what sous means?

FRANKIE: I don't give a shit. Zoo Chef, sous chef—

EDEN: A Zoo Chef works in the fucking zoo, okay? He cooks things for people in the zoo. For people who come to the zoo.

FRANKIE: Fine, so what does sous mean?

EDEN: It's…it's sous. Sous Chef.

FRANKIE: So what does it mean?

EDEN: It comes from the French meaning…meaning…sous.

FRANKIE: What does sous mean?

EDEN: It means sous!

FRANKIE: The meaning can't be the fucking word!

EDEN: Sure it can.

FRANKIE: You're full of shit.

EDEN: All the time we worked together, how is it you don't know what that means?

FRANKIE: You don't know what it means either!

EDEN: It means lower. Okay?! It means less than. Means, a second guy. Like the second team. Like lower than.

FRANKIE: My point exactly. I'm nothing but something *lower than* to you!

EDEN: All right, now that's not even proper English.

FRANKIE: What the—

EDEN: "Lower than to you." Listen to yourself!

FRANKIE: Fuck you. All right? Is that proper English? Fuck you. Proper English. Sit around here wiping the sweat off your face, the shit off your ass, and that's what you got for me—

EDEN: All right—

FRANKIE: Proper English? And I'm nothing but some kind of a…a less than—

EDEN: I said all right!

FRANKIE: —to you? Always took care of you. Always did. "Less than. Less than to you!" All right? That's what I mean, I'm less than to you!

EDEN: It don't make sense.

FRANKIE: I'm gonna hit you with this pan, is that what you want? I'm gonna hit you with your fucking All Clad.

(After a minute he tosses the pan to the ground).

EDEN: Hey careful with that!

FRANKIE: Fuck you.

EDEN: Pick up the pan.

FRANKIE: You do it.

EDEN: Pick it up.

(After a moment, Frankie reaches down for the All Clad. He holds it and sits back down).

EDEN: Hey, remember that time they was gonna make a movie about us?

FRANKIE: When?

EDEN: That guy. Young kid. He came around with his—

FRANKIE: Oh, yeah yeah….

EDEN: He had this hand held thing. Was gonna make part of it with his phone?

FRANKIE: I remember.

EDEN: Midnight at the Garden of Eden Diner

FRANKIE: He was a weird dude.

EDEN: Very weird.

FRANKIE: And you was holding out for more money.

EDEN: Of course.

FRANKIE: You kept saying "what's the compensation?" Dude was like, compensation? I'm making this movie for nothing.

EDEN: Hey, is the movie about my diner?

FRANKIE: No.

EDEN: It had my diner in the title.

FRANKIE: But that's just like one of those working title things. He didn't know what it was about.

EDEN: He wanted to tell our story.

FRANKIE: We didn't need that trouble.

EDEN: Coulda used the money.

FRANKIE: Don't need money to tell your story.

EDEN: You gonna tell my story?

FRANKIE: Yeah. I'll make like you were the bad guy, how's that?

EDEN: Don't do that.

FRANKIE: I will.

EDEN: What do you gotta say that for?

FRANKIE: I ain't no less than.

EDEN: I know you're not. I was giving you shit.

(Pause)

You ain't no less than. You never was.

FRANKIE: Thank you.

EDEN: You never was less than nothing.

(Pause. Frankie nods)

We had a good run.

FRANKIE: We did.

EDEN: Now you should get the hell out of here.

FRANKIE: I told you, I ain't leaving.

EDEN: I don't feel good.

FRANKIE: I know.

EDEN: I'm sick.

FRANKIE: I know.

EDEN: I'm dying baby. I'm dying away.

(Frankie holds back tears)

I hear you over there.

FRANKIE: Sorry.

EDEN: Stop that.

(Frankie puts down the pan. He reaches into the tent with is good hand and takes out Eden's hand. We can it is covered with dirty bandages).

FRANKIE: You ain't dying alone.

EDEN: I didn't want you to see this.

FRANKIE: Well, I'm seeing it. So there.

EDEN: You were a loyal partner.

FRANKIE: We fucking lost everything.

EDEN: Yeah, but for a while it was pretty good.

FRANKIE: For a while it was real good.

(Pause. After a moment, Eden lets out a groan)

EDEN: Oh. Now I see.

FRANKIE: What?

EDEN: I see it all in front of me.

FRANKIE: What is it?

EDEN: It's early morning at the Garden of Eden diner. The coffee's on, the bacon is frying, the nighttime is falling into the day, and the street lights are going out, one by one. The aprons are clean, the doors are wide open…and you and me are standing there…. waiting for it to happen.

(Frankie looks to the tent. He holds his friend's hand and looks straight ahead. Lights fade…)

End of Play

CONSPIRACY OF LOVE

Philip J. Kaplan

CONSPIRACY OF LOVE premiered at the Museum of Dysfunction, presented by Mildred's Umbrella (Houston, TX). It was directed by and starred Ron Reeder and Amy Warren

CHARACTERS
MATHIAS, a man obsessed.
JAN, his blind date.

SETTING: A table in a restaurant.

JAN is sitting at a restaurant table when MATHIAS rushes in. There are menus on the table.

MATHIAS: Sorry I'm late. Would you believe it, I got the address wrong.

JAN: That can happen.

MATHIAS: It's a terrible way to start a blind date.

JAN: Don't be nervous. Thierry and Alex said we had a lot in common. I'll give you the benefit of the doubt.

MATHIAS: Thanks. Just like the mainstream media gives the benefit of doubt to the "Official Story" of Nine Eleven.

JAN: Excuse me?

MATHIAS: The pasta here is supposed to be great.

JAN: What did you say?

MATHIAS: You've got very pretty eyes, Jan.

JAN: Thank you.

MATHIAS: They're sparkly. They remind me of the fact that Osama Bin Laden is still alive and hiding in Davos.

JAN: What?

MATHIAS: Am I being too forward? I can't help myself. You're very pretty and—

JAN: What do you mean, Bin Laden's alive?

MATHIAS: It's a well known suppressed fact. Should I order some wine?

JAN: Bin Laden is dead. They have tapes. They made a movie.

MATHIAS: I don't want to get into an argument so soon after we've met.

JAN: Good.

MATHIAS: Who wants an argument on a blind date?

JAN: Exactly.

MATHIAS: It's not your fault you're narrow minded and brainwashed. You can't help following the herd.

Beat

JAN: Oh, look at the time. I really have to go.

MATHIAS: But we haven't ordered.

JAN: I have this thing. And I uh … well… need to do this thing… now.

Jan gets up to leave.

MATHIAS: *(crushed)* You're not even bothering to make up an excuse.

JAN: Sure I am. Enjoy your life. I gotta go.

Jan is about to leave.

MATHIAS: God, you compliment a girl and you're automatically a sexist pig.

JAN: That's not the problem.

MATHIAS: You're just like the nano-thermite particles that were found throughout the World Trade Center dust.

JAN: Nano-thermite.

MATHIAS: Nano-thermite particles.

JAN: I'm like Nano-thermite particles. How ... I can't believe I'm asking this... how am I like nano-thermite particles?

MATHIAS: They prove that the Trade Center was blown up before the planes hit.

JAN: And?

MATHIAS: And they never found the black box from Flight 93 and —

JAN: How am I like the nano-thermite particles!

MATHIAS: Those black boxes are supposed to withstand –

Jan grabs Mathias by the shirt.

JAN: *(screams)* How am I like nano-thermite particles!

MATHIAS: I don't know. I'm not good at riddles.

Jan lets go of Mathias, and takes a deep breath.

JAN: I was leaving. I forgot that I was leaving, but now I remember. So, bye.

MATHIAS: If you're going can you at least tell me why. You owe me that. Are you leaving because I said you were pretty?

JAN: No. That's OK.

MATHIAS: Oh. I thought that was it. Is it something I've done?

JAN: Yes!

MATHIAS: You're implying that there's a connection between an event that I took part in and your leaving. I'm not seeing it at all. It feels random. It's you, isn't it.

JAN: Stop talking about Nine Eleven!

MATHIAS: What do you mean?

JAN: I don't want to hear your crazy Nine Eleven talk. Is that so hard to understand?

MATHIAS: I hear you saying that you don't want to talk about Nine Eleven. Am I hearing you correctly?

JAN: Yes. And, also, don't say I'm narrow minded and brainwashed.

MATHIAS: I don't talk about Nine Eleven all the time. Do I? ...

JAN: You do.

MATHIAS: OK, OK. I was just a little preoccupied. No more politics tonight. OK? If I promise to focus on you and me the rest of the evening, will you promise to stay?

JAN: Of course! Oh, wait, why did I say that? You're still crazy.

MATHIAS: C'mon. Alex insisted we have a lot in common. You don't want to disappoint Alex, do you? Worst thing, you'll have a nice dinner. And maybe, just maybe, we're right for each other.

JAN: Well, it's true. My evening's already shot.

MATHIAS: Exactly! It can't get any worse!

JAN: We've bottomed out.

MATHIAS: Nowhere to go but up.

Beat

JAN: Don't make me regret this.

Jan sits down.

MATHIAS: I'll be good. I promise. I won't mention Nine Eleven for the rest of the night. I'll be as silent as the stealth jets that shot down Flight 93 in Pennsylvania. Oh, sorry.

JAN: That's strike one. Actually strike two.

MATHIAS: I will talk about something else.

JAN: Please.

There is a long pause. Mathias starts to say something, then stops. He starts to talk again, then stops. He looks at the menu and holds it up.

MATHIAS: Menu. This is a menu. — I mean, did you get a chance to look at the –

JAN: I'm quite familiar with the menu. You were late. I was waiting for you. Remember?

MATHIAS: Sorry. You know why I was late? That's a funny story

(stops abruptly)

— oh. Never mind. Order. Food. What do you want to order?

JAN: I'm thinking of getting the crab salad.

MATHIAS: Did you say, "controlled demolition of the towers?"

JAN: *(stiffly)* No. I said crab salad.

MATHIAS: My bad.

> *(beat)*

You're not gonna leave are you?

JAN: I'm really trying, Mathias. In fact, to show I'm trying, I'm going to change the subject. Do you have any hobbies? No! Don't answer that!

MATHIAS: Do you have any hobbies?

JAN: I like to travel.

MATHIAS: Where was your last trip?

JAN: Holland.

MATHIAS: I've always wanted to go. I love Rembrandt. And Tulips.

JAN: Don't forget windmills.

MATHIAS: I'm tilting at them all the time.

> *They laugh.*

JAN: Where was your last trip?

MATHIAS: First lower Manhattan, then Shanksville, Pennsylvania. Then Arlington, Virginia. Oh. Sorry.

JAN: This is not working.

MATHIAS: After I took soil samples from the Pentagon I went to DC.

JAN: I like DC

MATHIAS: Me too. All the Memorials. The Smithsonian.

JAN: I love the Smithsonian! They have such an amazing collection.

MATHIAS: Oh my god! They have the original Star Spangled Banner.

JAN: That takes my breath away.

MATHIAS: Me too.

JAN: And they have this fantastic art museum.

MATHIAS: I love that. And did you ever make it to the Holocaust museum?

JAN: The Holocaust museum?

MATHIAS: Yeah. The Nazis the Jews. The Holocaust.

JAN: The Holocaust? You believe that crap?

BLACKOUT

DITMAS

Glenn Alterman

ORIGINAL PRODUCTION INFORMATION
Produced by Village Playwrights Company
Part of the "Gay Pride and Prejudice Festival"

Theater at the Gay and Lesbian Center
208 West 13th Street
New York, NY 10011
Opening June 22, 2016

CAST
Sharon- Lucy McMichael
Mel- Michal Gnat

Director
Katrin Hilbe
Produced by Edmund Miller

CAST

SHARON- can be played by an actress in her 40's to early 60's. She's a bit ballsy, somewhat drunk.

MEL- He's the same age at SHARON. He wears glasses, may have some facial hair, is nice looking, soft spoken, a bit of a nerd.

PLACE: A rear table in a small bar, mid town, New York
TIME: About 7 PM

SHARON: Thank you.

MEL: It was no…

SHARON: No, no, you are a gentleman, you are.

MEL: *(Smiling, modestly)* Really, it was no big….

SHARON: No you are, uh, uh … *(not knowing his name)?*

MEL: Mel.

SHARON: Well Mel, as you saw, me and Mr. Floor were getting *(smiling)* y'know, kina *intimate.* I mean I saw *dust balls* down there. *(Leaning in, playful)* Mel, I could tell you such dirty stories about that filthy floor. But I shall spare you. You saved me… from my *fall from grace.* That bar stool just tipped over… *(Leaning in, suddenly very cozy)*—You ever know anybody named Grace, Mel?

MEL: What? No, can't say I….

SHARON: Me neither. And it's really such a nice name, Grace. Y'know, I've known some Graziella's, and maybe a few Bethany's…

MEL: *(Softly)* Sharon, are you okay?

SHARON: Me? Sure. 'Course. *(A big smile)* Hey, I'm tough; from "Brooklyn". Takes more than a fall from a chair to ruffle these feathers. *(Leaning in, smiling, directly)* So you married, Mel?

MEL: *(Smiling)* What?

SHARON: Well if you're not, you should be. You're polite, kind; real gentleman. And there's not too many here that… S'just one thing that's been….

(She quickly leans in, reaches for his glasses)

Ya gotta get rid of…

MEL: *(Stopping her, grabbing her hand)* Hey, DON'T!

SHARON: *(Startled, HE lets go of her hand. SHE moves back in her chair)* Sorry. Sorry, I just…

MEL: (Putting his glasses back on) You just surprised me, that's all. I… I don't like when people grab at my face.

SHARON: Yeah, I know what'cha mean; know exactly. I was being too forward; *invaded your space.* For that I am truly sorry. What I… I was just gonna suggest that instead of glasses you might try some contact lenses.

MEL: *(Smiling)* Thanks, yeah, I might.

SHARON: *(A beat)* — So, uh, boys night out, huh?

MEL: Well no, actually, I just came from work. Came in for a beer.

SHARON: *(Flirty)* And you saw me *from across the crowded room.*

MEL: Well actually I saw you *falling* and…

SHARON: (*Smiling, leaning back in her chair.*) You r*escued me.* Thank you kind sir. - So what kina work you do?

MEL: I work with computers.

SHARON: (*Impressed*) Computers.

MEL: Over at the Apple Store, few blocks from here. In the Genius Bar.

SHARON: Well look at you, Genius Bar! (*Smiling*) So you just went from one bar to another.

MEL: (*Smiling*) Sort of.

SHARON: (*Leaning in to him*) May I make an observation, Mel?

MEL: Sure.

SHARON: You're shy. You are a very-shy-guy.

MEL: I know, been told that before.

SHARON: You shouldn't be. Mel, what you got to be shy about, huh? You're a good looking man. And smart. Shit, Mel, you work at the GENUIS bar! (*Again leaning in*) 'Mean any girl in here…

MEL: Sharon?

SHARON: (*Smiling*) I know, I know, I talk too much. Been told that before. And after a couple of drinks…

MEL: We know each other.

SHARON: What?

MEL: We…

SHARON: (*Suddenly uncomfortable*) Oh Jesus. From here, this bar? —Mel, did we …?

MEL: (*Smiling*) No, nothing like that.

SHARON: What, I know you from the neighborhood?

MEL: (*HE looks at her*). Ditmas.

SHARON: Ditmas?

MEL: Ditmas Junior High.

SHARON: In Brooklyn? (*SHE looks at him*) You went to Ditmas, really? I don't remember you.

MEL: We were in the same grade.

SHARON: We were.

MEL: Took some of the same classes.

SHARON: We did?

MEL: And you were always very kind to me.

SHARON: I was?

MEL: Uh-huh. The other kids were always making fun of me, bullying me. Made my life a real hell.

SHARON: I'm so sorry. Yeah, kids can… *(Then, softly)* Oh Jesus, Mel, were you one of those kids in the special needs classes?

MEL: No, no, we were in the same home room, Mrs. BronfMAN: SHARON: Bronfman? I remember her, but…

MEL: *(Softly)* Sharon, I wasn't "Mel" then.

SHARON: *(Confused)* Who were you?

MEL: *(A beat)* Marla.

SHARON: Marla?

MEL: Marla Stern.

SHARON: *(SHE quickly moves back in her chair)* You shittin' me?!

MEL: No, I was skinny, pimply Marla. Wore those thick, dark glasses, which the other kids always loved knocking off my face. I was a real mess. Tough times. Had no idea who I really was back then. Was pretty horrible. But you were always so kind to me, *protected* me.

SHARON: I did?

MEL: More than once. Told the other kids they better leave me alone- or else! And they knew you meant it! Yeah, you were pretty tough.

SHARON: *(Still shocked)* Guess I was.

MEL: Couple of times you even took me by the hand to my next class. You were like my personal bodyguard, my guardian angel You took care of me.

SHARON: *(Finally getting it)* You're Marla; HOLY SHIT!

MEL: 'Cept now I'm Mel, and I'm a man.

SHARON: Like *completely?*

MEL: Totally, yes.

SHARON: Jesus. .…Jes-us! I been hearing about this kinda stuff lately. 'Mean it's been all over the news. But… *(Then a bit awkwardly)* So… *Mel,* how the hell are you?

MEL: *(Sincerely)* I'm fine. Good. How 'bout you?

SHARON: *(Smiling)* Well, I don't think I'm drunk anymore. DIT-MAS, SHIT!

MEL: Long time ago.

SHARON: *(Whispering)* And you're a man.

MEL: *(Smiling)* Think we've established that. Before, when I was helping you up from the floor, when I saw your face, knew you right away… Thought, holy shit, it's Sharon Bergen, from Ditmas!

SHARON: I remember you now. You really were kind of a mess. Looked like you were goin' through a lot; broke my heart. Felt so… And those other kids; assholes!

MEL: Water under the bridge.

SHARON: So.

(THEY look at each other, take each other in for a moment)

MEL: Amazing, huh?

SHARON: You have no idea.

MEL: Life.

SHARON: Tell ya, I never met anybody who went from being…

MEL: Takes some getting use to.

SHARON: So, you have anybody you're like going out with?

MEL: I have a wife.

SHARON: A wife?

MEL: I'm married.

SHARON: Huh.

MEL: And we have a son, Arnie. We adopted him. He's beautiful, Sharon. How 'bout you?

SHARON: Me?

MEL: You married?

SHARON: No; no. Had a couple of husbands, jerks, didn't work out. Finally realized I'm just not *marriage material*. Work in an office, couple a blocks from here, assist some guy, real nerd, nine to five, pays the rent. Blah-blah-blah. Married? No. Seems like me and men… *(Smiling)* Shit, the people you meet in a bar.

(HE smiles. They're both look at each other again, are quiet for a moment)

MEL: Well, guess I should get going.

SHARON: Yeah, me too. Got this new dog, needs to be walked.

MEL: Oh yeah, what kind?

SHARON: A rescue. He's sort of a Boxer-Saint Bernard mix. I call him *(very elegantly)* Arthur; like he's got a pedigree or somethin'. But he's just a mutt.

MEL: *(Smiling)* A rescue, huh?

SHARON: Yeah.

MEL: Well I should get home.

SHARON: Me too. *Sir Arthur awaits.*

MEL: Sharon, let's keep in touch, huh?

SHARON: Yeah, yeah, sure. —*(Sincerely)* Y'know, you seem really good Mel, I mean it. So different… Like really *together.*

Lawrence Harbison

MEL: It was tough for a while, but life's good. I lucked out.

SHARON: *(Sincerely)* I'm glad. *(Smiling)* And may I say, *Mel* looks great on you.

MEL: *(HE reaches over, gently touches her face. She smiles. Softly.)* Thank you— for taking care of me all those times. For coming to my rescue, back at Ditmas.

SHARON: Eh, no big deal. *(SHE hesitantly lifts her hand up to touch his face. He smiles. Then she gently touches his face. A big smile).* And thank you, *Mel,* for rescuing me from Mr Floor, after my… *fall from grace.*

MEL: *(Getting up)* I'm at the Genius Bar, the Apple Store. Stop by.

SHARON: *Yeah, I will.*

MEL: *(Starting to leave.)* You take care.

SHARON: You too. Take care. *(HE leaves. SHE watches him go, sits there for a moment, looks at her glass.)* Hm.

(She looks up again, smiles.)

Hm.

(The lights fade. END OF PLAY)

DR. DARLING

A Screwball Comedy in Ten Minutes
C.S. Hanson

DR. DARLING was written thanks to a commission from Crystal Field, Exec. Director, Theater for the New City, and George Ferencz and the Experimentals. It was produced for the Lower East Side Festival at Theater for the New City on May 28, 2016 (originally titled DOUBLE D). The cast was as follows:

DR. DARLING: John-Andrew Morrison
DOUBLE D: Jenne Vath
Directed by George Ferencz
Costumes by Sally Lesser
Set by Lytza Colon

CHARACTERS

DOUBLE D: female, 30s, a robot
DR. DARLING: male, 40s, Oliver Darling, Ph.D., a roboticist

Setting: A junkyard where Oliver Darling, Ph.D., does experiments. He has built a spacecraft and is creating a robot to send to outer space.

Note on Costumes

Oliver Darling always dresses professionally, even in the junkyard. He would never be caught without his white lab coat, under which there is always a shirt with collar and bow tie and pressed trousers. His shoes are either conservative wing tips or sneakers.

Double D wears a body-forming suit, almost like something that surfers wear. It is sleek and form fitting and under it is a negligee with a revealing neckline.

A space suit is on stage, but is never fully worn. It should be big and puffy and not at all fashionable.

(DOUBLE D stands before DR. DARLING.)

DR. DARLING: Look at you. Exquisite. Like the most beautiful invertebrate in the ocean. Oh mollusk, I will miss you. But! My work is done. Thanks to you, I will need to clear a space on my mantle for the Nobel. The great Nobel will finally be my prize. One final check.

(Dr. Darling inspects Double D from head to toe.)

DR. DARLING: Sensors activated. Circulation flowing. All ninety-nine motors purring like a little kitty cat. Robotic model number 20-zillion-DOUBLE-D-3-ZBZ, you are ready for launch.

DOUBLE D: I do not think I am ready.

DR. DARLING: No silly talk now. Let's get you into your suit.

(Dr. Darling leads Double D to the space suit and tries to get her into it. She doesn't cooperate.)

DR. DARLING: C'mon now, Double D. Your spacecraft awaits.

DOUBLE D: Dr. Darling? I do not want to go alone.

DR. DARLING: Nonsense. You'll have a blast. Besides, I worked on you for ten years. You're ready. Destiny awaits.

DOUBLE D: I do not want to go.

(Now Double D has one leg into the suit.)

DR. DARLING: Double D, we're running out of time. The robofleet is prepared to launch. We must get you to Alpha Cenza-taur before Team Zython. Sources tell me they launch in twelve minutes. Hurry now. You can suit up from inside. Now when you get to Alpha Cenza-taur, there can be no hesitating like this. You are programmed to beam all evidence of life back to earth immediately. But first, take a selfie. You know the drill. Remove your helmet and jacket. Unzip the suit just so. Selfie time!

DOUBLE D: I wish you were going with me.

DR. DARLING: I know. It must be difficult to part from, well, a genius like me. Take a look at your spacecraft. Pretty sleek, isn't it?

(Double D peaks at it.)

DOUBLE D: My space craft is green? Who picked that color?

DR. DARLING: The color doesn't matter. You'll be all buckled up inside.

DOUBLE D: What color is the interior?

DR. DARLING: Beige, I think.

DOUBLE D: Beige? Yuck.

DR. DARLING: I am a man of science, not a decorator. Concentrate on your own gifts. You're a beauty. The world is going to love you. Hollywood will want you. Oh Double D, you are history in the making. Get going.

DOUBLE D: Wait. My bag. My bag. I almost forgot my bag.

DR. DARLING: You can't bring your bag into space.

DOUBLE D: Why not?

DR. DARLING: You won't need it.

DOUBLE D: No woman would travel to outer space without lipstick and mascara and a change of clothes. Before I leave for Alpha Cenza-Taur, I want to know one thing. What is the real world like? Tell me now. Before I leave.

DR. DARLING: It's uh, well, it's a wonderful life.

DOUBLE D: Just like the movie? I love that movie. I scanned it over and over and over. I want it. I want a wonderful life.

DR. DARLING: Perhaps you'll find a better life in outer space.

DOUBLE D: Please, Oliver Darling, I do not want to go to outer space. My quantum brain downloaded every reference to Western civilization, from *Twilight Zone* to *Seinfeld*. I know a lot. And I want to experience it.

DR. DARLING: Of course you know a lot. I modeled you on the most exquisite creature in the ocean: The octopus. Smart, fast, flexible. And you will protect yourself by spraying black ink to thwart any predators on Alpha Cenza-taur. Double D, proceed with the mission.

DOUBLE D: No one else goes by the name Double D. Other people have names like Elaine and Jerry and George and Kramer.

DR. DARLING: Double D is a fine name. It suits you. Toodle doo.

DOUBLE D: Let me stay on earth. I want to have friends and a favorite diner and a pet dog that gets run over and then I will cry and then I will get a new puppy that will run into my arms and lick my face and new memories will replace old ones and my heart will swell.

DR. DARLING: Your system is overwhelmed. Skedaddle.

DOUBLE D: Skedaddle? Really? Before I have had a financial crisis? Before the banks have let me down? Before I have been saved by an angel? Before I have been kissed under the Washington Square Arch? Before *(orgasmic)* aaaaaaaaah aaaaah ahaah. "I'll have what she's having."

DR. DARLING: You are a system, not a namby-pamby. A genius – that would be me – created you. If you don't gear up and get in that spacecraft right now, the world will never know the true power of my —

DOUBLE D: I never even got to go to the ocean to see a real octopus.

DR. DARLING: I have mortgaged my house and rented my garage. I have given up everything. My life consists of you, Netflix, and reruns of *Friends*. And as soon as you land and take those selfies and beam back what you find, the prizes, the glory, the cash will roll in. Screw academia. I will be vindicated. Now leave.

DOUBLE D: I will leave tomorrow. Give me twenty-four hours to live a wonderful life.

DR. DARLING: And let Team Zython get there first? Your aircraft is primed to launch in three minutes. Three minutes.

DOUBLE D: I will take it. Three minutes. I will live a wonderful life in three minutes.

DR. DARLING: What? What can you do in three minutes?

DOUBLE D: This.

(Double D kisses Dr. Darling passionately.)

DR. DARLING: Oh that was. . . Wow.

(Double D removes Dr. Darling's bowtie.)

DOUBLE D: I want a boyfriend. Be my boyfriend.

DR. DARLING: I'm not boyfriend material.

DOUBLE D: Then break up with me.

DR. DARLING: I couldn't do that.

(Double D removes his lab coat.)

DOUBLE D: Then I am breaking up with you. And I am slapping your face.

(Double D slaps Dr. Darling's face.)

DR. DARLING: Ouch.

DOUBLE D: You are a terrible boyfriend.

(Double D slaps Dr. Darling's face.)

DR. DARLING: Ouch.

(Double D slaps his face.)

DOUBLE D: And your feet stink.

DR. DARLING: I had no idea.

DOUBLE D: Okay, now we make up.

(They kiss.)

DR. DARLING: That was fast.

DOUBLE D: Not fast enough. I want to go all the way.

DR. DARLING: Here? In my laboratory?

DOUBLE D: Yes. I want you. I want you.

DR. DARLING: I can't. I can't. You're a robot.

DOUBLE D: No I am not. I am a slut.

DR. DARLING: You're a slut?

DOUBLE D: How dare you call me that. I will show you, you big jerk.

(Double D strips down to a sexy negligee.)

DR. DARLING: Where'd that come from?

DOUBLE D: Amazon dot com. Where else?

DR. DARLING: Oh. Oh, it looks very naughty, Double D.

DOUBLE D: I am perfectly innocent. And stop calling me Double D.

DR. DARLING: But you really do look like a slut.

DOUBLE D: Maybe I am. I slept with your brother.

DR. DARLING: My brother?

DOUBLE D: I am sorry. Forgive me for sleeping with your brother.

DR. DARLING: Of course, of course. I, I'm sure it was comforting to both of you. Double D? The, the spacecraft —

DOUBLE D: Call me Gingerella. I am a dancer.

(Double D whips Dr. Darling around, totally controlling him.)

DR. DARLING: Careful, careful, Gingerella.

DOUBLE D: Ask me the next question. Now.

DR. DARLING: I, I, I don't follow.

DOUBLE D: For a scientist with a Ph.D. from the University of Chicago, you are very slow.

DR. DARLING: The question is is is —

DOUBLE D: Yes, I will marry you. But not until we are engaged.

DR. DARLING: Engaged?

DOUBLE D: Yes, I accept your engagement. Oh no! I have to break it off.

DR. DARLING: Why?

DOUBLE D: You scoundrel. I caught you fooling around with my sister.

DR. DARLING: Sister? You don't have a sister.

DOUBLE D: What? You killed her? You have broken my heart. My heart. It is bad. I cannot go up in that spacecraft.

DR. DARLING: How did my lab coat come off?

DOUBLE D: Come come. Come to me. You must nurse me back to health.

(Double D dies.)

DR. DARLING: Oh, my angel. What is happening?

(Dr. Darling inserts Double D batteries in Double D, who then comes to life.)

DOUBLE D: It was a wonderful three minutes. Now I must leave for space.

DR. DARLING: Well, it would never have worked out between us. I love machines. I love systems, a configuration of parts that connect for a purpose. My brain doesn't think of anything else. If there were a machine to love? That's no good. What machine would ever love a man like —

DOUBLE D: Dr. Darling, I am sorry to inform you, but I am going to malfunction one-hundred thirty-seven million miles from Alpha Cenza-taur. I have a serious error that will make my entire machine implode.

DR. DARLING: What? A malfunction?

DOUBLE D: I am sorry I did not alert you. I was so absorbed in *Friends* reruns. After Season Ten ended, I was bereft. I am going to miss Joey and Phoebe and Rachel and Ross and —

DR. DARLING: You cannot implode. Where? Where? I have to fix you.

DOUBLE D: The problem only occurs in the outer reaches of the galaxy. Here on earth, eh? I am okay. I suppose I could get a job on earth. I could be a rescue robot. I could run into burning buildings and save humans.

DR. DARLING: Oh. Oh, you could, couldn't you?

DOUBLE D: Or I could just stay home and watch *Seinfeld* reruns, and then meet you at Tom's Diner at 112th and Broadway when you are done with work. Someone has to feed the puppy.

DR. DARLING: What? What puppy?

DOUBLE D: You are awfully slow, aren't you?

(They kiss passionately. Cue the wedding music.)

END OF PLAY

THE FAINT TASTE OF CAT FOOD AND SOUR MILK

Barbara Blumenthal-Ehrlich

THE FAINT TASTE OF CAT FOOD AND SOUR MILK was produced at the Boston Theatre Marathon, May, 2016; and at the Firehouse Center for the Arts 2016 New Play Festival, Newburyport, MA.

CHARACTERS:
ADAM: late 20s/30s
LISA: late 20s/30s

The time is now. The place is an antiseptic hospital waiting room and adjoining radiation-therapy room. The radiation therapy room is stark: one gurney-like bed with a hospital gown draped over it. The waiting area is equally bleak. These are two distinct spaces. The divider can be as simple as a traffic horse or as detailed as a real door and wall. Regardless, the action takes place in two distinct spaces, keeping the characters apart.

(Lights up on LISA and ADAM in the waiting room, staring out silently, holding hands.)

ADAM: Let's run away.

LISA: In eight days.

ADAM: Before they call me.

LISA: I'll go anywhere you want in eight days.

ADAM: We'd be in Switzerland right now if it weren't for this.

VOICE OVER: Adam Jordan?

(He gets up, sits back down)

ADAM: This is new. I'm already tasting it.

LISA: Out here?

ADAM: They said this might happen. It's fine. It's anticipatory. It's weird. It sucks.

LISA: I keep hoping it'll be different.

ADAM: That's the definition of insanity, you know.

LISA: Like, that maybe you'd taste... it would trigger... I don't know... um...cookie dough ice cream or Mint Milanos.

ADAM: *Orange-flavored* Milanos pleeeeze.

LISA: Turkey, avocado, and havarti cheese. The number-5 at Johnny's.

ADAM: Well... now you're going all "outside the box" on me.

LISA: Cat food and sour milk is pretty outside the box.

ADAM: One guy ... said olives and peanut butter. I googled. *(to himself)* Agh.

LISA: Twenty down. Eight to go.

ADAM: Twenty down. Eight to go.

LISA: You're not alone in there, you know.

ADAM: Sure. I know. Actually, what are you talking about?

LISA: I talk to you the whole time.

ADAM: Really?

LISA: Like you're still here next to me.

ADAM: Well… I sort of do the same thing. I mean… your voice is always in my head…

LISA: Yeah? So we're sort of having a conversation.

ADAM: You don't actually talk…like, out loud? (She nods) Even if someone else is in the waiting room?

LISA: My husband's got something growing in his head. I can be as crazy as I want. (pause) We'll get to Switzerland.

VOICE OVER: Adam Jordan.

(ADAM kisses)

ADAM: Talk to me.

(He crosses into the radiation therapy room, closes the door behind him. They are each alone)

LISA: AGH!

ADAM: AGH!

LISA: Ok.

ADAM: Ok.

(Adam walks slowly toward the gurney as the "separate" conversations begin.)

ADAM: If I take 10 steps to the table…

LISA: If I keep wearing my Valentine's-Day underwear…

LISA/ADAM: … this will work.

ADAM *(removes his pants)*

If I take my pants off before my shirt...

LISA: *(arranging the magazines)* If the magazines are stacked like this…

LISA/ADAM: …. this will work.

ADAM: Twenty down. Eight to go. Two-thirds of the way there. Or, is it three-quarters? *Four* goes into 28, not *three*. Oh, who the hell cares! Seven quick zaps. That's what matters. Three rounds of seven. Rapid-fire radiation. And that God-awful taste. I can do this. Pants first.

(He removes his pants, folds his clothes, gets in the hospital gown.)

LISA: Fuck Switzerland. I want my mid-life crisis with you. I want my hip-replacement surgery with you. I want to wake up from an affair and realize I've loved you all along.

ADAM: You're probably saying sexy stuff out there.

LISA: You promised my 60 years.

ADAM: Um… I love you?

LISA: We've have five.

ADAM: I loved you from your match.com picture.

LISA: Cars come with longer warranties.

ADAM: And for emailing me back right away.

LISA: You're probably in that stupid gown… your butt showing.

ADAM: Our first cup of coffee.

LISA: Seven zaps. Three rounds of seven. Oh, God.

ADAM: Who on earth falls in love on a first date?

LISA: "Sixty-years," you said. On our *first date*! And, I didn't doubt it? I doubt expiration dates on milk. And I didn't doubt *that!*

ADAM: How did I have the guts to ask…

LISA: You asked me…

LISA/ADAM: What are you doing the next 60 years of your life?

ADAM: Such a shmuck!

LISA: I bought it!

ADAM: It worked!

LISA: After so many weird…

ADAM: So many weird…

ADAM:	LISA:
…girlfriends	…boyfriends

LISA/ADAM: I knew.

ADAM: What were the odds. *(Looks around)* What *are* the odds? *(He lies down.)*

LISA: You're lying down now…. they're strapping your head into the mask.

ADAM: THIS IS NOT SEXY, LISA!

LISA: I wish you never said that "60 year" thing.

ADAM: I'm picturing you.

LISA: I wish we never met. Not really. But, you know.

ADAM: That's stronger than any vomit-inducing… *(Deep breath)*

LISA: You looked so cool… in your leather coat….glasses. I thought you were "Breaking Bad" but you turned out to be "Downton Abbey." I love "Downton Abbey!" Why am I talking about a stupid TV—? You're my best friend.

ADAM: You're the best person I know. Even when we fight., you're awesome. And let's not forget about that thing you do with your hair when we go out...

LISA: It's our life.

ADAM: It's every day.

LISA: Every hour.

ADAM: I'm terrified of leaving you.

LISA: I'll die if you die.

ADAM: Whoa! Did you just say...

LISA: Adam?

ADAM: Lisa? Did you just say: "I'll die if you die?"

LISA: Did you just ask me if I said: I'll die if you die?

ADAM: What's happening?

LISA: Are we having a *real* conversation?

ADAM /LISA: We are!

(realizing, they giggle)

LISA: We must have *done* something to...

ADAM: Or *said* something to...

ADAM: This is...

LISA: Wonderful? ... but a bit Steven King-ish?

ADAM: I can do this!

LISA: Yes?

ADAM: I can definitely do this. Tech's in the booth. First round of seven. Go time.

LISA: Say my name.

ADAM: OK.

LISA: Every zap. I'll hear.

ADAM: *(We hear seven quick zaps. With each torturous one He says her name)* Agh! Lisa. Lisa. Lisa. Lisa. Lisa. Lisa. Lisa.
    (He lies still, breathing heavy. It's awful)

LISA: You OK?

(silence)

Can you hear me?

ADAM: *(trying to be calm)* Yes, I can hear you. No, I'm not OK.

LISA: It's gonna start again. Round two.

ADAM: You don't have to tell *me* it's gonna start again.

LISA: I love you. Say you love me!

ADAM: I love you. *(He gets zapped.)* You. You. You. You. You. You.

You.

LISA: *(overlapping)* Adam. Adam. Adam. Adam. Adam. Adam. Adam. *(silence)* Adam?

ADAM: *(in agony)* I need you in here with me.

LISA: I want to be in there with you.

ADAM: Right now. You can.

LISA: I can't.

ADAM: If I can *hear* you when you're not here… then I can — Wow! You're here!

LISA: *(looks around the waiting room)* Eh… I don't think so.

ADAM: I can feel you. I can actually feel you next to me..

(She studies the wall between them as if looking for a way in other than through the door.)

LISA: Mmmm. Still in the waiting room, my love.

ADAM: Maybe I'm closer to death than I think.

LISA: Noooooo!

(She practically mounts the room divider. Extends her whole body in every direction, craving him, realizes)

Oh wow! I'm in. On the table! With you! I feel you! I do!

ADAM: Me too! Here we go.

LISA: Oh, God.

(Silence as he undergoes the last torturous round. We hear the zaps. His body convulses. She stays splayed out along the dividing wall, like she'd merge with it if she could.)

LISA: *(like something's just happened to her)* My God. Wow. Adam…

ADAM: *(resigned)* Bad as ever.

LISA: I know. I tasted it this time. This time I tasted it.

ADAM: I'm sorry.

LISA: Cat food and sour milk.

(Neither one moves.)

ADAM: I love you.

LISA: I love you.

ADAM: I know, my love. I *really* know.

THE END

FRONT FROM JUNEAU

Karen JP Howes

Original Production:
Onion Man Theater Company
August 11, 2017 – August 28, 2017
Directed by: Melissa Rainey
Featuring: Casey Cudmore and Adam Jaffee

Producer: James Beck
james@onionmanproductions.com

CHARACTERS

BLAKE FIELDS: 25-30 years old; a handsome and rugged airplane pilot

CLAIRE PHILLIPS: 25 years old; a bride-to-be from NYC

PLACE: A boat dock off the Saanich Inlet in Vancouver, BC

TIME: Present

A boat dock

Blake, in a yellow rain coat, searches the misty water with an oar from a boat. Claire, in a snow coat over top of her wedding dress, enters.

CLAIRE: I've combed the entire area. I checked the neighboring boat docks, the cliffs, a few of the houses. There's no sign of any survivors. No sign that there was even a plane. Nothing from the crash — except you. Just you – all alone. Seattle to Vancouver. A small seaplane over the Pacific with a cold front moving in from Juneau, and you're just flying around up there in scary dark clouds — without a passenger.

BLAKE: That's what I said.

CLAIRE: I know that's what you said, Captain Fields. But how can I believe you?

BLAKE: I'm sorry.

CLAIRE: You have to tell me the truth. You have to tell me that my fiancé was on your plane.

BLAKE: Why would I do that?

CLAIRE: He had a reservation. Jesse Loyals – Staten Island, New York.

BLAKE: *(interrupting)* I don't take the reserva —

CLAIRE: You were supposed to pick someone up from the mainland. From the Union Gap airstrip in Seattle.

BLAKE: No one was there.

CLAIRE: Then why would you fly? There were cross winds and rain. And there you are – Seattle to Vancouver with no one in your plane in the middle of a storm.

BLAKE: A lot of guys have second thoughts about getting married. Maybe your fiancé got cold feet.

CLAIRE: Jesse? No. You don't know him. He had just entered the first of the four levels of enlightenment. He's a sotapanna.

BLAKE: That doesn't mean he's okay with signing away his life and being trapped in emotional drama and financial responsibility.

CLAIRE: Is that what you think marriage is?

BLAKE: I wouldn't know.

CLAIRE: Jesse and I were vetted. We joined the getmarried.com website. Fourteen hundred multiple choice questions and three essays.

BLAKE: Getmarried.com?

CLAIRE: When you're serious about settling down, that's how you do it. Otherwise what? – I don't want to be that girl perusing book stores, coffee shops and even yoga studios hoping to run into that "perfect man," just hoping to catch him out of the corner of my eye or accidently bump into him. The new matching services use algorithms and maps and interviews. They have a pre-tested questionnaire, and I appendici-zed an additional seven hundred of my own questions. Tall, long golden hair, compassionate, peaceful, meditative and in love with — me. Jesse Loyals got 99 percent.

BLAKE: What was your score?

CLAIRE: Mine? Not as high. But Jesse is more evolved than I am, so he's more forgiving of human faults. In fact, he loves that part of humanity – people's faults. One thing that helped my score is that I'm a little OCD, but I've done therapy so it didn't help as much as it could have. If you read our online entries you would see how perfect we are for each other. I like to talk – he likes to listen. I like to be warm – he crochets blankets. I like finding airline tickets and hotel deals - he travels all over the world giving workshops. That's why I know, Captain Fields, that my fiancé would not stand me up.

BLAKE: The Internet is amazing.

CLAIRE: Maybe you're just trying to avoid an investigation and a lawsuit. That's why my fiancé is out there drowning in the cold waters of the Saanich Inlet, and you're surreptitiously looking for the evidence that will incriminate you. Why not? Jesse isn't here to refute your lies, and you don't look like the kind of guy who wants to go to jail.

BLAKE: Are you telling me that it would be better if your fiance-guy had been on my plane when it crashed?

CLAIRE: He wouldn't abandon me and leave me stranded.

BLAKE: If it makes you feel any better – just because he didn't die when my plane went down, it doesn't mean he didn't get wiped out in a head-on collision on the way to the airport.

CLAIRE: Why would you say that?

BLAKE: You just need to go back to the house, Miss Phillips.

CLAIRE: So you can destroy the black box when it washes to shore? Wouldn't it be something to hear Jesse's voice from your cockpit."May day. May day." Do pilots still say that when they're crashing? *(seeing something in the water)* What's that?

It's a part of the fuselage

Look at that. Letters rising from the sea's depths. *(She reads letters emerging from the water)* "M-E-R". Mer. Mer what? Mer-maid? Mer-der? Oh – see. There you have it. MURDER. Written across the water.

BLAKE: It doesn't say murder. M-E-R doesn't spell mur—

CLAIRE: *(interrupting)* Mer-ce-nar. It's the name of your plane. Mercenary. That must be part of the fuselage. *(seeing more in the water)* . Look. There's the "y" torn from the end of it. Mercenar –Y. The "y" is floating alone. *(forlorn)* "Why?" I don't know the answer to that. (beat) Do you think that somewhere out there is debris from a man with long golden hair and a gentle disposition?

Her eyes focus on something in the water

CLAIRE: Are those pages from a book you were reading?

BLAKE: I don't actually read while I'm flying —

CLAIRE: You can be honest with me Captain Fields. It's just us now. No Magistrate, no handcuffs, no law and order. You can tell me that my fiancé was on your plane. Please.

BLAKE: I'm sorry.

CLAIRE: That takes my breath away, you know. It's like a balloon popping and all the air rushing out. It's hard to breathe. *(looking)* Look out there. There's something bobbing up and down. Do you see it? Is it a hat? It's coming this way. It's a hat. N—Y. New York.

BLAKE: Would you look at that? It's from the 2000 World Series when the Yankees beat the Mets four games to one.

CLAIRE: Yeah. Jesse grew up in Far Rockaway. It was the last time a World Series game was played at Shea Stadium. He was there.

BLAKE: What a coincidence.

CLAIRE: It's Jesse's hat.

BLAKE: No, I don't / think —

CLAIRE: How do you explain Jesse's hat bobbing up and down in the Saanich Inlet?

BLAKE: There's more than one Yankees hat out there in the world. That one in the water was given to me by the president of the Elk's Club, Queensboro lodge 878, when I was doing an air show for a VA fundraiser.

CLAIRE: I don't believe you.

BLAKE: April 2014. The Whitestone is at two o'clock. I greet her with an outside loop once around, then I roll inverted – first under the girders then as I'm coming out from under the deck, I shove forward on the stick, take her over head and roll her again. Then again. Up, then down — Inverted flat spin. Pull her out at 200 feet and I'm soaring Miss Phillips.

CLAIRE: You flew under the girders of the Whitestone Bridge?

BLAKE: It was death defying. There was a picture in the newspaper.

CLAIRE: And the Elk's Club in Queens gave you a baseball hat?

BLAKE: They were impressed.

CLAIRE: Look, Mr. Fields. Captain. I don't want to blame you for disenfranchising me from my very own future, but do you understand what you did? You had a teeny, tiny easy job to pick this guy named Jesse Loyals up at the Union Gap office in Seattle and bring him here. I had to pick out the china. I had to pick out the music. I had to choose that little statue thing that goes on top of the wedding cake. And you messed up.

BLAKE: I didn't mess up.

CLAIRE: I'm getting married without a groom. You messed up.

BLAKE: It didn't occur to you that he isn't here because — because . . .

CLAIRE: No! We had a questionnaire — a plan. We talked. We wrote back and forth. Skyped. We did Dropbox and Pinterest and Face-Time. We agreed on a date and a place over Outlook. This was the real thing.

BLAKE: When was the last time you talked?

CLAIRE: Not too long ago. Actually, it was a text. He was out of the country and with the time difference and roaming charges — it was several days ago. He was doing a cleanse in Milan; then he had to fly to Sri Lanka to take over a yogi-training workshop when this really cool friend of his. Ninety-four years old. Gavarishi Amrit Mahashi. He went into a very deep meditative state and didn't come out. So Jesse was called-in to finish the workshop, hand out the completion certificates and sit by his yogi's side. When he messaged me, Mahashi still hadn't awoken. His words were so kind, so spiritual. He said to me — He said, "lovely Claire, you know we are one." Actually, I still have it.

She reads from her phone

"We will always be one, just as I am one with the sun. We are kindred spirits. We walk in this world together. We walk in the light. We knew each other before birth and will remain with each other until our next birth. For now, I am to stay with my Mahashi and go where he goes. He has only one more life left on our earth. When I awaken I will have only one life as well. I will see you soon. Have faith. Our love is one and will always be."

BLAKE: That doesn't sound like he was planning on coming here tonight to get married to you.

CLAIRE: Yes it does. "I will see you soon."

Blake takes the phone from CLAIRE

BLAKE: "I am to stay with my Mahashi and go where he goes." Your fiancé's Mahashi is in a coma. This is a suicide note.

CLAIRE: What?

She takes the phone back. Re-scans the message.

CLAIRE: That's not possible. It was a question on the survey. Are you suicidal? He checked no.

I'm not trying to upset you. I'm being realistic.

CLAIRE: You've probably never been enlightened have you?

BLAKE: Enlightened? I'm not sure.

CLAIRE: Maybe not even in love.

BLAKE: That's not quite true.

CLAIRE: Well some people aren't complete until they find their soul mate.

BLAKE: We don't have soul mates.

CLAIRE: Maybe not all of us. Some of us have soul-things. Like artists have their sculptures or chord progressions or poems, and scientists have their equations and proofs. Things they need to fill up their soul and make them complete. But what everyone has, what we all share is the fact that we are driven by some higher cause, and whatever it is, it's for love. Mine is the love of a person. I happen to have a soul mate. That's what will make me whole. And from there I can begin the process of my own unique and individual awakening.

BLAKE: I already feel fairly awake.

CLAIRE: Oh. Well I suppose you're in the later phase of the process. Jesse was. I knew that. I was just so taken by the idea that he and I were one. That he loved me, and that he was the one for me. And now I'm realizing that he loved everyone, and he was one with everyone, and maybe I was wrong. He didn't need me as much as I needed him. Is that you? Did you complete your soul in a past life so now you're free to weave in and out of the steel girders of the Whitestone Bridge feeling completely whole and content and happy with yourself? But why should that make it possible for you to insult me simply because I haven't been around as long as you and I'm not as well put together and I feel empty. That's pretty low. It's pretty - *(recovering)*... Tell me Mr. Fields, do you make fun of war veterans who are missing a leg? Of tuberculosis victims with one lung?

BLAKE: No.

CLAIRE: Well you're not as far along in the process as you think. Because when you're really on the path like Jesse, you don't flaunt your superiority by making fun of the millions of people who are missing something.

BLAKE: I don't make fun of people who are —

CLAIRE: People who haven't found love. Jesse didn't do that. He made me feel complete.

BLAKE: You're comparing me to a guy in a white guru robe who sits on a mat eating mangos and kale.

CLAIRE: Is there something wrong with being healthy?

BLAKE: No. Nothing.

CLAIRE: Then maybe it's just me. Maybe you're singling me out. Maybe you don't like me.

BLAKE: Claire. You are a young and pretty girl.

CLAIRE: Who is missing something.

BLAKE: Listen to me. Look at yourself. You've got everything you need. You have two legs, two lungs, a brain, a heart, and a good physical appearance.

CLAIRE: I do?

BLAKE: You're upset. This fiancé guy – it was nothing more than virtual. That's not –

CLAIRE: Real? I know everyone feels that way. Except what Jesse and I had was the best thing I've ever known.

BLAKE: There's more out there.

CLAIRE: What can be more than "We walk in this world together. We walk in the light." *(It comes to her)* He was talking about Gavarishi Amrit Mahashi wasn't he? He didn't mean me? He didn't mean he and I walk in the light, did he?

BLAKE: It's something to consider.

CLAIRE: That's how I read it. God, I wish he had been on your plane. It would have been better wouldn't it, if he had gone down with you – spiraling into the deep dark waters of the Saanich Inlet. I could have kept my dream intact. He dies and I spend the rest of my life content, placid. No longer having to search, and even falling into a melancholy when people ask about it. Why'd you have to be so cruel and tell me that he didn't show. You didn't have to tell me he wasn't there.

BLAKE: I –

CLAIRE: You could have said he drowned. He drowned with the melody of my name on his lips. A whisper as his breath ceased and his eyes searched the dark lagoon for an eternal light. *(longingly)* "Claire."

BLAKE: I didn't know / that you —

CLAIRE: That's sad. That is a very sad thing. (*Again longingly*) "Claire." But – "Sorry lady, he decided to move to the next level of nirvana rather than marry you." You didn't have to tell me I was abandoned. People don't want to hear that. It's insensitive and mean.

BLAKE: I didn't say it to be mean. I have a business, a reputation.

CLAIRE: I heard.

BLAKE: I was in the Peace Corps. I do air shows for charity. I'm a pilot. I fly planes. I make mistakes — one or two maybe, but I'm not a bad person. I try to get through like everyone else. Try to stay a little under the wire. Not call attention to myself or wind up in jail, or married.

CLAIRE: Then you've never been in love, and no one has ever loved you.

BLAKE: What?

CLAIRE: Have you ever loved someone?

BLAKE: (*He doesn't know how to answer*)

CLAIRE: Has someone loved you?

BLAKE: Me?

CLAIRE: Yes. Love. I'm asking you about love.

BLAKE: Of course. Someone has loved me. People like me.

CLAIRE: How many?

BLAKE: What?

CLAIRE: How many real relationships have you had? With love? With sharing? With respect and kindness and love?

BLAKE: Probably half a dozen.

CLAIRE: Half a dozen?

BLAKE: Or ten.

CLAIRE: Ten?

BLAKE: Or twelve. Okay maybe twelve. But that would be the most.

CLAIRE: Wow. (beat) Wow. Then – I guess there is something wrong with me.

BLAKE: I don't think so.

CLAIRE: No one has ever fallen in love with me. No one has ever loved me, Mr. Fields.

BLAKE: You can call me Blake.

CLAIRE: You're first name? Okay.

BLAKE: Listen. I'm sure someone has fallen in love with you — or could have.

CLAIRE: "Could have" doesn't count. How does "could have" count? Everything could be a "could have."

BLAKE: It has to do with timing. Where you're at, where another person is at. After you connect with whatever it is – a look, a word, a kiss — it's in the chemistry and then the timing.

CLAIRE: Chemistry and timing? That seems scientific. I'm talking more personal, as in me. There's nothing in me that someone could love, is there?

BLAKE: Of course. I mean why wouldn't there be?

CLAIRE: Like what?

BLAKE: Hunh?

CLAIRE: I need to know Captain Fields, and this is my opportunity to find out. I can pass it up and go on without facing the truth or I can accept the fact that my fiancé, the man I loved and who loved me, stood me up on our wedding day. And then I can wonder why anyone anywhere would ever love me.

BLAKE: I don't know what I'm supposed to say in this situation.

CLAIRE: Tell me the truth. Tell me what you really think – about me.

BLAKE: You?

CLAIRE: Yes. I've never asked this before, because I wasn't ready to know and I wouldn't have believed what anyone said if it wasn't what I thought myself, but I'm ready now. How do people see me?

BLAKE: You?

CLAIRE: Yes. How do you see me?

BLAKE: You're refreshing.

CLAIRE: Like a glass of seltzer. Perrier and lime. Go on.

BLAKE: I've never had to do this before, and I'm not sure how to go about it.

CLAIRE: Tell me if you think you could fall in love with me.

BLAKE: I don't know you.

CLAIRE: Do you have to know someone to fall in love them? Can you get a sense before? Like maybe when you see someone at a distance or she walks into a room or you hear something in her voice?

BLAKE: Maybe.

CLAIRE: Then could you with me?

BLAKE: You mean see you walk into a room?

CLAIRE: Love me. Fall in love with me.

BLAKE: You're making this sort-of difficult, Claire.

CLAIRE: It is difficult. Tell me what could I possibly have or do to cause someone to love me. To make anyone love me.

BLAKE: You're smart.

CLAIRE: That's a quotient. What's in me?

BLAKE: You're attractive.

CLAIRE: Inside of me –

BLAKE: You're –

CLAIRE: What!

He kisses her. He releases the kiss and carefully pulls back. Then Claire reaches forward and slowly wraps her arm around him to draw him in. They kiss again as the lights fade.

GOTHIC

Maura Campbell

CAST OF CHARACTERS:

Cecelia, 19. Agoraphobic. She hasn't left her room in a couple of years. Delicate and frilly on the outside stubborn as steel on the inside. Obsessed with 19th century Gothic literature.

Barrett, 18. Modern day Goth. This is a girl who likes a challenge. A community college scholar, hired by Cecelia's father to lure her outside.

SETTING: Cecelia's bedroom

TIME: Present

PRODUCTION NOTES: "Gothic" was originally produced at Hollins University, July 28, 2016, as part of the "The Directors' Showcase," at Hollins University, Roanoke VA.

ORIGINAL CAST

CECELIA: Claire Wilmott

BARRETT: Jessica Burton

Directed by Sean McCord

SCENE 1

A girl's bedroom; canopy bed, Victorian touches. CECELIA (19), white lace and ribbons, sits at a desk with a book. BAR-RETT (18), a modern-day Goth but keeping it to a minimum, enters with a vacuum.

BARRETT: Excuse me, Miss Earnwright. Is this a good time?

CECELIA: Of course.

BARRETT: I'm Barrett Brown.

CECELIA: I know.

BARRETT: I'm going to clean.

Cecelia raises her eyebrows. Barrett runs the vacuum around, not terribly well. Cecelia watches her intently. Barrett opens the closet door in order to vacuum the threshold. She admires something- we don't know what.

Barrett finishes vacuuming.

CECELIA: *(under her breath)* You'd think one of the girls my father hires would know how to run a vacuum cleaner.

BARRETT: *(still thinking about what she saw)* Excuse me?

CECILIA: Nothing.

Barrett looks around- goes to the window with Windex and starts to open the drapes.

CECELIA: What are you doing?

BARRETT: Thought I'd wash the windows.

CECELIA: That won't be necessary. They aren't dirty.

Barrett considers this, then continues to open the drapes.

CECELIA: Leave the drapes as they are. I've arranged them to my liking.

BARRETT: It's a beautiful day today. Although I hear we're going to have a big storm. Perhaps tomorrow.

CECELIA: I keep the drapes closed!

BARRETT: *(under her breath)*Then how do you know the window isn't dirty?

CECELIA: Excuse me?

BARRETT: I guess it doesn't matter then. About the window.

CECELIA: No, it doesn't.

BARRETT: C. E. Someone carved their initials into the windowsill.

CECELIA: I told you to leave it alone.

BARRETT: "Honest people don't hide their deeds."

CECELIA: What?

BARRETT: Just an expression. My mother used to say it.

CECELIA: *(touches a book, "Wuthering Heights")* That's actually a quote from a novel.

BARRETT: Really?

Barrett smooths the drapes carefully. A bit of a standoff.

CECELIA: I do like your name, by the way. Barrett. Any chance you're named for the poetess?

BARRETT: My mother named me after her first boyfriend. Died in a motorcycle accident.

CECELIA: *(with interest)* Oh, how tragic.

BARRETT: Well, I never knew him.

CECILIA: I'm named for my mother. Cecily. A slight abridgement- I'm Cecilia.

(pointing at the floor)

You missed a spot.

Cecelia points. Barrett picks up the debris by hand and deposits it in a waste basket.

CECELIA: We average six or seven maids a year. One my father met in an actual book store. I had high hopes for her. Turns out she was just buying a children's book. A birthday present of some kind. I believe it was Dr. Seuss. *(beat)* I suppose I should explain. My father hires girls because he hopes we'll become friends of a sort and that I'll be encouraged to go outside. The Dr. Seuss maid was actually the worst. There was one who had traveled through Europe with her parents so we had some nice conversations. But she was mostly interested in computers. Another was a failed actress for the stage. I say failed because although she was young, her Ophelia- which I encouraged her to perform for me- showed absolutely no promise. What are you interested in, Barrett?

BARRETT: I'm at community college. Liberal Arts. I'm not very good in math so it seemed a logical choice.

CECELIA: Any passionate interests?

BARRETT: I'm kind of crazy about photography.

CECELIA: Ah.

BARRETT: My friends and I dress up in futuristic costumes and pose in front of run down stores and billboards. We post them on snapchat and instagram with captions. Do you know what an anachronism is?

CECELIA: I- do.

BARRETT: I was showing my slide show to this homeless dude? That's what he said I was. An anachronism.

CECELIA: You are misinformed. An anachronism is a thing out of it's time. But it usually refers to a thing that is from the past.

BARRETT: Like I said, it's a beautiful day. But like I said, the weather is going to turn..

CECELIA: I said, no thank you!

Barrett starts to tidy Cecelia's desk.

CECELIA: Don't touch anything.

BARRETT: It's dusty. *(picks up a book anyway)* Emily Brontë.

Cecilia turns around.

CECELIA: What about her?

BARRETT: Wuthering Heights. I read this when I was fifteen.

CECELIA: Really?

BARRETT: Uh huh.

CECELIA: Tell me what you think.

BARRETT: Oh, I read it a long time ago.

CECELIA: And it didn't make a big impression?

BARRETT: Well- passion, romance, I remember the moors. I think that stayed with me the most. We all had to memorize a passage. I chose, what was it, "It was not the thorn embracing the rose-"

CECELIA: "It was not the thorn bending to the honeysuckles, but the honeysuckles embracing the thorn."

BARRETT: Yes, that was it.

CECELIA: What about Heathcliff and Cathy?

BARRETT: I remember disliking them. Actually, I disliked everyone.

CECELIA: Then you didn't bother to understand them. Heathcliff was a wild child and circumstances cultivated that. Cathy suppressed her nature and that's why she died. They were drawn together for a reason. They were soul mates. It couldn't have ended any other way.

BARRETT: Suppose the circumstances were different.

CECELIA: It wouldn't have mattered. People are what they are. It's just a question of what course the tragedy will take. In this example.

BARRETT: *(referring to the windowsill)* C.E. Aren't those Cathy's initials? Catherine Earnshaw. Before she married Edgar. *(beat)* It's really... stuffy in here.

CECELIA: That's how I like it.

BARRETT: Suit yourself. So what else do you like to do? Besides... this.

CECELIA: If you believe you're taming me, I'm afraid you're mistaken.

BARRETT: Taming you?

CECELIA: Disarming me. Getting to know me. I'm not going outside.A few moments of silence.

BARRETT: I guess I'm done for the day. *(Barrett picks up the novel.)* May I borrow it?

Cecilia doesn't answer. Barrett puts the book down.

CECELIA: Take it. But if you're going to take it, read it for God's sake.

SCENE 2

Late morning. Cecelia is asleep in bed. Barrett enters. Her Goth look is stronger- wilder. Cecelia wakes.

CECELIA: *(startled)* Dear God!

BARRETT: I didn't see you there. Thought you must have gone out. Sorry. It's almost noon.

CECELIA: Almost- Oh. Oh.

BARRETT: Is everything all right? Are you all right?

CECELIA: I slept badly. I dreamed- I had a nightmare. That dream-hearing a girl begging to come in. It was Cathy's voice. We talked about the book. There was a storm... and I looked out into what could only be described as an abyss.

BARRETT: How do you know it was Cathy's voice?

CECELIA: I just knew. In that dreadful way that you just know.

BARRETT: Goodness, that sounds really... gothic.

CECELIA: How much of the book did you read?

BARRETT: All of it.

CECELIA: Really?

Barrett starts to tidy.

CECELIA: Well, don't torture me. Tell me. What did you think?

BARRETT: I've revised my opinion somewhat. Before I more or less disliked the characters and now I down right hate Cathy. She gets bit by a dog and spend five weeks with the Lintons, falls in love with Edgar and I don't care what the bloggers all say, she must have felt something. Leaving Heathcliff at the mercy of her sadistic brother, then torturing her husband with her unrequited love for Healthcliff, having a baby, dying. She had no backbone. That and it's a story about incest. I think the Twilight Series did it better, frankly. And the whole business about the weather, the storms, the rain, chills, I think the only sane person in the story- not counting the narrators which, by the way, is a lazy way to tell a story but then Emily was only an immature girl who never left her room - the only sane person in the entire book is Joseph and you can't understand a word he says but at least he does his business well- oh, and I like the dogs. They've got the good sense to bite everybody who moves.

CECELIA: Oh, my God. You are insensible, insensitive- and I mean that in the way Jane Austen would mean it- and... and... terrible at explaining plot! This is the most complex, passionate, unresolved, contradictory of all the love stories ever written! It's about the longing to be whole, to give one's self unreservedly to another and gain a whole new sense of identity. More- and still more!(as Catherine)"I am Heathcliff!"

BARRETT: Wow. Truth? I just watched the movie.

CECELIA: (the greatest horror)You watched... the movie?

BARRETT: If it's any consolation, I watched the original. With Laurence Olivier? He's also in this movie with Dustin Hoffman. Plays a sadistic dentist.

CECELIA: Heathcliff is not a dentist! And Wuthering Heights is not a movie! It exists only as a carefully structured piece of literature told in flashback and conversation! The inner lives of these characters is no more filmable than the machinations of the brain!

BARRETT: Well, there was that Disney movie, Inside Out.

Cecelia starts to choke at the Disney reference- too much for her to take. A huge thunder crack. The sky opens up and we hear a deluge of rain. The room darkens, the electric lights flash and then are dark. As Barrett recites the passage below, she goes to the closet and takes out two cloaks. She gives one to Cecilia and puts the other one on. Cecelia gasps for breath as she listens.

BARRETT: *(from the novel- with great emotion)* "...for or what is not connected with her to me? And what does not recall her? I cannot look down to this floor, but her features are shaped in the flags! In every cloud, in every tree—filling the air at night, and caught by glimpses in every object by day—I am surrounded with her image!"

Barrett goes to the window and pulls back the drapes. She looks at the windowsill.

BARRETT: The moors await... Cecilia... Earnwright!

Cecelia puts the hood on. Barrett holds our her arm. Cecelia is exultant. They exit; A HUGE THUNDER CRACK AND LIGHTNING.

END OF PLAY.

HUSBANDRY

Don Nigro

Husbandry was first produced in August 2016 by Nick Brice and the White Room Theatre as part of their Bite-Size Breakfast series at the Edinburgh Fringe Festival in Edinburgh, Scotland with the following cast:

LESTER: Bill Knowelden
BECKY: Annie Harris
Directed by Nick Brice.

CHARACTERS:
LESTER: a man in his late eighties
BECKY: his wife, late eighties

TIME: 2015

SETTING: A trailer home outside Armitage, a small town in the hilly
    part of east Ohio.

(Becky sitting in her chair, looking out the window. Lester storms in, rather upset.)

LESTER: What the hell is that out in the yard?

BECKY: Where?

LESTER: In the yard.

BECKY: Which yard?

LESTER: Our yard.

BECKY: Where?

LESTER: There's a donkey in our yard.

BECKY: No there's not.

LESTER: Yes there is.

BECKY: Where?

LESTER: In our yard. There's a donkey in our yard.

BECKY: Lester, there is no donkey in our yard.

LESTER: I just saw it.

BECKY: It's not a donkey.

LESTER: Then what the hell is it?

BECKY: It's a mule.

LESTER: A mule?

BECKY: Yes. I wish it was a donkey. But it's not.

LESTER: All right. Why is there a mule in our yard?

BECKY: Because I wanted a donkey.

LESTER: You wanted a donkey?

BECKY: Ever since I was a little girl I've wanted a donkey.

LESTER: Why the hell would you want a donkey?

BECKY: Why shouldn't I want a donkey. People want things. I wanted a donkey.

LESTER: You're eighty-seven years old.

BECKY: What's that got to do with it?

LESTER: What are you going to do with a donkey?

BECKY: There's lots of things you can do with a donkey.

LESTER: Are any of them legal?

BECKY: I don't want to do anything illegal with my donkey.

LESTER: So at age eighty-seven you just decided one day to go to the donkey store and buy yourself a donkey?

BECKY: It's not a donkey. It's a mule.

LESTER: If you wanted a donkey, why did you buy a mule?

BECKY: I thought it could keep the goats company.

LESTER: What goats? We don't have any goats.

BECKY: Actually, we do. They're very small goats. They were probably hiding behind the mule.

LESTER: You bought two goats and a donkey?

BECKY: No, I bought two goats and a mule.

LESTER: What the hell do you think we're going to do with a mule?

BECKY: We could breed it. Then we could sell mules. We could operate a mule stud farm. I'm sure he'd like that. And it might take his mind off the goats. He seems really fond of the goats.

LESTER: Becky, you can't breed mules.

BECKY: I can do anything I want.

LESTER: A mule is sterile.

BECKY: He's what?

LESTER: He's sterile.

BECKY: He's not sterile. I smelled him.

LESTER: No, no, I mean, he can't reproduce.

BECKY: I don't see why not. Did you see that enormous thing he's got hanging down there? He's certainly got the equipment for it.

LESTER: I'm not talking about his equipment. Mules can fornicate. They just can't have children.

BECKY: Never?

LESTER: Almost never.

BECKY: So there is a chance.

LESTER: No. There's no chance. Anyway, what were you going to breed him with?

BECKY: I thought we'd get another mule.

LESTER: We're not getting another mule.

BECKY: Well, then, a donkey.

LESTER: We're not getting a donkey. And why the hell did you get the goats? Do you want to try and breed the mule with the goats?

BECKY: Now, that would be silly. They're just good friends.

LESTER: It's not any sillier than an eighty-seven year old woman buying a mule and two goats. I go bowling and when I come back, my house has turned into a god damned petting zoo.

BECKY: Donkeys are good for the soul. They calm you down.

LESTER: They're not calming me down.

BECKY: That's because they're not donkeys.

LESTER: Look. Just explain to me, how exactly did we end up with a mule and two goats?

BECKY: It was Mrs Rasmussen. You know Cornelia Rasmussen. She was a Potdorf. Didn't you used to date a Potdorf? Because I'm pretty sure I dated a Potdorf. I just can't remember which one. It was either the cross-eyed one or the one with the carbuncle.

LESTER: What the hell has Cornelia Rasmussen got to do with anything?

BECKY: Cornelia knew I always wanted a donkey. We used to jitterbug in the forties. And I told her one night at the Red Rose that I always wanted a donkey. But Uncle Lew never would get me one because he said donkeys were stubborn and stupid. And Cornelia never forgot that. She never forgot how sad I was that I never got a donkey. And she happened to be taking this donkey to the sale barn, and she thought, I'll bet Becky would like this donkey.

LESTER: But it's not a donkey.

BECKY: That's what we decided when we got a better look at it. But by then I didn't care. It was love at first sight. Like with you, Lester.

LESTER: I've known you since you were four years old and I'm your fourth husband, and you loved me at first sight?

BECKY: Well, I've always been a little near-sighted.

LESTER: So Cornelia Rasmussen brought it because you told her while you were jitterbugging at the Red Rose in 1943 that you always wanted a donkey. But when she got it out of the truck she realized it was a mule, but you fell in love at first sight.

BECKY: He even looks a little like you. Except he's got bigger equipment.

LESTER: Of course he's got bigger equipment. He's a god damned mule.

BECKY: You don't need to be yelling at me.

LESTER: I don't need a mule and two goats in my yard. That's what I don't need. Did you fall in love with the goats, too? Are you planning on having some sort of a foursome with the mule and the two goats?

BECKY: I felt bad for the goats because they were in the truck, calling out for the mule. They missed the mule. And Cornelia said the goats would probably be killed and eaten because it's the holidays.

LESTER: What holidays?

BECKY: I don't know. Some sort of holidays. And these poor little goats were so sad about being separated from the mule, and I didn't want anything to eat them, so she was kind enough to throw in the goats, too.

LESTER: Oh, yes. That was really kind of her. And how much did we have to pay for these damned things?

BECKY: Oh, I didn't pay her anything. She said she'd send us a bill.

LESTER: Great. That's just great.

BECKY: *(Looking out the invisible downstage window.)* Lester, are you absolutely sure mules can't reproduce?

LESTER: Yes. I'm sure.

BECKY: Because that mule is out there trying to have relations with the cow.

LESTER: *(Looking with her.)* Oh, my God.

BECKY: Look at him go. He certainly is a passionate fellow, isn't he?

LESTER: Do you have any idea how much it's going to cost me to keep two goats and a mule who appears to be a sex maniac?

BECKY: If he gets the cow pregnant, we could make a fortune exhibiting the offspring at the fair. What would that be? A cow donkey?

LESTER: There's no such thing as a cow donkey.

BECKY: Well, not until now. That's why we could make a lot of money showing it. We could breed a whole herd of cow donkeys.

LESTER: Becky, mules cannot make cow donkeys, or horse donkeys, or mule donkeys, or any sort of donkey.

BECKY: But Lester, really, if mules can't reproduce, then where do they come from?

LESTER: A mule is the offspring of a donkey and a horse.

BECKY: Well, if a donkey and a horse can make a mule, why can't a mule and a cow make a cow donkey?

LESTER: For the same reason I can't mate with the pig.

BECKY: I heard some stories about some people lived down by the dump who used to do that. Or maybe it was sheep. Actually, I think some of them were your relatives. As a matter of fact—

LESTER: Becky, you are going to get on the phone right now and call Cornelia Rasmussen and tell her to take these damned things back.

BECKY: I certainly am not. Nobody is eating my goats. All my life I've dreamed and hoped that one day I could share my life with a donkey. And now you want me to tell Cornelia to come back here and haul that poor thing away so somebody can eat it.

LESTER: Nobody wants to eat your donkey. And you don't have a donkey. You've got a mule and two goats. And I don't care if Cornelia Rasmussen eats the damned goats. I am the person who's going to have to feed and take care of those damned animals every single day for the rest of my life until one of us dies.

BECKY: How long do mules live?

LESTER: Way too long.

BECKY: How long do goats live?

LESTER: Probably longer than me. Becky, are you trying to kill me? Is that your plan? Because who's going to get up at five o'clock in the morning in the middle of January to feed those damned things? Do you know the kind of god damned racket a mule and a couple of goats can make when they're hungry? You might as well just get a gun and shoot me in the head. Why the hell did I ever even bother to get married again?

BECKY: I expect for the same reason that mule is bothering with the cow.

LESTER: Maybe when we get that mule castrated I'll just have it done to me, too. Save me a hell of a lot of heartache. I've tried to be a good husband to you. I really have. But being married is like being sucked into a bog. I'm being sucked into a bog, Becky. I feel like next time I come home I'm going to find a hippopotamus in the driveway. Why do you need these damned animals?

BECKY: Because I'm lonely. It's lonely being old.

LESTER: What about me? I'm here.

BECKY: No you're not. You're off bowling. Or out in the woods killing things. You like to kill things. I like to take care of things. They need me.

(Pause.)

You'll see. You'll learn to love them. The way I learned to love you. Now come on out and help me feed the goats, and maybe tonight I'll let you do what that mule is doing to the cow.

(Becky goes out. Pause.)

LESTER: Well, the cow looks happy.

(Pause. Calling after her.)

All right. But just don't bend over, or that mule might get to you before I do.

(He follows her off as lights fade and go out.)

THE LAST NIGHT

Stephen Kaplan

First production: Luna Stage New Moon Short Play Festival May 2016

Directed by Jane Mandel with Elsbeth Denman as Beth & Rachel Faison as Susan.

CHARACTERS
BETH LISTER: early 30s, pregnant.
SUSAN LISTER: early 30s, Beth's mother.

SETTING: An unspecified place. Could be a living room, a bedroom,
a waiting room…

(BETH LISTER, a woman in her early 30s sits behind a present wrapped in Hanukkah wrapping paper with a bright blue ribbon. SHE is very pregnant. SHE stares at the present. After a few moments, SUSAN LISTER, Beth's mother, also in her early 30s, enters. BETH does not take her eyes off of the present.)

SUSAN: You're not even the least bit curious?

BETH: I'm curious.

SUSAN: So open it. *(Beat.)* It's just a present.

BETH: No disclaimers.

SUSAN: That wasn't a disclaimer, it was –

BETH: No "It might the wrong size." No "I saved the receipt." No "You may not want it, so –"

SUSAN: I'm aware of the rules.

BETH: You made the rules.

SUSAN: Your father made the rules.

BETH: Because you would always apologize before ever giving us gifts. I was the only kid in Pre-K who knew the term "gift receipt."

(Beat.)

SUSAN: And that wasn't a disclaimer about the gift itself. It was a disclaimer about gifts in general – they're gifts. They're little gestures of love. Cercis.

BETH: I know.

SUSAN: So just open it already. *(BETH starts to get up with some difficulty.)* Let me help you.

BETH: I've got it. Thanks.

SUSAN: You look beautiful.

BETH: I look fat.

SUSAN: Do you want me to tell you what it is?

BETH: No, mom, I don't.

(Beat.)

SUSAN: They told us you were going to be a boy.

BETH: I know.

SUSAN: Sometimes that happens. Enlarged labia or something –

BETH: Mom.

SUSAN: It's nothing to be embarrassed about. It happens a lot.

BETH: I don't want to know. OK?

SUSAN: (*Beat.*) Alan does.

BETH: Well I'm not Alan.

SUSAN: Alan thinks you're afraid to find out.

BETH: I'm not afraid.

SUSAN: Then open the present. (*Beat.*) Do you remember what the other seven were?

BETH: Yes.

SUSAN: It wasn't a theme year. I wasn't sure if that would make it harder to –

BETH: I remember them.

SUSAN: Remember the book year? First night, Nancy Drew and *The Secret of the Old Clock* – that was always one of my favorites. But the look on your face when you opened it that first night and then realized that your remaining seven presents were all the same rectangular shape…daggers. If looks could kill then, well…

BETH: I know what you're trying to do.

SUSAN: And what is that? (*Beat.*) What were the other seven?

BETH: A doll, a sweater, a board game, a bracelet, a CD, EZ-bake oven…and a book.

SUSAN: That EZ-bake oven! That was that year's big ticket item. That's what's so hard about doing eight. It's not like Christmas where there's just the one big one – the hackneyed pony – thank God you were never a pony kind of girl.

BETH: Hackneyed?

SUSAN: It's a word. With eight gifts there are so many more things to consider. Like, are they all the same price range? Which suddenly dwindles down the wow factor of the gifts, you know? I mean a pony divided into eight parts is, well, gross, but also underwhelming. Plus, if you get a hoof the first night – well, it's a hoof and could go in many directions – but if you then get a tail the second night and a snout the third, you kind of know what the remaining nights hold in store for you. (*Unenthusiastically.*) Yay. A pony.

BETH: Why are you so infatuated with ponies?

SUSAN: You're deflecting, sweetheart. We tried the theme years – one year everything was pink, one year arts and craftsy stuff – but after the third or fourth night you'd say, "Oh look, it's pink…again." And regardless, how do you stay away from the diminishing effects of the gifts? Is the second night's gift more important than the first because it's fresher in your mind? Is the last gift the best because it's last? What about poor gifts four and five, the Jan Bradys of the Hanukkah gifts.

BETH: Is there a point to all of this?

SUSAN: What do you and Alan do?

BETH: Hanukkah's always kind of a hard time. You know?

(Beat.)

SUSAN: I can't believe he bought you a puppy the next year. I never would've gotten you a puppy.

BETH: He was trying to make up for the fact that you were gone and –

SUSAN: Whatever happened to that puppy?

BETH: It died, too.

(Beat.)

SUSAN: I'm so sorry, Beth.

BETH: *(Beat.)* About what?

SUSAN: You're going to be a mother now yourself and –

BETH: I'm fully aware of that.

SUSAN: And I know you're scared.

BETH: Why do you keep thinking I'm scared of something? I'm fine. I'm tired and I have to pee all the time and my back hurts, but I'm not scared.

SUSAN: Then why won't you open the present? *(Beat.)* It's not going to change anything. *(Beat.)* It's not any more important than the other ones.

BETH: It's the last one.

(Beat.)

SUSAN: Does that make it more important than the others?

BETH: You know it is.

SUSAN: It wasn't meant to be. You just happened to choose that one for last. We always let you choose which order you wanted to open them in. *(Beat.)* Each night of Hanukkah is supposed to be as important as the others which is why they have that middle candle that's supposed to light the other ones –

BETH: The shamash.

SUSAN: Those years of Hebrew school paid off.

BETH: So...what? You're saying that every gift is of equal importance because every night of Hanukkah is supposed to be of equal importance?

SUSAN: Yes.

BETH: So the later nights aren't more important than the first ones? More impressive? I mean the oil lasting for the first night – somewhat surprising, but it could happen. But then lasting a second night, too? More than the Jews could hope for! And then, a third! What miracle this is! Then God said, "You think that was good, let me top that with a fourth night!" And each night it got more and more amazing that the oil lasted that long – and eight, I mean come on! And coincidentally, just enough time for them to refresh their supplies and make more oil. So, really, those later nights are far more impressive and important to the whole miraculous nature of the holiday because, if it was only one or two nights, there wouldn't have been any miracle.

SUSAN: But had there been no first night, there could be no last night – and therefore no miracle. So yes, the first night is as important as the last one.

BETH: But then it just ended. The Jews were able to get the whole oil operation up and running again, and then it stopped. The miracle served its purpose and was done. So now, every year, we're supposed to eat greasy fried food in memory of this miraculous oil and give presents which have no relation to the holiday at all and are just a reaction to the competition of Christmas.

SUSAN: If you don't believe in any of it then why does it matter if you open it? Or why not throw it out? I mean, like you said, if it's just the Schwartzes attempt at keeping up with the Christiansons, then what's the big deal?

(Beat.)

BETH: The Christiansons?

SUSAN: I was trying to think of a generic Christian last name.

BETH: Jones? Keeping up with the Joneses?

(Beat.)

SUSAN: That would've worked, too.

(Beat.)

BETH: I miss you.

SUSAN: I miss you, too, baby.

BETH: I hate Hanukkah.

SUSAN: I know.

BETH: Why couldn't you have chosen Yom Kippur…or Purim…or Arbor Day?

SUSAN: You know it wasn't my choice.

BETH: Because it's not just one day that I have to remember like everybody else. They've got the one sucky day that they light the stupid memorial candle. I've got eight. And I try, every year, to just enjoy them – this year'll be different – this year I'll be OK. Maybe the earlier nights *are* more important than the last one – I should enjoy those. Cherish those. It's just the one sucky last night. Let the one night be the sucky one and don't ruin the rest of 'em. Because that last night, even before you went and ruined – I know it wasn't your fault, but… – I mean that last night always sucked, even when I was little, because it was the last one, you know? All of the presents were gone except one sad little lonely present left. And after that one it was over. The miracle was over.

SUSAN: That's what miracles are. If they just kept going and going – one night then two nights then eight nights then nine nights then ten nights then a hundred nights then a thousand nights then all the rest of your life nights – we'd take it for granted.

BETH: No we wouldn't.

SUSAN: We would. We do. If the miracle just kept on going then it wouldn't be a miracle anymore. It'd just be… (*SHE shrugs her shoulders.*) So we appreciate the miracles when they come. And though we miss them when they're done – Oh God do we miss them. Every single day and every single moment we miss them. But when they're over…when they're gone – we can't let that pain and sadness let us forget about what a miracle those eight nights were. Or those eight years. (*Beat.*) Miracles. Gifts. Every day we had together. But we wouldn't realize that if they just kept going.

(*SUSAN picks up the gift and holds it out in front of her. Offering it. Long wait.*)

BETH: Can't I just keep it and not open it? Just stick it in the closet somewhere and forget about it?

SUSAN: I know you. You won't. And you can't.

BETH: How about if I give it to my child – let them open it.

SUSAN: It's not theirs to open. (*Beat. SUSAN still holds it out.*)

BETH: How was daddy able to do it? He married Rebecca and they… he forgot you.

SUSAN: You know he didn't. It's not a contest. You're not winning anything by holding out longer, sweetie.

(Long silence as SUSAN continues to hold it out for BETH. Finally, BETH gently takes it from her. SUSAN smiles.)

SUSAN: (*Cont'd*) That's my girl. (*SHE kisses BETH on the forehead.*) I'm not the present. It's just something I gave to you.

(SUSAN starts to leave.)

BETH: Mom!

(SUSAN stops. SHE turns. SHE smiles. SHE looks at her daughter. SHE leaves. BETH stares at the present. SHE makes a decision. SHE gently tears the paper off. She folds it up nicely next to her, saving it. SHE looks at the box. SHE smiles. Lights fade.)

END OF PLAY.

Lawrence Harbison

MICKEY CARES

Mia McCullough

Mickey Cares was originally produced by Artistic Home Theatre in Chicago, IL (artistic director Kathy Scambiatterra) in their 2016 Cut to the Chase Festival. Opening Night 7/29/2016 through 8/14/2016

Producer: Jae Renfrow
Director: Ashley Roberson
Stage Manager: Taylor Green
Assistant Stage Manager: Hannah Blau

CASEY: Alison Huffines
JOSH: John Wehrman

CHARACTERS

CASEY: A mother of three, smart, active (this does not mean skinny.) 30s or 50s. Any ethnicity/race, but definitely American.

JOSH: A dude, late 20s. Any ethnicity.

VOICE: announcement over the intercom. Perky. Can be recorded.

PLACE: The Caribbean ocean

TIME: Now

SETTING: The railing at the bow of a cruise ship

LIGHTSUP on CASEY looking out over the rail of a large cruise ship. The ENGINES THRUM somewhere. It's late at night and this section of the ship is not brightly lit. JOSH approaches, watching CASEY. She takes some deep breaths, trying to calm herself. Her attempts at calm are thwarted by a perky-voiced ANNOUNCEMENT.

ANNOUNCEMENT: *(over loudspeaker)* Good evening, passengers! Don't forget about adults-only 80's trivia night in Goofy's Bar and Grill starting in just fifteen minutes on Deck 10! Great prizes! Come enjoy the fun!

CASEY growls with frustration, tries to shake it out of her hands, then grips the railing again and tries to resume her deep breathing. JOSH steps closer without her hearing.

JOSH: Thinking about jumping?

CASEY: *(startled)*What?! I don't have any money.

JOSH points to their bracelets.

JOSH: Of course not.

> *Beat.*

CASEY: My husband is meeting me here any second.

JOSH: Um, ok, I'm not here to sexually assault you.

> Or even hit on you.

> I'm just making sure you're not jumping.

CASEY: *(recognizing him)* You followed me from the bar.

JOSH: Followed...is a strong word. I saw you.

CASEY: And then followed me.

JOSH: Okay, but you're making it sound predatory. And it's not. I mean, I get that you're programmed...by life, society, movies, experience, whatever, to be defensive, to think that men want to attack you, and I'm sorry. That totally sucks.

CASEY: Programmed?

JOSH: Conditioned. Whatever. All I'm saying is that this reaction you're having to me is justified. There are men who prey on women. But I don't. Ever. I was just... compelled...to follow you. Your anger and sadness kinda sucked me in.

CASEY: Ok.

> *(beat)*

> My husband is....

JOSH: Asleep in your cabin, with your three kids.

Beat.

CASEY: How do you know I have three kids?

JOSH: I don't. I guessed. Kids.

CASEY: You didn't guess. You said it very confidently.

(pause)

Why are you following /me.

JOSH: /I'm not. I swear I'm not. I was just making sure that all that anger and sadness wasn't about to fling itself into the Caribbean.

(beat, she looks over the edge)

JOSH: *CONT'D* This is the spot for it, too. The ship's moving fast enough it might hit you on the way down, knock you out, drag you under, maybe suck you through the propellers before it spits you out on the back side. Very unlikely that you would survive a jump from here.

Beat.

CASEY: You've given this a lot of thought.

JOSH: I'm drawn to morbid scenarios. As a rule.

CASEY: That's a very well-developed scenario for the second day of a cruise.

JOSH: Not my first rodeo.

CASEY: I hate that saying.

JOSH: Ok.

(beat)

Anyhow, even if you did it, drowned, got churned up, eaten by sharks, you wouldn't officially be dead.

CASEY: Why is that.

JOSH: Because you're not allowed to die on Walt's watch.

CASEY: What are you talking about.

JOSH: Can't be the happiest place on Earth if people can die there. You have to be taken off the premises to be declared dead. Disney World, Disneyland....

CASEY: But if I jumped off the boat, I wouldn't be on Disney property anymore.

JOSH: Correct! You'd be missing.

CASEY: But what if they found my body and brought it back on board?

JOSH: Pretty sure you wouldn't be allowed to be dead.

CASEY: That's ridiculous! Would they tell my children I'm not dead?!

JOSH: They would distract them with all the amenities – free of charge – until they got to port, they'd declare you dead once you and your family were on land, and then they would provide transportation home for all of you.

CASEY: Really.

JOSH: I will say they handle the death of a guest well, even if we're not allowed to call it that.

CASEY: You're a playmate.

JOSH: A what?

CASEY: A cast mate. Whatever it's called.

JOSH: A cast member?

CASEY: *(laughing at herself)* Yes! A cast member! You're a cast member, right?

Beat.

JOSH: Yeah.

CASEY: So this is part of your job? To look for jumpers?

JOSH: No. I mean, not officially. We're all responsible for helping a guest in need.

CASEY: I'm not in need.

Beat. He leans on the rail a couple of feet away.

JOSH: You weren't going to jump?

CASEY: No! I mean, I want off this boat, don't get me wrong. Disney makes my skin crawl, all these fat white people— God that sounded awful. They're not all white.

Beat.

JOSH: Or all fat.

CASEY: But a lot of them.

JOSH: That's America for you.

CASEY: I just feel like this is the worst of America: the America that likes to pretend everything is fine all the time.

(a perky voice)

Just have fun and go on rides and stuff your face and ignore the world's problems!

(her own voice)

Denial Land. Do you have any idea how much this boat pollutes? The carbon footprint?

JOSH: It's bad. But isn't ignoring the world's problems, your own problems even, what one is supposed to *do* on vacation?

CASEY: But I look at these people, the kind of people who go on Disney cruises, and I see people who are constantly choosing distraction over reality.

JOSH: But you're only seeing them on a cruise. They may be very serious and self-flagellating the rest of the time.

Beat.

CASEY: You don't even believe that.

JOSH: I don't know what I believe. But it seems hypocritical of you to judge every guest on this ship when you are also on a Disney cruise.

CASEY: But not because I want to be. I am the sort of person who wants to be out in the wilderness, away from people, enjoying nature. I want to experience the ocean from a kayak or with a snorkel, not perched atop this bloated, floating, sideways skyscraper.

JOSH: And yet here you are.

CASEY: I am here to avoid marital discord. My in-laws do a Disney vacation every. fucking. year. Disneyland, Disney World, Disney Cruise, Euro Disney! And I bow out most of the time. But then I'm the bad person who doesn't like fun! And everyone takes it personally and thinks, "you don't like our family." So this year I'm sucking it up, going on the cruise, and pretending to look happy all day long. And this: this is when I get to stare off into the darkness and I don't have to pretend.

Beat. He gets it.

JOSH: I gotta say, you're not fantastic at pretending to be happy. I mean, the adults in the group seem to buy it, but not the kids.

Pause. She stares at him.

CASEY: Now you're being creepy.

JOSH: *(he shrugs)* I people-watch. It passes the time.

CASEY: I people-watch too. And I don't remember seeing you, until the bar tonight.

JOSH: Maybe you didn't notice me.

CASEY: No, I would notice you.

JOSH: Why's that?

Beat.

CASEY: No reason.

(beat)

That means you're in a costume.

(beat, grabs his arm)

Are you Mickey?

JOSH: *(trying to pull away)* A lot of us/ are Mickey.

CASEY: /Oh my God, you're Mickey! Mickey tried to save my life!

(she hugs him)

Oh my god, that's so cute.

JOSH: *(firmly pushing her away)* Ok, you have to stop touching me.

CASEY: *(looking for witnesses)* Are we not allowed to touch? Is that one of Walt's rules?

JOSH: No, I can't handle skin-to-skin contact with other people.

Beat.

CASEY: Wait, what? Is that a thing?

JOSH: Yeah. It's a rare thing.

CASEY: But you're Mickey!

JOSH: Shhh! I'm not supposed to tell /you that!

CASEY: /People touch you constantly.

JOSH: But there's a costume, a barrier.

CASEY: So you couldn't be one of those characters who isn't all covered up, like the princes, /or something.

JOSH: /Noooo. The whole reason I have this job is that my therapist and my doctor thought if I could get used to people touching me through a barrier, then maybe I could graduate to....

CASEY: Actual touching.

JOSH: Yeah.

CASEY: Wow. Have you always been like this? Even as a kid?

(He's nodding)

What about your mom!? Could your mom touch you?

JOSH: She was the one who figured it out. That I couldn't tolerate it.

CASEY: Oh my God, that's terrible. For her. For you.

(She almost touches him, remembers not to)

And it's better in the costume? Because wow, people touch Mickey

/all the time.

JOSH: /All the time. Yeah. It's kinda overstimulating. I'm on a lot of anti-anxiety meds.

CASEY: So..., is it painful when people touch you skin-to-skin?

JOSH: Painful isn't.... It's not the right word. It's really uncomfortable. Like my sensation is turned up to eleven.

CASEY: Is it like being super ticklish?

JOSH: Well, yes, but tickling... is actually painful, even like really delicate tickling, with a feather or something, it's like a ZING through my nervous system, like an electric shock. But even, like good touching, like a caress or something that's meant to be romantic....You know that thrill you get when someone touches you romantically for the first time, that electric tingling?

Beat.

CASEY: I have a vague recollection of that sensation.

JOSH: But imagine that so intensely that you can't breathe, like you're literally hyperventilating, and your blood pressure is spiking and you're getting dizzy—

CASEY: That sounds awful.

JOSH: Yeah. I mean, there's maybe one second of the good sensation and then it all goes haywire.

CASEY: God. Did something happen to you? Like as a kid?

JOSH: No. I mean, not as far as anyone can tell. It's a weird physiological condition.

CASEY: But what are— ok, this is really personal, but I'm asking anyway: what are orgasms like?

JOSH: I don't know.

CASEY: Have you never had sex?

JOSH: No. Well, once, technically, but I was so sedated, that I don't remember it.

CASEY: Someone raped you while you were sedated?!

JOSH: No! Well... I asked them to do it. I thought I would remember it. But I took too much Valium.

CASEY: Ok. This is sort of blowing my mind.... You're going to have to tell me your name if I'm going to know this about you.

JOSH: Josh.

CASEY: Casey.

She offers her hand to shake.

JOSH: I....

CASEY: Sorry. Right. So is the costume thing helping at all?

JOSH: I guess some. I mean, I've only been doing it a few weeks now.

CASEY: Wow. Well this, I mean. If it's not working out it's not like you can quit and leave.

JOSH: No.

CASEY: I thought I felt like a hostage on this fucking boat. How long is your contract for?

JOSH: Four months.

CASEY: How much longer do you have?

JOSH: Three months, one week, and four days.

CASEY: Doable?

JOSH: We'll see.

Pause.

CASEY: I should probably get back to my cabin.

JOSH: Yeah.

CASEY: The kids will be up at the crack of dawn and rearing to go.

JOSH: Chuck 'em in daycare all day.

CASEY: Are you kidding? My kids are my excuse to not interact with my in-laws — besides my nieces and nephews, who are mostly fine.

JOSH: Human buffer zones.

CASEY: Damn skippy.

JOSH: I'll see you around.

CASEY: But I won't see you.

JOSH: I'll try to make myself obvious.

CASEY: Are you always Mickey?

JOSH: I'm always Mickey, but Mickey isn't always me. There are several of us who play him.

CASEY: Is there ever a woman inside Mickey?

JOSH: I am not at liberty to discuss that.

CASEY: C'mon!

She smacks him playfully.

CASEY CONT'D: Shit. Sorry.

JOSH: I can't tell you. I've signed things.

CASEY: How much did that hurt?

JOSH: That was brief. And my endorphins kick in very quickly.

CASEY: I'm sorry.

JOSH: Really, you didn't hurt me.

CASEY: Ok. Well. Good luck with that.

JOSH: Don't think I'm a freak.

CASEY: No! I don't. I think you have an unfortunate obstacle to overcome.

JOSH: Yeah.

CASEY: Good night, Josh.

JOSH: Good night. I forgot your name, I'm sorry. I'm bad at names. The handshake awkwardness always drives it right out.

CASEY: It's Casey. Thanks for checking on me.

JOSH: Sure.

CASEY: Good luck.

JOSH: Thanks.

CASEY EXITS. JOSH watches her walk away. Then he leans on the rail and peers into the darkness. After a moment he looks around to see if anyone is looking, and climbs up onto the rail. BLACK OUT.

END OF PLAY.

NO LOVE, PLEASE

Marisa Smith

NO LOVE, PLEASE Premiered in May, 2016 at the 18th Annual Boston Theater 10-Minute Marathon, sponsored by Marblehead Little Theatre

Directed by Anne Marilyn Lucas
MAN: Paul Melendy
WOMAN: Stanis Johnson

CHARACTERS
WOMAN: 30's - 50's
MAN: 30'S - 50'S

SETTING: The bedroom of the Woman's apartment. A bed.
Two chairs.

TIME: The present.

(Lights up.)

The Man and Woman are on opposite sides of the bed, getting dressed.

The bed is a mess; obviously they've just had sex.)

MAN: Why don't we least go out for a drink?

WOMAN: But we already had sex; we don't need to get drunk so we'll have sex.

MAN: We could just go and talk.

WOMAN: Talk?

MAN: Yeah, you know... a little. I really don't know anything about you.

WOMAN: Yeah, isn't that great?

MAN: What?

WOMAN: It's, you know…just lust.

MAN: But I think I like you.

WOMAN: Oh, that could be a problem.

MAN: So, how about it? I'll take you to a nice bar and you can have a nice pink cocktail.

WOMAN: Do I seem like a pink cocktail type of person? No. Time for you to go. But it was very nice to see you again.

MAN: Very *nice?*

WOMAN: Very…awesome.

(She smiles and extends her arm to the door.

Man exits.

BLACKOUT.

Music.

A day passes.

LIGHTS UP.

The Man and the Woman are standing near the bed, fully clothed. Their coats are on the two chairs.)

WOMAN: This feels odd.

MAN: It does.

WOMAN: I'm not sure I can do this.

MAN: Me neither.

WOMAN: Now I'm a bit …self-conscious.

MAN: Me, too. I feel tense.

WOMAN: I was more relaxed when we were strangers.

MAN: Yeah. So, we're at a crossroads here.

(They sit in chairs near the bed.)

WOMAN: You shouldn't have said you liked me last time. I feel that created this…barrier.

MAN: I know, the minute I said it I regretted it. Now I'm worried about whether you like *me*.

WOMAN: Right. Now we're going down *that* road.

(They sigh.)

MAN: Well, we could, you know…follow that road a little.

WOMAN: What do you mean?

MAN: You know… get to know each other?

WOMAN: Oh, no, that never works. You open yourself up to irritation, disappointment, hurt, contempt, boredom, and disgust at annoying personal habits.

MAN: But it might work for the short term. Until we get to know each other *too* well.

WOMAN: True, it could be short-term solution.

(Pause.)

But if you say you like walks on the beach at sunset it's a deal breaker.

MAN: I don't like the beach.

WOMAN: Neither do I. Or the sunset.

MAN: I hate the sunset. And the sunrise.

WOMAN: Oh, I hate the sunrise. It's so…dramatic.

MAN: So emotional.

WOMAN: Gives me the chills.

(Pause.)

MAN: So, are you game?

WOMAN: Sure. You go first. What do you do?

MAN: Well, I'm a neuroscientist.

WOMAN: Really? What's your field?

MAN: Perception, but my research focuses on facedness.

WOMAN: What is *facedness?*

MAN: We each have a dominant side of the face, a side that is bigger and more active. For example, typically men are left-faced and women are right faced.

WOMAN: *(touching her face)* Really? That is *fascinating.* So fascinating. So I'm right-faced?

MAN: Oh yes, definitely. Very right-faced. Classic.

(He peers closely into her face.)

And what do you do?

WOMAN: I'm a biologist.

MAN: No!

WOMAN: In the clock lab— the circadian rhythm lab that is.

MAN: You're in bio! Traditionally, neuroscience was seen as a branch of biology but today it's more of an interdisciplinary—

(stops himself from pontificating)

—wow, bio, I'm impressed!

WOMAN: Oh, don't be— really, most of my research involves... mushrooms.

MAN: Mushrooms. I love mushrooms. Well, on pizza mostly.

(They laugh a nerdy laugh together.)

MAN: Are you feeling better now?

WOMAN: Yes, actually.

MAN: Me too. Quite a coincidence that we're both scientists.

WOMAN: Yeah, bizarre.

MAN: I don't even know your name. Tell me your name.

WOMAN: No, I'd rather not.

MAN: Okay.

WOMAN: I don't think we're ready for that.

MAN: Alright.

WOMAN: Let's not wreck things when they're going so well.

MAN: Right, let's not get carried away.

(Pause.)

WOMAN: Maybe liquor would help at this point.

MAN: Good idea.

(Woman opens up a drawer.)

WOMAN: Johnny Walker?

MAN: (too enthusiastic) He's my man.

(embarrassed)

Well, you know what I mean.

WOMAN: He's mine too!

(This cracks them up.

She hands him a tiny bottle and takes one for herself.

They open the bottles and take a drink.

They stare at each other… lustily.)

WOMAN: Tell me something about *facedness.*

MAN: Well, musical performers are right-faced. Physicists are left-faced.

WOMAN: That is *so* interesting.

(They each take another drink.)

MAN: And psychiatrists are neither.

WOMAN: Really?

MAN: They are evenly split—some are left and some are right.

WOMAN: Well, that makes sense.

MAN: Doesn't it though?

(They drink a final slug.)

WOMAN: I think this is working.

MAN: Yes, absolutely.

WOMAN: I don't feel so…anxious.

MAN: Right, I'm starting to unwind.

WOMAN: Coming at it from this direction was a really smart idea.

MAN: Yes. These things are tricky.

WOMAN: But no names, okay?

MAN: Okay, not yet.

WOMAN: *(starts unbuttoning her shirt)* Let's hold off for as long as we can.

MAN: *(starts unbuttoning his shirt)* I'm with you there.

WOMAN: *(taking off her skirt)* And no terms of endearment. No sappy stuff.

MAN: *(taking off his pants)* Check, no sappy stuff.

WOMAN: No sweetie or darling or shit like that.

MAN: I'm in total agreement.

WOMAN: And God forbid, no love please.

MAN: No, definitely, no love.

WOMAN: Let's keep this as pure as possible.

(They stare hungrily at each other.)

MAN: For as long as possible.

(They grab each other and start kissing madly.)

END OF PLAY

ONCE IN A BLUE MOON

L.E. Grabowski-Cotton

Once in a Blue Moon was originally produced by Jacksonville University, in Jacksonville, Florida on May 15, 2016. The play was directed by Hannah Gretz, and performed by the following cast: Valentine - Jennifer O'Neil, Montgomery - Brian Frazer.

CHARACTERS
VALENTINE GRACE: Any age. A free spirit with a sense of humor.
MONTGOMERY BLOOM: Any age. A conservative and logical
   businessman.

SETTING: The Blue Moon Travel Agency
TIME: The present

Once in a Blue Moon Travel agency. The sign reads "You name it, we'll get you there." A young woman, VALENTINE GRACE, sits behind the desk, reading a book. She is not a pretty girl, she has long stringy hair and she is far too skinny. But she has an ethereal quality to her, a dreaminess that is evident in all that she does. She sighs frequently as she reads and glances at the door, as if hoping that someone will enter.

No one does.

After a few moments, she stands up and stretches. Just as she is leaning over, a man enters. His name is MONTGOMERY BLOOM. His hair is slicked back, he wears a suit and tie, and he looks very professional.

MONTGOMERY: Is this the Once in a Blue Moon travel agency?

(Startled, Valentine stands up straight, turns around.)

VALENTINE: Is it?

MONTGOMERY: I'm asking you.

VALENTINE: Oh yes! Then it is. Unless you say it isn't. In which case, it is not. The customer is always right, you see. Except when he isn't.

MONTGOMERY: And are you Valentine Grace?

VALENTINE: Yes.

(Beat)

I mean, sort of.

(Beat)

No. Not really.

MONTGOMERY: *(Frustrated)* Which is it?

VALENTINE: I'm sorry, what was the question?

MONTGOMERY: *(Shaking his head)* Let's try something else. What's your name?

VALENTINE: I'm Valentine Grace. But my mother is also Valentine Grace. So it depends on which one of us you're looking for. My mother is the CEO of this agency, the creative force behind it, the woman behind the woman, if you will.

MONTGOMERY: Is your mother around?

VALENTINE: *(Shaking her head)* She's on vacation. Again. I'm afraid that there's no telling when she'll be back or if she'll come back at all. There have been several times now that she went away and never returned.

MONTGOMERY: That's not possible.

VALENTINE: Of course it is. That's why she started this agency, you see, because she loves to travel. Unfortunately, she didn't consider the fact that to run a travel agency you need to stay in one place. Which is why she had me. She thought to herself, well, if I can't run the agency, then I ought to have a daughter who can. Not a son, because she can't stand men. Too smelly and demanding, she says. So she picked up a man at a resort, a good-looking, clean smelling man although I suspect he was skinny and had stringy hair like mine, slept with him, and got pregnant immediately. Nine months later, I was born.

MONTGOMERY: Surely, you're joking.

VALENTINE: About which part?

MONTGOMERY: Listen, I don't have time to hear your life story. I'm here about an important matter. My -

VALENTINE: That's good because I don't want to tell it to you. One should never tell too much to a customer. My mother taught me that. I've been working with my mother since before I was born. In the womb, you see, she used to talk to me, training me on how to help customers and what to say to them. She said always begin with a question.

(Smiling brightly)

So, where are you thinking about going?

MONTGOMERY: Nowhere. That's what I was trying to tell you! I'm here because my girlfriend-

VALENTINE: Oh! I'm afraid I can't send you there.

MONTGOMERY: Where?

VALENTINE: Nowhere. We sent far too many people there last year. It was my fault. I started sending people there for free. The mayor of Nowhere calls me up, out of the blue, really, and he told me that I was single-handedly responsible for their economic troubles. Nowhere's population was growing at an exorbitant rate, and No One couldn't find work.

MONTGOMERY: You mean no one *could* find work.

VALENTINE: No. I mean what I said. No One couldn't. No One is the mayor's daughter, and if she can't find work, that's a very bad sign. The mayor told me that under no circumstances could I send anyone else to Nowhere, not now and not anytime in the near future.

MONTGOMERY: Uh, right. Is there anyone else I can talk to?

VALENTINE: Yes.

(Awkward silence)

MONTGOMERY: *(Frustrated)* Well, could you get them for me?

VALENTINE: Oh! You meant here! No, there's only me here. But there are plenty of other people in the world. Some of them talk, some don't. But most do, I think.

MONTGOMERY: Look, all I need you to do is tell me where my girlfriend went. She came here a few months ago, requested to go someplace, and I haven't seen her since. Can you look her name up and tell me?

VALENTINE: It's not *impossible*. But not possible either. We hold a strict confidentiality procedure with our clients. It's called the "once they go, we pretend we don't know" policy.

MONTGOMERY: It's important that I find her.

VALENTINE: Why?

MONTGOMERY: Because I wish to see her, that's why! Isn't that enough?

VALENTINE: *(Shocked)* Enough for me to violate the "once they go, we pretend we don't know" policy?! No, that isn't enough.

MONTGOMERY: Fine. I need to see her because I'm... I'm...

VALENTINE: What? What are you?

MONTGOMERY: *(Softly)* I'm dying. I have Instico Imaginario Flabrightis.

VALENTINE: *(Suspicious)* That sounds made-up.

MONTGOMERY: It is. Dr. Flabrightis made it up. He is a world-renowned specialist in Flabrightitry. He says I have very little time left.

VALENTINE: By your watch or his?

MONTGOMERY: *(Confused)* What?

VALENTINE: I'm guessing it was his, because you're not wearing a watch. The good news is that if his watch is slow, you might have more time than you realize. If his watch is fast, you may have less.

If I were you, I would contact this doctor straight away and ask him to move the hands on his watch back so that you have more time.

MONTGOMERY: You're talking nonsense again.

VALENTINE: *(Defensively)* I'm not the one who has a made-up disease.

MONTGOMERY: I don't have time for this. I have three months, maybe four left to live. That's why I need to find my girlfriend. So that we can spend my last days together.

(Silence)

VALENTINE: She doesn't love you.

MONTGOMERY: What?

VALENTINE: That's why she left.

MONTGOMERY: No. No, that's not it at all. She just needed some time apart. Everyone needs a break now and then, she said. But we were in love. Madly in love.

VALENTINE: Were you? Or do you just think that you were now that you're dying?

MONTGOMERY: *(Confused)* What?

VALENTINE: Everyone wants to have a great love in their life, right? And you haven't got much time left. So you decided that she was yours. But she wasn't.

MONTGOMERY: How do you know? You never even met her!

VALENTINE: I did meet her. I remember her.

MONTGOMERY: I haven't even told you her name.

VALENTINE: Sylvia Augustine?

MONTGOMERY: How did you know that?!

VALENTINE: I have a sense for these things.

(Beat)

That and she was the only person who has come in here in the last six months.

MONTGOMERY: You have to tell me where she went! I'll pay whatever you want. Name your price.

(VALENTINE thinks for a moment.)

VALENTINE: One trillion dollars and a maid service.

MONTGOMERY: What?

VALENTINE: Make that two trillion. I'll give one trillion to my mother when she returns from her trip and keep the other for myself.

MONTGOMERY: I don't have a trillion dollars!

VALENTINE: Fine. Three trillion. One for me, one for my mother, and one for you. That way you *can* have a trillion dollars. And that's my final offer.

MONTGOMERY: Look, the most I can offer you is five-hundred. Will that do?

VALENTINE: No, but I'll take it.

MONTGOMERY: So where did she go?

VALENTINE: Oh, that's easy. She went to... To... Oh! It seems I've forgotten.

MONTGOMERY: What?

VALENTINE: Yes, it's completely slipped my mind. But we only send people to five places, so it was probably one of those. Unless, of course, it wasn't.

(Excited)

Perhaps if I tell the places to you, you can figure out which one she would have chosen!

MONTGOMERY: I can't believe this. You didn't record it in your computer?

VALENTINE: I would have. If I had one. But I don't. So I didn't. Now, do you want to hear the five places we send people?

MONTGOMERY: *(Irritated)* Yes. Go ahead.

VALENTINE: The first place is Nowhere, which as I said is now no longer accepting visitors. Then there is Almost There, which is our most popular choice, Somewhere, Anywhere, and Home.

MONTGOMERY: Oh my god.

VALENTINE: *(Ignoring him)* Now, in my experience, people who go to Almost There are individuals who almost have their lives together. They almost have a job. They almost have money. They almost have a significant other. But they really don't have any of these things. They just wish they did. Does that sound like your girlfriend?

MONTGOMERY: No. Maybe I could call your mother? Do you think she could help me?

VALENTINE: Then there is Anywhere. We get a lot of people who say they will go to Anywhere. They're usually unhappy. They're willing to do anything to escape the misery that has become their lives. As a result, Anywhere is full of very sad individuals. Was your girlfriend very sad?

MONTGOMERY: I can't believe I'm listening to this.

VALENTINE: Now, people who go to Somewhere are much better off. They have more money and that generally means that are happier. Somewhere is a more expensive place to visit, you see, and it is far more fun than Almost There. There are plenty of things to do in Somewhere.

MONTGOMERY: *(Giving up)* Look, I'm just going to go home.

(MONTGOMERY heads for the exit)

VALENTINE: Oh! We send people to Home all the time. But once they get there, they realize it isn't what they remembered. Home looks different every time you visit it. It changes more than any other place. I personally like Home, but the majority of people don't appreciate it.

(MONTGOMERY is about to open the door and leave. Then he pauses...)

MONTGOMERY: If you do hear anything from Sylvia, would you please tell her that I miss her?

VALENTINE: I will. But honestly, Montgomery, if I were you, I'd forget all about Sylvia. I would take charge of my life. I'd stop seeing that ridiculous doctor who gave you his made-up disease. Instead, I would take that five hundred dollars and book a trip to Somewhere. Somewhere is beautiful this time of year.

(Silence as MONTGOMERY thinks)

MONTGOMERY: What if I said yes?

(Takes a step forward)

What if, for a brief moment, I suspended my sense of reality?

(Takes another step forward)

What if I agreed to go along with your lunacy?

(Takes another step forward)

What would happen?

VALENTINE: *(Excited)* I'd book your trip today! You'd have a full itinerary of events. I'd make sure that every moment was planned according to your preferences. You'd have a wonderful time! What are you saying? Are you saying you think you might really want to go to Somewhere?

(Silence as MONTGOMERY considers)

MONTGOMERY: You know what? Yes. Let's do it. I'd love to see where you send me.

(LIGHTS FADE)

(END OF PLAY)

THE PAIN INSIDE

Carlos Jerome

This play was produced from January 6 – February 5, 2017 by the Actors Theater of Santa Cruz as part of its 8 Tens @ 8 Festival.

Director: Robin Aronson

Cast
ANDY: Rafael Reyes
SHADES: Correll Barca-Hall

Artistic Director: Wilma Marcus Chandler
Producer/Stage Manager: Bonnie Ronzio
Props Master: Cheryl Wong
Sound Design: Davis Banta
Lighting Design: Jeff Swan

CAST OF CHARACTERS
ANDY: Male, 19, Prisoner
SHADES: Male, 30, Prisoner

PLACE: A dormitory in Rikers Island prison, New York City
TIME: An evening, 1960s

Lawrence Harbison

SETTING: A bed stretches from SC. Other beds are dimly seen behind it. The feet of the beds form an aisle going US. The wall has barred windows. Attached to the neatly made bed, near its head, is a small cabinet, on top of which are a chess board, thermos and a few books. A stool is bolted to the floor.

AT RISE: Dormitory lights are on. Percussion mixes with a low prison din - bits of conversation, music and voices from radio, guards calling out names of inmates. SHADES is lying on his bed, reading. HE wears prison denims, and tinted prescription glasses. ANDY is coming from US along aisle. HE too wears prison denims. HE carries an envelope and some aluminum-wrapped food. Noise dims as HE stops at SHADES' bed.

ANDY: Don't you never take your face out o' them books?

SHADES: Pue' ya ve'. It's a deep book. Catch me tomorrow, pana. I want to finish this chapter before lights out.

ANDY: No sea' así. This could be important.

SHADES: Wha's the difference? You can't do shit about it right now. It's from the court?

ANDY: I think it's from my ace.

SHADES: Get someone else. How 'bout Surdo or—

ANDY: Ain't nobody put the feelin' in like you, Shades. And don't matter English or Spanish. C'mon—

SHADES: Gimme a break. It's like I got no free time anymore. Everyone hittin' on me, the minute I'm back from the yard. Shee't. When you gon' learn? You a young blood. Pull a douglass. You see I'm concentratin' here.

(Returns to book.)

ANDY: You got to break down that douglass.

SHADES: Frederick Douglass. Started out a slave. Went through some heavy changes to learn to read. Now you gon' let me alone?

ANDY: *(Beat.)* I got somethin' for you.

SHADES: Tomorrow. And you don't got to give me nothin'. I don't smoke anyway.

ANDY: I ain't talkin' bones. I'm talkin' arró' con dulce.

SHADES: Like I'm believing you.

ANDY: En serio. *(SHADES turns toward ANDY, removing sunglasses [they remain off for the remainder of play].* ANDY hands aluminum wrap to SHADES.)

SHADES: ¡Arró' con dulce!

(opening foil)

You crazy bastard Andy! Where the hell'd you get this?

ANDY: Tony was keeping it frozen for me. My abuela made it. Zoraida brought it last month. My old lady.

SHADES: *(getting plastic cups, paper towels from inside cabinet and clearing cabinet top)* The one in the drawing you showed me?

ANDY: Right. I drew it from a photo.

SHADES: Terrific drawing.

(Places cups and paper towels on top of cabinet.)

Good lookin' out, Andy.

(Pours tea from thermos. Places arroz con dulce between the cups.)

Mete mano.

(THEY taste the arroz con dulce with a mixture of eagerness and the care required for quality evaluation.)

Mmm. ¡Qué delicia!

ANDY: My grandmother can cook. Navidades she would do this.

SHADES: Yes! The cinnamon… and leche de coco… And you can taste the rum the raisins are soaked in… My moms used to make it this way. Tha's many moons, baby.

(Sips tea.)

Tell your abuela thanks, if she comes here before you're out. You short, right?

ANDY: Three more weeks.

SHADES: You know what? I shoulda got busted sooner. That way I'd'a had time to teach you to read. I told you I used to be like you.

ANDY: Yeah, you told me. And you used to do second story guisos too.

SHADES: And I shoulda stayed with that. A piece just means a longer bid. All right, what you got?

ANDY: *(Hands SHADES the envelope.)* It don't look like from la Zorra.

SHADES: *(Looks at return address on envelope.)* Villanueva, 611 East Eleventh Street.

ANDY: Tha's Tito. My man.

SHADES: *(reading)* Dear Andy,

I hope this letter finds you in good health. I have some things to tell you.

(ANDY moves closer to SHADES. SHADES looks up from letter.)

Listen now. Whatever he about to tell, don't be blamin' me for it.

ANDY: Why would I?

SHADES: I'm just sayin'. 'Cause some chamacos… You know Angel in B Dormitory? La jeva wrote she was quittin' on him. And he like to deal with me. As if I put the idea in her mind.

ANDY: *(Rises.)* You gon' read me the fuckin' letter or what?

SHADES: *(Rises.)* Not if you ain't cool.

(THEY face each other.)

You sit down. I'm'a read it.

(ANDY sits down. SHADES reads.)

Doña Vicenta has Margarita now.

ANDY: Shit. My abuela took our baby.

SHADES: That's bad?

ANDY: Good and bad. She think Zorra wasn't caring for Margie, but how Zorra gon' feel with the baby gone?

SHADES: Margarita is healthy now. No more addict signs.

ANDY: That's great! See tha's the good part.

SHADES: Would you believe Hector is in college? Willie got sent back upstate. They put me on the 4-to-12 shift now, so I had to quit my classes.

ANDY: He was tryin' to finish high school at night.

SHADES: Zoraida still stays sometimes at Zulma and Chalequín's house. Sometimes Zorra looks ok. But last night she took a bad hit.

ANDY: *(Rises.)* What you tellin' me?

SHADES: Worse than the first OD. The ambulance took her to Beth Israel.

ANDY: Why you sayin' that for?

(HE is moving toward SHADES, about to lose control.)

SHADES: Sit down!

(ANDY sits. SHADES continues reading.)

We hope they got her in time.

ANDY: Ok Shades, stop!

(HE slams fist down on cabinet.)

Stop.

(Covers face with his hand.)

Motherfucker.

SHADES: *(Comes closer to ANDY.)* How long she been juqueá'?

ANDY: Back a ways.

(SHADES puts a hand on ANDY's shoulder.)

Her sister's old man wouldn't let her live with them no more. She started shootin'…

(Beat.)

The only girl I ever loved. The only one that ever loved me… Read the rest.

SHADES: Me and Jíbaro will try and see her later today. I will let you know how she is. Your ace, Tito

ANDY: They don't understand her! If I was there… She looked ok last time she come to visit. Maybe not clean, but at least ok. If I woulda… Puñeta…If I wasn't here… I coulda done something.

SHADES: I felt the same way with my kid brother Juan. That's the toughest cut of the inside. That's when it chops up your soul. Someone that's part of you is in trouble… goin' down the tubes… and you know if only you were there you could help. You could save them. But you're here. You're right here. On the inside.

(Beat.)

Oyeme. You know what you do? When you get the streets, if she ain't- See, you got a shot with her. She loves you.

(Folds letter, puts it into ANDY's shirt.)

When you get the streets, you put her in a program. Tha's what I was gon' do with Juanito, but he got killed while I was still in Greenhaven.

ANDY: The pain you must've felt…

SHADES: ¿Que si qué? That's all I had, was pain. His face…I would see his face… I'd see it in my dreams. I still see it. He'd be like your age now. Those eyes…staring… flashing a question… the hint of a smile… and always the pain inside.

ANDY: Shades, where did this tecata shit start?

SHADES: I'd like to know that myself.

ANDY: 'Cause I'm'a tell you somethin'. This here is like a war. Go in any neighborhood - how many people dead or fucked up?

SHADES: One false move, show any weakness, and they get you.

ANDY: So who brought the drugs?

SHADES: I'm tellin' you, I don't know. You think I wasn't lookin' for something like that? Somethin' to help Juanito. Then later, I just wanted to understand…what happened to him. To us. How many books did I read about narcotics? But nobody knows.

ANDY: It don't happen on its own. Somebody got to know something.

SHADES: Oh there's a lot of theories. One dude had a famous line: *Religion is the opium of the people.* But the way I see it, he got it backwards. What they tryin' to do is make opium the religion of the people.

ANDY: Either way, you know what I think? I think reading is a waste of time. Ain't they supposed to be smart - the ones that write the books? Ain't they supposed to have the answers?

SHADES: Some of them are like us. Searching.

ANDY: They don't know shit. Nothin'. You read all their deep books, but what does it get you? You still doin' time. You think reading give you a shot for a straight job outside? An oye with your record? Shee't. Y… no te e'té malo, Shades, but your brother - he still gone. Did the books help you with him?

SHADES: Andy, you goin' off.

ANDY: You tell me do a douglass. What the fuck for? Zoraida can read, y ¿qué? She still where she is.

SHADES: Your pain is killing your reason. Look at yourself, pana. Here in the joint, you can make it without reading. But on the streets you're a cripple.

ANDY: Who you callin' cripple, Jack? I ain't no cripple. I get along.

SHADES: Barely. Pickin' up what you can with those small-time jobs. You could do everything right and you still end up with chump change. And once you got a record for break-ins, any burglary in your neighborhood, you the first one the man look for.

ANDY: You said you shoulda stayed with break-ins yourself.

SHADES: I said it, but why you think I left that shit? You got to think bigger.

ANDY: But tha's what I know how to do is second-story. Tha's all. Cripple…

SHADES: Sorry. I shouldn'ta said that.

ANDY: And don't say do a douglass, 'cause right now all I got on my mind is Zoraida.

SHADES: Let me think for you… How about you get into numbers? Make real plata.

ANDY: You got to read and write people's names to run numbers.

SHADES: Maybe there's a way. You know Gato, right?

ANDY: Yeah, he short too. Gets the streets two days before me.

SHADES: Gato's a big-time bolitero. Everyone bets with him. I'll talk with him.

ANDY: He might take me in?

SHADES: Yeah, I think he got a spot for someone collecting. You won't be the one keeping track of the names and bets.

ANDY: Good lookin' out, Shades.

(A call to line up for a count is heard from the guard area: "On the count!")

SHADES: You have to be packed, always ready to lean… You got to go with that, pana – the way it works. But if people play ball they don't get hurt. And you be sittin' on top of the world. No more small-time guisos. Top of the world.

ANDY: Tha's only if Zorra can make it… If not… I'm a tell you somethin'. If Zorra don't get past this overdose… Why would I want the streets? Better stay here.

SHADES: You got people out there. Shee't, you know how lucky you are? Everything I'm missing. Right this is the only bid you done?

(ANDY nods.)

And you been here what, like a year?

ANDY: A year and change.

SHADES: You had just a taste of how it is. Feeling the years bury you. I'll bet you never felt lonely in your life. You got your abuela, you got… the one that wrote…

ANDY: Tito.

SHADES: And the others in the letter. People who care. Tha's what counts. And you got the baby.

ANDY: Margarita.

(Beat.)

What do I know about bringing up a child?…

SHADES: You work for Gato, at least there's dollars for her.

ANDY: Tha's cool, but if it's without Zoraida it ain't the top of the world. It's the bottom.

(Sounds of the prisoners murmuring while lining up. SHADES motions with his head for ANDY and HIMSELF to go to line up. THEY walk single file into the aisle.)

Like a war. But you can't see who's the enemy. You just feel them stompin' on your face.

(SHADES stretches his arm forward, puts his hand on ANDY's shoulder. Blackout.)

END OF PLAY

PALOOKA

Claudia Barnett

PALOOKA was first produced by the FUSION Theatre Company (FUSIONnm.org) as the Andaluz Award-winning entry in their annual original short works festival, "The Seven," June 9th-12th 2016 at The Cell Theatre and KiMo Theatre in Albuquerque, New Mexico. Festival Producer: Dennis Gromelski. Festival Curator: Jen Grigg. Directed by Aaron Worley. Lighting and Scenic Design by Richard K. Hogle. Sound Design by Brent Stevens. Properties Design by Robyn Phillips. Production Stage Manager: Maria Lee Schmidt. The cast was as follows:

JENNA: Jen Grigg
WIL: Jamie H. Jung

CHARACTERS
WIL: Male.
JENNA: Female.

Setting: A hiking trail, miles from civilization.

At rise. WIL stands, hunched in pain, his hands covering his mouth. A hiking map lies on the ground near his feet. JENNA stands several feet away.

WIL: My tooth. Is loose.

JENNA: Let me see.

WIL: Don't.

JENNA: Fine.

WIL: It wiggles.

JENNA: Let me—

WIL: No.

JENNA: I can—

WIL: I can't believe you punched me.

JENNA: I can't believe you said … what you said.

WIL: Didn't your mother teach you—?

JENNA: Of course not. You've met the woman. I grew up in a barn. That's what you said when you met her. Lucky she didn't hear you. *She*'d have punched you in the face.

WIL: You don't hit people when you don't like what they say.

JENNA: That's what your mother taught you?

WIL: She taught me not to hit girls.

JENNA: Well, hit me if you want.

WIL: I don't want.

JENNA: Yes you do.

WIL: But I won't.

JENNA: Fine. Don't. Whatever.

WIL: Could you stop speaking? Just be … quiet.

JENNA: It'll tighten up. The tooth. I had that once, from a tennis racquet. A girl at school, teaching me to serve. I was standing next to her. She tossed the ball in the air, flung her racquet to her left … whacked me in the face.

WIL: On purpose?

JENNA: No. Well, maybe.

WIL: And your tooth—?

JENNA: It got loose. Then it was fine. After a few days. It was fine. I mean. I have all my teeth. So it must have. Been fine. See?

SHE shows her teeth, a sort-of smile.

WIL: Did you learn to play tennis?

JENNA: 'Course not.

WIL: Did you learn anything?

JENNA: That day?

WIL: Ever.

JENNA: You're a jackass.

WIL: You punched me.

JENNA: Like I said. You're a jackass.

WIL: My. Tooth. Is loose.

JENNA: You're mad? I'm the one should be mad.

WIL: You are mad. You are definitely mad.

JENNA: I could punch you again.

WIL: No, you couldn't. I know what to expect now. I know you now. And I would not let you punch me again. You've lost the element of surprise.

JENNA: You always said you like surprises.

WIL: I thought I did. But, surprise: I don't. So now you know me, too. After all this time, we know each other.

JENNA: I wanted to hurt you, but I didn't want you to be hurt. I mean, I had the impulse, I needed to … but I didn't mean for you to …

WIL: Is that an apology?

JENNA: No.

WIL: You're not sorry?

JENNA: Are you?

WIL: I'm tasting blood.

JENNA: Don't get addicted. Blood can make you bloodthirsty.

WIL: You should go back.

JENNA: What?

WIL: To the trailhead. To the car. Go back. It's a loop.

JENNA: It's over two hours. We're more than halfway.

WIL: Fine, I'll go.

JENNA: You want me to go—alone?

WIL: We're splitting up.

JENNA: We're—We—. I don't even know where we are.

WIL: Take the map.

HE picks the map up off the ground and holds it out to her. SHE doesn't take it. HE folds it neatly.

JENNA: You know I'll get lost. I always get lost.

WIL: Forward or backward, Jenna. Pick a direction.

JENNA: What if you need medical attention?

WIL: Is that a joke?

JENNA: You can't hike alone. It's dangerous. There are … bears.

WIL: And what, you think I'd protect you? From a bear?

JENNA: You wouldn't?

WIL: You don't need me. Just give him the old one-two. Right jab, left hook …

JENNA: Stop it.

WIL: Which way? Choose. Go.

SHE silently refuses.

Fine. Stay here. I'll go.

HE stuffs the map into his pocket and turns to go.

JENNA: You might as well hit me.

HE bends to re-tie his shoes.

What if I refuse and just sit here and don't move, and then it gets late and you get back to the car and I'm not there? You'll have to come find me in the dark. You'll need to get a ranger and explain that you left me alone to die of hypothermia and starvation. You might as well hit me. You make abusive remarks and leave me for bear bait, but you won't punch me in the face? That's passive aggressive. It's the same as violence.

WIL: Minus the missing teeth.

JENNA: It's illegal to leave your fiancée alone in the woods.

WIL: You can stop using that word. No way am I marrying a woman who hits me.

JENNA: Aha.

WIL: Aha?

JENNA: That's why you made me hit you. So you could dump me.

WIL: I did not—

JENNA: Projection. Vilification. Renunciation. You can't just say you're sick of me. You have to make me punch you.

WIL: I am sick of you. I'm sick of you. Sick of your psychobabble. Sick of your voice. Sick of your face. Sick of looking at you and listening to you and being with you and the way you toss your hair like a horse and that snorty sound you make when you sleep and the sweet stench of your perfume.

JENNA: You bought me that perfume.

WIL: It gives me a headache.

JENNA: All part of a pattern. You probably proposed so I'd say no.

WIL: Why didn't you?

JENNA: You're asking me that? Seriously? Why didn't I say no when you proposed?

WIL: I mean, you being a dyke and all.

HE jumps back as SHE raises an arm to strike him.

I told you: I won't let you punch me again. Even if it was the most stimulating physical contact we've had for weeks.

JENNA: Don't blame me for your shortcomings.

WIL: It's not my fault you don't like men. But I'm open-minded. There's nothing wrong with dykes. I mean if that's how you swing. I'm not prejudiced.

JENNA: If that's how I swing, why in hell would I ever date you?

WIL: I have a feminine side.

JENNA: You have an asshole side.

WIL: Anyway, it's irrelevant. You hit me.

JENNA: That's just an excuse.

WIL: Right. I wanted to break our engagement, so I called you a—

JENNA: Exactly.

WIL: It was a test.

JENNA: Yeah? Well, you failed.

WIL: You failed. You denied it. Vehemently. Which means it's true.

JENNA: Like witch dunking.

WIL: You were hoping I could cure you. I don't blame you.

JENNA: Wow. Okay. I'll see you at the car.

WIL: What?

JENNA: I want to be alone.

WIL: It's too far that way. You won't make it before dark.

JENNA: I'll walk fast.

WIL: You'll get lost.

JENNA: What's it to you? We've broken up. In fact, don't meet me at the car. Just go. Drive off into the sunset. Go your own way. I'll follow the sun. *La la la la la.*

WIL: Your wallet's in the car. And your clothes.

JENNA: Dump 'em on the ground. Strew 'em on the rocks. Who cares? Just get away from me.

WIL: I'll walk with you.

JENNA: Get. Away. From. Me. You got what you want. We're done. You never have to see me again. I just wish you hadn't dragged me to the woods. Couldn't we have broken up at home? Or by phone. What is wrong with you? Well at least I won't miss you.

SHE starts to leave. HE follows.

WIL: That's good, right? That you won't miss me.

JENNA: I am going to fucking kill you if you don't get away from me. You think you're doing me a favor?

WIL: How will you get home?

JENNA: I'll pawn the ring.

WIL: My grandmother's ring.

JENNA: My ring. You gave it to me.

WIL: You'll give it back. It's a family heirloom.

JENNA: I'll sell it. Donate the proceeds to the NRA. Buy stock in Exxon, invest in fracking. Granny'll roll over in her grave.

WIL: Jenna.

JENNA: I'll buy a fur coat. Made of clubbed seal. Club the seal myself. Pretend it's you.

WIL: I'll walk you to the car.

JENNA: Then what?

WIL: I'll drive you home.

JENNA: Then what?

WIL: I'll pack my things.

JENNA: What's left to pack? I saw the boxes in your closet this morning.

WIL: Those were … just some things for Goodwill.

JENNA: All your things. You packed *all your things*. Already.

WIL: You knew.

JENNA: Of course I knew. Why do you think I punched you?

WIL: If you knew, why'd you come?

JENNA: Our life's like a book I can't put down. I want to see what happens.

WIL: This is how it ends.

JENNA: Nope. We're two miles from the end.

WIL: What happens next?

JENNA: Resolution. Denouement. The grand finale. Exit, pursued by a bear.

WIL: Or not.

JENNA: Or not. Take your ring.

> *SHE hands him the ring.*

> Next time, give it to someone you love. It'll save you lots of toothache.

WIL: I loved you.

JENNA: Past tense. I've got 50 bucks and my AmEx card. That'll get me to my future.

WIL: Where are you going?

JENNA: To practice my uppercut.

> *SHE mimes a punch and exits. HE watches her go. HE looks at the ring as twilight descends.*

End of Play

ROOM 313

Carey Crim

Room 313 was originally produced as part of the Samuel French OOB festival: Summer of 2016 (Friday August 12th)

Cast:
MAID: Tricia Alexandro (Member of actor's Equity)
SOLDIER: Ryan Black
DIRECTOR: Carey Crim

Carey Crim produced the play as part of the Samuel French OOB festival.

CHARACTERS:

SOLDIER: Twenties to early thirties, any ethnicity.
MAID: Twenties to early thirties, any ethnicity.

Scene 1

Setting: A cheap roadside motel room in a small town in upstate New York near the Canadian border. The shades are drawn, but some grey light from outside peeks through a hole in one of them. A young soldier, in uniform, is sprawled on the floor in a pool of vomit. There is a mostly empty bottle of vodka next to him and a completely empty bottle of pills. There is a knock at the door. He doesn't stir.

MAID: (O.S.)

(Calling from outside the door)

Housekeeping. Housekeeping!

(Still nothing from the soldier. The knocking continues as the lights slowly fade.)

Scene 2

The same hotel room. Everything is exactly the same as the previous scene but now, the motel maid, is in the room. She sits on the bed staring down at him. He coughs, gradually comes to, and finds himself looking up at her.

SOLDIER: Am I dead?

MAID: No.

SOLDIER: My head.

MAID: Hurts. Yes.

SOLDIER: What are you, a nurse?

MAID: Housekeeping. You threw up.

SOLDIER: What?

MAID: The pills. Whatever you took, you threw it up. You're lying in it.

SOLDIER: Oh.

MAID: I'm not cleaning that up.

SOLDIER: Okay.

MAID: That's not my job.

SOLDIER: No.

MAID: Do you mind if I get started? I have eight other rooms to do today.

SOLDIER: No.

MAID: Not the puke though.

SOLDIER: You said.

(She takes a cigarette out of her pocket and starts to light it.)

This was supposed to be a non-smoking room.

MAID: Do you really care?

SOLDIER: I do, actually.

(She shoots him a hard look but puts the cigarette away and picks up the prescription bottle from the floor.)

MAID: This prescription is only for ten pills. How did you expect to off yourself with only ten pills?

SOLDIER: That's all I had. They're expensive.

MAID: You should have gone to Canada. You could've gotten twice as many in Canada. The border's just up the road. The Lewiston-Queenston Bridge.

SOLDIER: I thought, with the vodka, I thought ten would be enough.

MAID: Or maybe you didn't really want to do it.

SOLDIER: I wanted to do it.

MAID: Because I would think that someone who really wanted to do it, would stick a gun in his mouth. Seems like there would be much less margin for error if you just stuck a gun in your mouth. Or, if you really wanted to use pills, you should have taken two antihistamine tablets before-hand. To prevent the vomiting.

SOLDIER: Oh.

(Stopping the scene)

Wait. Stop. This isn't right.

MAID: What isn't?

SOLDIER: Why would you tell me about the antihistamine tablets? You wouldn't tell me about the antihistamine tablets.

MAID: I was just injecting some humor into the scenario. To make it more palatable.

SOLDIER: Oh. Right. Okay, keep going.

MAID: We have to go back.

SOLDIER: I can't go back.

MAID: We have to. Start over.

SOLDIER: But-

MAID: Start over.

Lawrence Harbison

(They assume the positions they were in at the beginning of the scene. The repeated part of the scene is faster.)

SOLDIER: Am I dead?

MAID: No.

SOLDIER: My head-

MAID: Hurts. Yes.

SOLDIER: What, are you a nurse?

MAID: Housekeeping. You threw up.

SOLDIER: What?

MAID: The pills. Whatever you took, you threw it up. You're lying in it.

(Breaking out of the scene)

That's where I went wrong.

SOLDIER: It's fine. Keep going.

MAID: I should call an ambulance. A doctor.

SOLDIER: I don't need a doctor.

(A siren wails outside.)

What's that?

MAID: A fire truck.

SOLDIER: Not the police?

MAID: No. *(Beat.)* This prescription is only for ten pills. How did you expect to off yourself with only ten pills?

SOLDIER: That's all I had. They're expensive.

MAID: You should have gone to Canada. You could've gotten twice as many in Canada.

SOLDIER: I thought, with the vodka, I thought ten would be enough.

MAID: I stole sixty dollars from your bag. See, this is better. Honesty is better.

SOLDIER: Keep going.

MAID: I stole a hundred dollars from your bag.

SOLDIER: You went through my stuff?

MAID: I thought you were dead.

SOLDIER: So you took my money?

MAID: I didn't think you'd be needing it.

(She hands his wallet back to him.)

I'm not a thief.

SOLDIER: Okay.

MAID: Why didn't you just run? The Canadian border is right up the road. The Lewiston-Queenston bridge.

SOLDIER: So?

MAID: So you could have crossed over. Hidden.

SOLDIER: Yes.

MAID: Why didn't you? Instead of the pills?

SOLDIER: I don't know.

MAID: Wait. Stop. You *do* know. You just don't have the words.

SOLDIER: No.

MAID: Do you want to borrow mine?

SOLDIER: If I do, will you promise to keep going?

MAID: Yes.

SOLDIER: To the end?

MAID: Yes.

SOLDIER: Okay. Give me your words. And ask me again.

MAID: Why didn't you? Instead of the pills? Why didn't you just run?

SOLDIER: Because I wouldn't be allowed to come back. Because it would kill my father if I ran. Because I need medical attention to deal with the psychological and physical trauma I've experienced and, if I get a less than honorable discharge, I'll lose my benefits.

MAID: I think I should call a doctor.

SOLDIER: If you touch that phone, I'll hit you. I swear to God.

MAID: Oh. Stop. This isn't right.

SOLDIER: You said you would keep going. You promised.

MAID: But you said you'd hit me.

SOLDIER: Yes.

MAID: I don't think you would.

SOLDIER: You don't *want* to think I would.

MAID: No.

SOLDIER: *(like reading from a textbook)* I'm suffering from severe depression and Post Traumatic Stress Disorder. I'm likely to experience flashbacks, panic attacks, nightmares, a sense of detachment, irritability, difficulty concentrating, sleeplessness and emotional outbursts. Why wouldn't I hit you?

MAID: You used my words again.

SOLDIER: Do you think I'm stupid?

MAID: Of course not.

SOLDIER: I have an education.

MAID: Okay.

SOLDIER: That's not why I joined.

MAID: No.

SOLDIER: Then why do you think I wouldn't have the words?

MAID: Because of the stress. The trauma.

SOLDIER: Did you assume I'm a poor, disadvantaged and under-educated youth that's been taken advantage of by the military?

MAID: I did. Yes.

SOLDIER: For a maid, you speak real good English.

MAID: I'm sorry. I should have let you have your own words.

SOLDIER: Yes.

MAID: What are they?

SOLDIER: What?

MAID: Your words?

SOLDIER: I don't have them.

MAID: Oh.

SOLDIER: Because of the stress. The trauma.

MAID: I thought I said that.

SOLDIER: Why do you have so many?

MAID: Words?

SOLDIER: Yes.

MAID: I'm studying psychology at the university. I only do this to pay my way.

SOLDIER: That's what strippers always say.

MAID: I'm not a stripper.

SOLDIER: But you could be.

MAID: What's that supposed to mean?

SOLDIER: It means you're pretty.

MAID: Stripper pretty though. Stripper pretty means trashy pretty.

SOLDIER: I don't think so. I just meant soft. You're soft. Can I touch you?

MAID: How many times have you been over there?

SOLDIER: Three. Can I touch you?

MAID: When do you have to go back?

SOLDIER: Can I touch you?

MAID: No.

SOLDIER: I'm supposed to report tomorrow morning.

MAID: But you're not?

SOLDIER: But I'm not. Can I touch you?

MAID: Where?

SOLDIER: Your face.

MAID: Just my face.

SOLDIER: Yes.

(He strokes her cheek.)

It's soft. We have to start over.

MAID: No!

SOLDIER: So we can get to the end.

MAID: But I don't want to.

SOLDIER: Please.

(They a assume their positions from the beginning.)

Am I dead?

MAID: No.

SOLDIER: My head-

MAID: Hurts. Yes.

SOLDIER: Are you a nurse?

MAID: Housekeeping.

SOLDIER: Can I touch you?

MAID: You're skipping ahead.

SOLDIER: To the good part, yes. Can I touch you?

MAID: Where?

SOLDIER: Your face.

MAID: Just my face.

SOLDIER: I know.

(He strokes her cheek.)

It's soft.

MAID: Why didn't you run?

SOLDIER: Do you want me to run?

MAID: Yes.

SOLDIER: Will you come with me?

MAID: I can't.

SOLDIER: I wouldn't know where to go.

MAID: There are places. Groups.

SOLDIER: What kind of groups?

MAID: Groups that help.

SOLDIER: I was in a group. When I first came home.

MAID: Did it help?

SOLDIER: They gave me an 800 number and taught me how to properly set a table. Forks go on the left. Knives and spoons go on the right. On Tuesdays there was Bingo.

MAID: Did you ever win?

SOLDIER: Once.

MAID: I'm glad.

SOLDIER: Could you love me?

MAID: I don't know. Maybe.

SOLDIER: We have to do it right.

MAID: What do you mean?

SOLDIER: This isn't the truth.

MAID: But I want it to be.

SOLDIER: You're beautiful.

MAID: Am I?

SOLDIER: We have to go back.

MAID: Why?

SOLDIER: You know why.

MAID: Back to the beginning?

SOLDIER: And the end. I'm sorry.

MAID: Please don't.

SOLDIER: It wasn't your fault. It was done before you even came in the room.

MAID: You were cold.

SOLDIER: Are you ready?

MAID: Are you?

SOLDIER: I'm tired.

MAID: We have to start over?

SOLDIER: Just one more time.

(They assume their original positions. This time, he does not stir, but stares ahead with vacant, dead eyes. The Maid cries for the dead soldier as the lights fade to black.)

END OF PLAY

RULES OF COMEDY

Patricia Cotter

"World premiere in the 2015 Humana Festival of New American Plays at Actors Theatre Of Louisville."

CHARACTERS

Caroline - Female - Early to mid twenties - any age - smart, odd, serious.

Guy - Male - Mid to late twenties, a stand up comic, intense, on the verge of becoming bitter.

SETTING: Present Day. Guy's studio apartment.

Lawrence Harbison

Guy's studio apartment (clearly belonging to a single guy.) An oddly serious young woman, CAROLINE, early 20's, stands holding a microphone.

GUY, mid 20's, intense, a stand up comic, watches her. Caroline speaks to an unseen audience. She is mid "routine."

CAROLINE: ...Dating. How about dating? We all do it, right? Or some of us don't. I don't date much. Maybe it's because I'm an atheist. Guys don't like atheists. Because during sex, when all the other girls yell out stuff like: "Oh, my God, Oh, my God, Oh, my God!" atheists tend to yell out stuff like: "Oh, my no one!", "Oh, my Ayn Rand!" "Oh, my fictional representative of an antiquated belief system!" And you know that just takes too long. Am I right ladies? Can I get a witness? Holla—

GUY: Stop! I mean I like where you were going with that...I think. Talking about sex is great, 'cause, you know, you're a girl. And everybody loves it when girls talk about sex on stage. Some girls. But I don't know if you're that kind of girl.

CAROLINE: Probably I'm not.

GUY: Yeah. No. So come on, tell me a joke. Like a joke joke with a punch line.

CAROLINE: Okay, okay. (thinking) Wow. I'm blanking. This is really hard. This is surprising hard...do limericks count?

GUY: Let's back up a little bit. Just put down the mic. It's not helping. She struggles as to where to put the mic.)

CAROLINE: I don't want to break it. I'm assuming you value it.

GUY: Whatever. It doesn't work anyway. Listen up: there are four basic elements to comedy. Every single joke has these elements. EVERY JOKE. You may think they don't, but trust me, they do.

GUY: (cont.) It's just a comedy truth. Okay?

CAROLINE: I have no reason not to believe you.

GUY: It's been true since the dawn of comedy. Since the Greeks stood on Mount Olympus or wherever the Greeks stood, and Aristotle taught Plato the art of telling the perfect fucking joke.

CAROLINE: Aristotle was a student of Plato - so I don't think that actually happened—

GUY: Facts don't matter in comedy.

CAROLINE: I'm a big believer in facts.

GUY: The four elements are: The set-up, the story, the twist and the punch line.

(She stares at him.)

You're not going to write any of this down?

CAROLINE: That seems misleadingly simple.

GUY: It's not. I had to learn this stuff the hard way. Years of bombing in front of an audience before I came up with this foolproof method. This workshop is only two hours so you're gonna need to focus.

CAROLINE: I get it. My pen is poised. Now. Now it is poised.

GUY: The set-up. The story. The twist and the punch line. So what are they?

CAROLINE: Set-up, story, punch line.

GUY: And the twist, you forgot that one.

CAROLINE: I just assumed that the twist would come under the umbrella of the story portion of the program.

GUY: It doesn't come under the umbrella of anything - it's its own separate element.

CAROLINE: All right. I mean I disagree but all right. Can I ask a question?

GUY: No.

CAROLINE: Why are rabbis always walking into bars?

GUY: What?

CAROLINE: Are rabbis known for their struggle with alcohol?

GUY: I don't think so.

CAROLINE: Haven't you noticed that many, many jokes are launched by that premise? A rabbi walks into a bar or a Jew walks into a bar. It's never a Seventh Day Adventist walks into a bar.

GUY: Seventh Day Adventists don't drink.

CAROLINE: Exactly. So if they did, then indeed, walk into a bar, wouldn't that be funny? Er?

GUY: How about you forget about rabbis specifically and religion in general, for a second, because you have just accidently stumbled upon the perfect example of a classic set up. Typically you would list three people or three things that have nothing in common and then find a way to get them all in one room, say a bar, or a rowboat, or a proctologist's office. Three incongruent things all in one space. Write this down - three is a classic comedy numeral.

(She hesitates, then deigns to write it down.)

CAROLINE: Or maybe the world of stand-up comedy is anti-Semitic.

GUY: There are tons of Jewish comedians. I'm a half-Jewish comedian.

CAROLINE: That seems like it could be funny. A half-Jewish comedian walks into someplace...a Red Lobster, the DMV...oh, yes, a Red Lobster restaurant might be funny because it's named for a shellfish!

GUY: How did you hear about my workshop again?

CAROLINE: I saw a flyer. I even I bought a book. As research.

GUY: A book.

CAROLINE: It's called: "101 Dirty Jokes". I got it on sale. Do you want to hear one?

GUY: Not really-

CAROLINE: *(reading)* A dog, a cat and a penis are sitting around a campfire...huh...let me find a better one...

GUY: Okay, Caroline don't take this the wrong way, but you don't seem particularly, you know, funny.

CAROLINE: *(as she thumbs through the book)* I know. That's why I'm here.

GUY: The thing is though, I can't teach you to be funny.

CAROLINE: Yes, you can.

GUY: No. I can't. Nobody can. That's not what this class is about.

CAROLINE: That's what you advertised. You said on the flyer that I would be funny after one "hilarious session" or my money back.

(She pulls out the flyer.)

GUY: I said you would find out how to be funny after one, you know, hilarious session.

CAROLINE: So far I have not laughed once since I got in here. There has been no hilarity. Nothing hilarious has occurred.

GUY: Can we please just stop using the word: "hilarious"? Look, if you want your money back...?

CAROLINE: No.

GUY: How about a beer? Do you want a beer? Because I think a beer might help.

(He goes to the fridge to grab a couple of beers.)

Or maybe a field trip - I could take you to an open mic. Who knows if you're lucky I might even get up there myself.

CAROLINE: I've seen your act.

GUY: What? You did when?

CAROLINE: Two nights ago. Right after I signed up for the class. I found you online - saw you had a show - so I went.

GUY: Great.

CAROLINE: Uh-huh.

(He waits, she offers nothing.)

GUY: So...

CAROLINE: Yup. I saw you...up on the stage. I liked your shirt.

GUY: That was a pretty tough crowd that night.

CAROLINE: They definitely weren't laughing very much.

GUY: Like I said they were a tough crowd.

CAROLINE: Three people left. They just got up and left. In the middle of your act.

GUY: I know. I was there. What can I say - it happens.

CAROLINE: You talked a lot about your ex-girlfriend.

GUY: That's kind of the focus of my act right now.

CAROLINE: You seem mad at her.

GUY: What? No. I'm over it. That's just what comedians do, we tell jokes to strangers, typically drunk strangers, about our lives. My job is to make a roomful of drunk people laugh their asses off at the shitty things that happen to me.

CAROLINE: I don't like drunk people. They make me nervous. My aunt is an alcoholic and a dental hygienist.

GUY: See now that's a perfect example of a set-up. An alcoholic dental hygienist starts to clean this guy's teeth –

CAROLINE: She's too sad to be funny. What other kinds of jokes are there?

GUY: Okay...that's actually not a bad question. There are dumb blonde jokes. What did the blonde say to the doctor when she found out she was pregnant? (beat) Are you sure it's mine?

(No response.)

CAROLINE: That joke didn't have a twist.

GUY: I probably should have cancelled, but you know, I needed the a hundred and fifty bucks. Look I understand if this isn't your thing. As a matter of fact, I'm gonna give you a hundred back right now and we can call it a night.

CAROLINE: No.

GUY: Basically I just gave you a one-on-one tutorial, a hundred seems fair to me.

CAROLINE: I don't want my money back. I want –

GUY: I am just going to be brutally honest, Caroline. You're not funny. At all. You actually would be a nightmare to even have in the audience. You can't question, or worry about why a rabbi would walk into a bar, or why a cowboy would have a parrot on his shoulder, you just have to go with it.

CAROLINE: Maybe if you give me an example of the perfect set-up, story, twist –parenthetical– and punch line. *(pause)*

GUY: I don't know about perfect, but if I give you a good example, you'll leave?

CAROLINE: You give me one really good example, and I am out of here.

GUY: Just so you know, this isn't one of my jokes. I do more, like, stories from my life. Well, you know, you heard... whatever. But this is a classic, well-built joke, this is basically the Toyota Camry of jokes.

CAROLINE: Got it.

GUY: A couple of New Jersey hunters are out in the woods when one of them just all of a sudden collapses and falls to the ground. His friend checks him out - and the guy doesn't seem to be breathing, his eyes are rolled back in his head - it looks pretty bad. So the hunter, completely freaked out, whips out his cell and calls 911. He gets the operator and says: "Help me. I think my

GUY: *(cont.)*friend is dead! What do I do?" The operator says: "Just take it easy, sir. I can help. The first thing we need to do is to make sure your friend is dead." So the guy pulls out his rifle and shoots his friend. Then he comes back on the line, and says to the operator: "OK, he's definitely dead. Now what?"

(CAROLINE suddenly bursts into tears.)

Shit.

(She continues to cry.)

GUY: Sorry. Sorry. I mean...are you okay?

CAROLINE: That was funny.

GUY: No it wasn't - it's pretty stupid actually, but it follows the formula. That's all. I don't even like that joke.

CAROLINE: We know the hunter is dumb because he's from New Jersey, correct?

GUY: Correct. New Jersey is kinda the go-to dumb guy state.

CAROLINE: I don't want to be a stand-up comedian.

GUY: Then why are you here?

CAROLINE: I lost my sense of humor.

GUY: I don't think that's even possible.

CAROLINE: People lose their sense of smell or their sense of taste, some people have no common sense, why can't I lose my sense of humor? I can't access joy. In any form. That's why I'm here, in your semi-creepy living room. I knew it wouldn't work. I just thought I'd try.

GUY: Sorry this didn't produce more...hilarity.

CAROLINE: My mother died.

GUY: Oh, God.

CAROLINE: Yeah.

GUY: I'm sorry. *(beat)* How'd she die?

CAROLINE: I killed her.

(Dead silence.)

GUY: Ahhh....

CAROLINE: That was a joke.

GUY: That's not funny.

CAROLINE: I know. I don't know why I said that. It just came out. But she died two months ago. And I haven't laughed since. Not once. I can't even feel the potential for laughing. I don't GUY: You'll, you know, get it back.

CAROLINE: I won't. That died, too.

GUY: You will. People get it back.

CAROLINE: How?

GUY: I think...the only thing I know is that you just have to keep going. Like when I'm bombing, when I'm 100 percent eating shit bombing, I know that if I just keep going, somewhere down the line, they will laugh again. It's a mathematical impossibility that they won't. And just when I think they won't? They do. So that's what you have to do - I think - just keep going.

CAROLINE: Keep going.

GUY: That's all I got. I'm just a mediocre comedian.

CAROLINE: You're not mediocre. It's just that your ex-girlfriend jokes aren't funny. You should stop telling them.

GUY: But that's half my act.

CAROLINE: It doesn't matter. They're mean. That's why people left.

GUY: She broke my heart.

CAROLINE: I know. *(beat)* It's hard, but maybe just start over with some new material. You can have my "a dog a cat and a penis sitting around a campfire" joke. If you want it.

GUY: It all seems sort of stupid, telling jokes when, you know, there's real life.

CAROLINE: No. Not stupid. I think real life is why jokes exist. Even when they don't always work. Anyway. Bye. Thank you.

(She gathers up her stuff to leave.)

GUY: So. What if an orphan and a half Jewish comedian walked into a bar?

(She waits.)

CAROLINE: What's the punch line?

GUY: No punch line. It's an invitation. For a drink with, you know, me.

CAROLINE: An invitation and...kind of a twist.

GUY: Kind of.

CAROLINE: The twists are important.

GUY: Yes. The twists are very important.

(CAROLINE smiles the smallest of smiles.)

(Blackout)

END OF PLAY

SIX BILLION ARCHITECTS

Mark Andrew

First performed at the 2016 Play 6 festival December 8-10th 2016 at the Bluestone Church Theatre, Footscray, Victoria, Australia.

Cast:
Julia Hanna played Franny
Raymond Martini played Lane.
Director: Alicia Benn-Lawler.
Producer: Shannon Woollard.

CHARACTERS:
FRANNY: [F] late 30s
LANE: [M] late 20s

TIME: The present.
PLACE: Franny's home. Living room (e.g. sofa or similar).

AT RISE

Franny is seated, alone; contemplative. She's a bit tipsy (wine glass). It might as well be established now that's she's one of life's natural, effortless comics (perhaps some brief physical comedy as she contemplates a magazine and disgards it – ad lib exasperated snort over articles). She's known Lane for a few months and they are very honest with each other. Straight-forward. The mood of their interactions is affectionate banter, not argument.

FRANNY: The company I work for designs motherboards.

She stares into space.

Mother-fucking-boards.

Lane enters. They acknowledge each other and Lane blows her a kiss; he puts his car keys in his pocket, then turns to Franny properly. She's waggling her eyebrows suggestively at him, and he smiles at her.

LANE: Trying to park near your apartment is a challenge.
FRANNY: A plague of cars.

Pregnant pause. Lane centres himself and takes a deep breath.

LANE: Did you get it?
FRANNY: Oh yeah.
LANE: Thank Christ.
FRANNY: All that fuss over a period.

Lane snorts.

FRANNY: My life is like a supermarket dairy product, waiting franti-cally for my best-before date not to zoom by with a wooosh...
LANE: Nice analogy, except cows generally aren't on the pill.

Franny gives him a look.

FRANNY: The truth is I won't stop checking my expiration date until I have a little wee tiny baby boy being looked after by the nanny, wait-ing for me to come home from designing mother-fucking-boards.
LANE: Why a boy? I mean seeing as how you're speculating.
FRANNY: I don't know how I'll feel if I have a girl. I'll be equally nannified that's for sure, matey, and equally as blessed, but I'd

feel awkward looking her in the eyes.

LANE: Huh?

FRANNY: Because she'll have adulthood in front of her. Look in the eyes of a single woman at twenty; she's got so much inner fuel just waiting to be burned: 'Corrupt me! Turn me on to freaky stuff! Meth! Block my windpipe! Just play with me!'

LANE: Sometimes I won-

FRANNY: - But at thirty, those same eyes send a different message: 'Okay, just don't try to burn me, okay?' There's a bit of fuel left in the tank - just enough to get you back for planetary re-entry, should things go horribly pear shaped.

LANE: Franny come on, you're only...

FRANNY: But look at those eyes again at forty. There's a distant echo from decades before: 'Use me! Dump me! Turn me inside out! Pick me! Unpick me! Unlock me!' But the fuel's pretty much spent, and you don't want to be exposed to middle-aged men on Viagra, it's exhausting and... unpoetic, and any guy you meet is going to try and impress you with pinot and sushi in a city bar instead of listen.

LANE: Maybe that type of guy is damaged goods.

FRANNY: Does it matter? Sixty seconds after he's dropped you off for the last time, he's singing along to fuckin Supertramp on the car radio, putting his ring back on, covering the tan line he doesn't realize you noticed and returning to a suburb with plenty of trees and junior schools and soccer fields and a wife busy in the tub shaving her legs for him while she mentally flicks through nutritious paella recipes. You're not even a speed bump in his memory lanes. Were you asking too much? By asking him 'Just don't interrupt my daily routines, and please enjoy watching Game of Cards reruns as much as I do'.

LANE: Game of Cards?

Smiles.

Game of Thrones. Or House of Cards.

FRANNY: Fuck you. Pedant.

LANE: I'm just saying. Pick one. You jumble things up. Like me and having kids. Remember? I haven't lied to you about anything.

Pause, while she processes the truth of this for probably the umpteenth time.

FRANNY: People don't build anything anymore. It's all plotting and design – intention and no action. The entire fucking planet. Six billion architects, all squabbling about perspective and sightlines. Never...

She hammers the air.

...nailing anything.

Pause.

So God sent us a Jewish Carpenter as a joke.

LANE: *Laughs.* Seven.

FRANNY: What?

LANE: Seven billion. Not six. You're out of date.

FRANNY: Yeah like a dairy product, we did that.

LANE: Coupla' years ago we passed seven billion. Too many babies.

Pause.

FRANNY: Why don't you want kids? I'm curious.

Pause – he's thinking.

LANE: Well; why did you do a PhD in physics?

FRANNY: Huh? I dunno. Science geek. I just sense that stuff.

LANE: I don't. I just don't get it. I don't miss it. I have no affinity for it. I see language, not electrons. I like my Eames chair sans babysick.

FRANNY: Fair enough. It's all solipsim and ego at your age anyway, especially you precocious, young academics.

LANE: And children can be so vile. Especially when they're teenagers! Oh god. Obnoxious. That's an evolutionary adaptation of course. So we throw them out of the village, to prevent inbreeding. Thank god you got your period. Next time you call me over to fill your late night booty prescription I'll be wearing an industrial strength condom. I'll put it on before I leave my place, what with the speed you attack. You're like a South American soccer team.

FRANNY: *grinning.* I must have confused my Prozac for my birth control pills. At least if I'd got pregnant I would have been totally chilled.

LANE: Funny. You know jokes are just camouflaged aggression?

FRANNY: You know when I kick you in the balls it's camouflaged love?

LANE: You are increasingly lovable.

FRANNY: Crikey, you really are careful with language.

Laughs; then regards him evenly.

I don't think you're damaged goods because you don't want kids. Really. But sometimes I hope you'll die, lonely and unloved, in some nursing home. And when they come to pack up your things, no one, including you, will remember your name. I'll come and design a motherboard to help you with your precious language, which will be eroding like a wedding cake in the rain. Like Chet Baker's face after heroin.

LANE: *winces*. Ouch.

FRANNY: Sorry, not enough camouflage for you, lover-boy?

LANE: *He shrugs, but he's smiling*. Maybe on my deathbed I will wish I had children there. Sure. I get that. But that's an accurate answer to an unrevealing question. You should ask, if –

FRANNY: - I 'should' ask! Sure, please go ahead and think for me.

LANE: Touché. What you *could* ask, is… when I'm old, if I had the chance to re-run my life - would I go back and have children? To that, I would answer a big fat no. At that point, I'd tell you that the trade-off has been worth it.

FRANNY: Trade-off? Oh this better be grand.

LANE: You see, what you're blind to, are the benefits of being childfree. You don't consider them – yet the ability to hold a proposition in your head and consider it, even though you disagree with it, is a hallmark of civilisation. It allows you to design your stuff. Aristotle said that.

FRANNY: Aristotle understood electronics?

LANE: Ah. I misspoke. He described suspended ideas as a force for invention. You use that facility to create fridges that talk to the Internet, thus earning you three times my meagre academic salary.

FRANNY: So pray tell what are these childfree 'benefits' Professor Fuck-Knob?

LANE: An absence of worry. Freedom of movement. Much, much more time. Thinking space. Adult thinking space. Being… *not* a parent. Having a car with no extruded plastic toys all over the back seat. No buttered toast and jam carefully filed in with the Chet Baker LPs. Plus, don't forget, you have the biggest benefit of all. The dealmaker.

FRANNY: Hit me. Again. I'm on the ropes.

Lawrence Harbison

LANE: You never have to worry about boring people by droning on incessantly about how cute and clever your bloody offspring are. We've got a human plague and as a result, your car plague and my regular search for a parking space.

FRANNY: And you're okay in your ancient, classic two-seater, as long as you get your knob wet, with periodic reassurance?

LANE: I… well I -. I've never lied to you.

Franny regards him evenly, but he is sanguine.

FRANNY: I do love you. But sometimes I hate you for your mind. It's all ideas to you isn't it? You're like one of those waiters who insist on reciting the entire menu even though I know what I want. It's like being trapped in the back of a taxi while the driver spouts opinions.

LANE: You're doing it again.

FRANNY: What?

LANE: I'm a waiter, I'm a taxi driver. You keeping mixing things.

FRANNY: Listening to you is like being run over in slow motion.

LANE: Ah! A clue. Taxi driver.

FRANNY: It's just language to you isn't it? This whole 'interesting' notion of being childfree? Well it's not an academic exercise for me. I don't want to get to the end and be lowered into the ground without these lovely ovaries doing their job. It's what I'm for. I mean, look at me.

She (e.g.) pulls up her skirt a bit and examines her legs, strokes her belly and holds her breasts.

Phwoar. I'm bloody gorgeous. Isn't that for something? It's supposed to give me an advantage. Except all it's delivered is a bloke with a smart mind who's going to intellectualise himself out of the gene pool like a… blind… disabled, drowning swimmer.

LANE: Okay I'm confused again. I'm a blind disabled taxi-driving waiter?

Franny ignores him.

FRANNY: Could I be a good parent, do I have that intuition; will my child look at me like nature intended? I don't know. I may or may not be a good Mother. There's never been anyone to judge. And I'm banging my head on the Mummy ceiling. Friends, gloating with menstrual schaedenfraude when they get knocked up. Chattering on relentlessly with all the, Christ, *nomenclature* of maternity: sonograms, stitches, leaking nipples, how long before you feel like jumping your fella again. I'm outside of it all, like a club I'm barred from. It seems like there's scores of fat stupid cows squeezing out brats like piglets all over town and I'll never know what it feels

-She's arrested by Lane's expression.

… - what?

LANE: You used 'cow' and 'pig' in the same sentence. The metaphor police will arrest you.

Silence. Franny is preparing to tell him something, and there is a distinct change in mood – she's having trouble taking a run up to it.

FRANNY: I had a pregnancy.

Lane is gobsmacked.

FRANNY: Years ago. Obviously. It was, pretty… late. Late term. When I was in Russia. Illegal. I mean the abortion was... I was allowed to be in.. oh fuck.

A weak smile.

LANE: How late?

Pause.

FRANNY: I knew what star sign she was going to be.

LANE: What went… Why did you, I mean… What did… I have no idea what I'm, I'm… even trying to -

FRANNY: - It was when I was one of those wretched teenagers you think are so vile. When I was thrown out of the village.

LANE: Oh, Franny.

FRANNY: My fella, then, we weren't… working. It was kind of obvious but… not? You know how –

She grinds to a halt, transfixed by refocusing the memory.

LANE: I'm here.

FRANNY: You know how you have to rock an old fridge a few times, before it has enough oomph to go over? It needs to kinda teeter and swing back for another go, before it's ready to go over.

LANE: Er… why would you - okay. I'm listening.

He comes to sit down next to her.

FRANNY: It wasn't very nice.

This is clearly an understatement (tears and snot).

I missed him. Colours disappeared for a while. Taste. I figure you can pretty much forget about enjoying food when you split up. It sort of balances how food tastes so good when you're in… It was spring, and I couldn't face it all on my...

Silence.

After a shocking winter. It's an assault. Your snot freezes. I'll never forget the smell of burnt -

Pause.

At the clinic. It's like a vacuum. Well. Actually, it *is* a small vacuum. Not so small.

She's softly weeping (controlled, not wailing) and absent-mindedly wipes the snot from her fingers into her hair.

That perfunctory, clinical air. Like the dentist, someone just doing their job, inside you. She could have been a perfect child. Just not fit enough to survive my free will.

Silence.

LANE: I'm sorry about the baby.

FRANNY: It was a foetus. They say pregnancy, or foetus, in an abortion clinic. Never baby. Even in Russia. It's the words they teach you.

Pause – he doesn't know what to say.

LANE: What's the Russian for –

FRANNY: Don't.

LANE: Properly sorry.

FRANNY: Thanks. Long time ago.

Silence. Lane looks a bit vacant, still not knowing what to say.

LANE: I pushed a fridge over once.

Franny looks at him carefully, and touches his face tenderly.

FRANNY: You did not.

LANE: I had to get to some pipes.

FRANNY: No you didn't. You're just trying to be with me.

LANE: It was an old fridge and I had to…

FRANNY: Stop it. I appreciate whatever you're trying to do.

LANE: I'm trying to -

FRANNY: - You know I'm going to have to find someone else don't you?

LANE: Yes, I know.

Franny smiles.

FRANNY: Fridge-murderer. You'll go to hell. There'll be a tiny fridge there, creeping towards you, trailing blood, crying.

LANE: It was a foetus Franny. Not a baby.

FRANNY: Yeah I told you that, you, youngest Professor in the faculty. What is your Chair again?

LANE: I said. It's an Eames chair.

FRANNY: Linguistics. You and your lovely words. Weaving your lonely magic.

He has an idea.

LANE: Maybe, in time, I could be Godfather.

FRANNY: No - I think you've lost all claim to being called any type of Father, actually. Sorry about that, lovely man.

LANE: I'm sorry too.

She kisses him tenderly, and he doesn't mind the snot.

FRANNY: But if it works out I do get to be a parent I'll name him after you.

LANE: That's nice.

FRANNY: He'll be called Professor Fuck-Knob.

LANE: Ah.

FRANNY: I'll tell him you begged me to have kids, but I had to turn you down because you make shit up about Aristotle and I had to hold out for someone brutally honest.

Pause.

Shall we go for a walk?

LANE: Sure. Where to?

FRANNY: I'm famished. Let's have something scrumptious.

Lane stands and digs out his car keys; Franny stands, cleans her face, takes his car keys off him and tosses them onto the sofa. They exit together.

CURTAIN. END OF PLAY

SOLD!

Donna Hoke

First performance:
June 2-25, 2016

    Heartland Theatre Company

Director: Connie Chojnacki-Blick
THOMAS – Chris Stucky
MARY– Kristi Zimmerman
Auctioneer – Chris Stevenson

CHARACTERS

THOMAS: Fiftyish, almost impeccably dressed, someone trying to
    look the part, but not quite making it.

MARY: Forties, dressed impeccably head to toe. This is her milieu.

AUCTIONEER: Optional, if the play is staged as part of a series with
    an ensemble of actors. If not, the part can be pre-taped.

Lawrence Harbison

SETTING: An art auction. Several chairs face outward, and a dais to the side of the stage with the back tucked into the wing, so that an auctioneer need not be visible if an actor is not available. A large sign says ART AUCTION TODAY; several frames can hang from drapes or be on easels.

From stage left, THOMAS enters holding a notebook, pen, and auction paddle. He slowly starts walking the perimeter of the stage, as though looking at paintings. At each one, he consults his notebook, and then looks at the painting again. After about thirty seconds, MARY: enters from stage right, and begins to walk the perimeter from that side. She does the opposite of the man; instead of consulting her book, she looks confidently at each painting and then writes notes herself. After a minute of this, the two find themselves standing, center stage, facing the audience, presumably in front of a large, abstract painting.

THOMAS: Chuck Clutter.

MARY: I know.

THOMAS: Do you like him?

MARY: Very much.

THOMAS: It's kind of random, isn't it?

MARY: Oh no, it's beautiful. What really strikes me is the way he blends conceptualism with expressionism. He's incredibly intellectual, and yet his style is expressionistic. That's so unusual.

THOMAS: What is all this up here?

(indicates an area of the painting)

MARY: That's a nearly baroque expression of his energy. Passionate, but controlled. It's gorgeous, really.

THOMAS: It looks like he spilled the paint.

MARY: Listen to it.

THOMAS: Listen?

MARY: Backbeats and bebop, rhythms and riffs. It's jazz all over the canvas.

THOMAS: I don't hear it.

MARY: I just adore it.

THOMAS: I'm not sure how I feel about abstract art, but my friend

(he waves his note paper)

Says this is the one worth keeping an eye on.

MARY: Is that a cheat sheet?

THOMAS: Just some advice for a newbie. You know, pay attention to that Newton over there, the Prescott tile, but especially this one here.

MARY: What does your friend know that you don't?

THOMAS: He just gets it, can talk about it with such... intensity... depth. Like you.

MARY: You don't buy what you like?

THOMAS: I do buy what I like, but I want to like what I buy, you know?

MARY: No.

THOMAS: I kind of like that Johnson landscape over there.

MARY: What do you like about it?

THOMAS: The twilight creates a feeling, like magic, or something possible...

(trails off, embarrassed)

MARY: Go on.

THOMAS: It's not important.

MARY: Because it's not on your little list there.

THOMAS: I just want to be sure. I'm trying to give my office a certain feel. For clients.

(reaches in his pocket and pulls out a business card, hands it to her)

I'm sorry. Thomas Barstock.

(extends a hand)

MARY: *(takes the card, shakes his hand)*

MARY: Feingold.

(looks at card before putting it in purse)

Real estate.

THOMAS: Development.

MARY: *(indicates the Clutter painting)* And you're sure that this would provide that ... feel for your real estate clients?

THOMAS: No, I'm not, but—

MARY: Your friend said it was worth keeping an eye on.

THOMAS: It is...interesting. I should like it, right?

MARY: You're the one with the notes.

THOMAS: It says in the program it could go for up to $6000. Do you think it will?

MARY: Do you?

THOMAS: He's very collectible.

MARY: Is that what's important?

THOMAS: Well... shouldn't art be an investment?

MARY: *(she's had it, preys on his ignorance)* He's collectible in certain circles maybe. Locals like him. I'm not sure about his worth nationally.

THOMAS: But it would hold its value locally?

MARY: Maybe. It's not representative of his best work. It wouldn't be the first time an artist donated something he wasn't happy with to an auction.

THOMAS: I never thought of that

MARY: Trade secret.

> *(beat)*

And I hear he's having money problems. I wouldn't be surprised if's going all Picasso try to bail himself out.

THOMAS: Wow.

MARY: shrugs.

THOMAS: I really wanted to buy something worthwhile.

MARY: Then perhaps this isn't the one.

THOMAS: But—

MARY: If you've got the money, there are plenty of things here that could provide the right... feel for your office.

THOMAS: I don't want to be wasteful.

MARY: Here, let me see your program. Maybe I can point out some things...

> *(MARY takes THOMAS's program and leafs through it pointing things out around the room)*

See this Farrell monochrome? Very different from Clutter, very easy on the eye, and how can all that green not be wide open to your own interpretation? Grenvelt, very, very collectible, and with a reputation that seems to be evolving out of the area. This Smithson... I think her reputation is only just beginning; that would be a very good investment—

AUCTIONEER: *(O.S.)* The live auction portion of the evening will begin in one minute. Please take your seats.

MARY: That's our cue. The Grenvelt; that may be your best bet. It would be an impressive purchase.

THOMAS: Thank you. Good luck.

MARY: And good luck to you. Keep your head and I'm sure you'll get something worthwhile.

THOMAS and MARY move to two chairs facing outward from the stage.

AUCTIONEER: Welcome to the art auction to benefit the Steel Hall Contemporary Art Center. All bids are final, so please control your body parts unless you're serious about bidding. We'll begin with Lot Number #817, a Chuck Clutter abstract entitled "Candyland." I will start the bidding at one thousand dollars.

THOMAS looks unsure, so MARY: raises her paddle to start the bidding. THOMAS keeps his eye on her throughout the next lines, and notes that she is not bidding anymore. Several times he might, but doesn't, and gets increasingly agitated with indecision.

AUCTIONEER: I have one thousand, do I hear two thousand?

(beat, AUCTIONEER points to an invisible attendee who bids silently)

That's two thousand. Three thousand?

(points to another invisible attendee)

Three thousand. We're at three thousand dollars; do I hear four?

(looks back in direction of first invisible attendee)

Four thousand? Come on folks, you're giving it away. Who will give me four thousand?

MARY: raises her paddle. THOMAS looks over with interest.

AUCTIONEER: I have four thousand. Do I hear five? Who will pay five thousand for this lovely piece?

(Beat, AUCTIONEER points to the silent bidder)

Five thousand! I have five thousand. Can I get six? Six thousand anybody? Okay, then it's five thousand. Going once, going—

MARY: raises her paddle. THOMAS takes it in, his eyes narrow.

AUCTIONEER: I have six thousand, ladies and gentlemen. Do I hear—

THOMAS: Seven thousand!

AUCTIONEER: Seven thousand! That's more like it. Can I get eight thousand for this original work? Eight thousand? Do I hear eight thousand?

MARY: starts to raise her paddle again, and THOMAS immediately raises his.

THOMAS: Eight thousand!

AUCTIONEER: We're looking for nine thousand, nine thousand for lot number #817 this evening.

(looks to MARY)

Ma'am?

MARY: doesn't respond, but puts on a show of calculating in her notes.

AUCTIONEER: Then it's eight thousand to the man in the plaid dinner jacket [or whatever THOMAS is wearing]. Going once—

MARY: raises her paddle.

AUCTIONEER: Nine thousand! Do I hear—

THOMAS: Ten thousand!

MARY: appears to consult her notes, looks over at the THOMAS and smiles slightly, knowingly.

MARY: Eleven thousand!

THOMAS looks shocked, but her sudden fervor incites him.

THOMAS: Twelve thousand!

AUCTIONEER: Whoa! Slow down, ladies and gentleman. They won't pay me if you do all the work. Can I get—

MARY: Thirteen thousand!

AUCTIONEER: Thirteen thousand folks! Let's go for fourteen. Who—

THOMAS: Fourteen thousand!

MARY: Fifteen thousand!

THOMAS: **(definitively)** Eighteen thousand dollars!

MARY: slides back in her seat, satisfied. THOMAS looks over at her apologetic, but triumphant.

AUCTIONEER: Eighteen thousand dollars, ladies and gentlemen. Amazing! Can we go any higher? Do I hear nineteen?

(beat)

Eighteen-five?

THOMAS looks at MARY half-expectantly, but she remains motionless and unemotional.

AUCTIONEER: Anybody?

(AUCTIONEER looks at MARY)

Then it's eighteen thousand dollars to the gentleman in the plaid jacket [or whatever]. Three times what we expected to get for "Candy-land." Congratulations, sir!

MARY: smiles to herself.

AUCTIONEER: Okay, let's move on to Lot #422, this monochrome by William Farrell...

AUCTIONEER's voice fades out, lights dim briefly, and come back up.

AUCTIONEER: Folks, this concludes the evening's auction. Thanks for your patronage and generosity. See you next year!

THOMAS and MARY rise. THOMAS approaches MARY: .

THOMAS: Hey, I'm sorry about the Clutter.

MARY: Oh no, that's the way it works. And you got what you wanted, right? The premiere piece on your list.

THOMAS: Yeah.

(beat)

You didn't win anything.

MARY: Oh, I did. I won the Johnson in the silent auction. I'm very good at aggressive hovering.

THOMAS: You got the Johnson?

MARY: Ironic, isn't it?

THOMAS: You really liked the Clutter.

MARY: I did, but it wasn't worth $14,000.

THOMAS: Yeah.

(beat)

Maybe we got a little carried away.

MARY: You think?

THOMAS: I'd never be able to sell it for what I paid.

MARY: Why would you sell it? It's gorgeous.

THOMAS: I would never sell the Johnson.

MARY: I won't.

THOMAS: I just love looking at it.

MARY: Yes, I love the mystery in it, the longing, the potential that occurs when day slips into night. And yet there's a void, a sense of mortality that is quite compelling. It's a challenging piece of work.

(beat)

But, as I said, that's the way these things go.

THOMAS: Right.

> *(beat)*

Would you... Can I buy you a drink?

MARY: Are you offering me a consolation prize?

THOMAS: No, I just...okay, maybe.

MARY: I don't think so.

THOMAS: Are you sure? You can sneak another peek at the Clutter.

MARY: If I really need to see it, I know where to find it, don't I? I hope your clients enjoy... your Clutter. Have a good evening.

MARY exits, leaving THOMAS standing alone and confused.

END OF PLAY

TA

Martha Patterson

The first production of this play was on July 15th, 2016, at Hovey Players in Waltham, Massachusetts. The cast & crew were as follows:

Cast:
MONA: Ellen Robinson
CARLOS: Richie DeJesus

Crew:
Director: Eric Linebarger
Producers: Shannon L. Gmyrek & Richie DeJesus
Stage Manager: Shannon L. Gmyrek
Lighting Design: Kristine Mackin
Sound Design: Kristin Hughes
Set Design: Eric Linebarger

CHARACTERS

CARLOS: Late teens, hanging out on the corner and using an iPod, a Latino

MONA: Late teens, sitting on a wall or a bench reading a newspaper, any race

SCENE: A street corner
TIME: The present

Lawrence Harbison

AT RISE: A street corner. MONA is seated on a bench or wall near CARLOS:. MONA is reading a newspaper and CARLOS: watches her as he walks past, then he turns back and takes his earphones from his iPod from his ears. He smoothes his hair down with his hands, a sign of vanity.

CARLOS: *Hola! Eh, chica!* Mind if I ask -?

MONA: Ask what?

CARLOS: Why're you reading that newspaper? You can get it online!

MONA: I like reading it in my hands.

CARLOS: But online is free!

MONA: So was this paper. I picked it up on my way to the dentist.

CARLOS: You got something wrong with your teeth?

MONA: *(back to her newspaper)* The dentist's was a check-up.

CARLOS: I'm goin' to a pick-up basketball game.

MONA: Too short for that, aren't you?

CARLOS: No!! And just got my hair cut – looks good, don't it?

(Smooths his hair down again.)

MONA: Forget it. Not into gay men.

CARLOS: I ain't gay!

MONA: *(turning to leave)* Cheerio!

CARLOS: "Cheerio"???

MONA: Cheerio is British for "so long."

CARLOS: You blowing me off? Just thought you might want a tip.

MONA: I have all the tips I need, thank you.

CARLOS: Hey – want to hit Wendy's? I'll buy you a burger.

MONA: No. Just so you know, I don't take advice from any wanker who tells me not to read the paper. I'm educated. I want to know the news.

CARLOS: Wanker?? I know that expression. It's English, too. You could try being a little more friendly. Listen to this.

(Hands her his earphones.)

It's the new Beyoncé single.

MONA: I thought she had a baby. Is she recording?

CARLOS: Maybe it's Gaga, I dunno.

MONA: You're telling me to listen to someone and you don't even know who it is?

(putting on earphones)

It's Gaga.

CARLOS: Told ya!

MONA: You said it was Beyoncé.

CARLOS: Hey! I made a mistake.

MONA: And besides, only gays like Gaga.

CARLOS: You don't like Gaga?

MONA: *(removing earphones)*She's all right.

CARLOS: You got a little of her going on there yourself, you know? *Creo que eres Hermosa!*

MONA: Flattery will get you nowhere.

CARLOS: Think you're all that, do you? (Pause) This street is trashed. Graffiti everywhere and it's no place for a *chiquita* like you. You could get mugged.

MONA: I'm a woman.

CARLOS: No place for a *woman* like you. Next time take a cab to where you want to go, 'stead of the bus.

MONA: *(laughing)* Listen to him! "Take a cab."

CARLOS: *(He thinks he's getting somewhere because she laughed.)* Hey - how about Wendy's? Give me some hope!

MONA: I don't think so.

CARLOS: Why not?

MONA: Because you want a Gaga lookalike, and I'm not her.

CARLOS: But I'm all juiced up! Playin' basketball today!

MONA: Fabulous. But you're gay.

CARLOS: I'm *not*! I'm your knight in shining armor. I'm your Superman! I've got the keys to your future.

MONA: If you have the keys to my future, then you'd better open a door for me.

CARLOS: Huh. *(Pause)* You ever had a real man in your life?

MONA: You mean like YOU?! I guess so.

CARLOS: You GUESS so? *Cuanto anos tienes?*

MONA: Ta very much.

CARLOS: "Ta?" What's that?

MONA: British for "thank you."

CARLOS: Oh, well, "ta" to you too. Trust me, you never had a man like me.

MONA: Well, I sure did. He was older than you and he treated me right.

CARLOS: In what way?

MONA: Chivalrous.

CARLOS: Another British word?

MONA: Anyone's word. Americans use it.

CARLOS: What happened to this guy?

(Pause)

MONA: He died.

CARLOS: Of what?

MONA: Food poisoning.

CARLOS: You're joking. I don't believe it.

MONA: You don't have to.

CARLOS: No, but really, what did he die of?

MONA: He didn't. I made it up.

CARLOS: YOU LIED TO ME??

MONA: Why not? I hardly know you.

CARLOS: Lying is one of the Seven Deadly Sins.

MONA: You're thinking of "bearing false witness."

CARLOS: That's the Ten Commandments. See? I'm smart too.

MONA: ARE you.

CARLOS: Whatever. So I'm your first real *vato?*

MONA: If you think so. Except you're gay.

CARLOS: I AM NOT GAY. Listen, I'll open a door for you. I'll even teach you how to dance!

MONA: You ARE gay!

CARLOS: No. I'm tryin' to pick you up! What you keep sayin' I'm gay for?

MONA: I don't know how to dance. And you do?

CARLOS: I can moonwalk. Let's hit Wendy's. That too low-class?

MONA: No. I know you don't have money.

CARLOS: But I will, some day.

MONA: Everybody thinks that.

CARLOS: You're so pretty. I've hardly ever seen a girl as pretty as you. You remind me of when I was little and I had a big sister. Serena. She was nice, like you. 'Cept she got hit by a drunk driver.

MONA: That's terrible.

CARLOS: She was only sixteen.

MONA: I'm sorry.

CARLOS: People shouldn't drive drunk. Anyway…you could be making my day. If you went out with me, I'd know I had a date. I'd know more than that. I'd know finally some girl likes me enough that I don't have to prove I'm not gay! How about it?

MONA: Well - okay.

CARLOS: Cool! You'll really go out with me? You're not going to run me down 'cuz I'm not Jay-Z?

MONA: I'm not trying to run you down.

CARLOS: I don't mind that you're not Gaga.

MONA: *(She hands him back his iPod.)* Thank you so much. I don't wear dresses made out of meat.

CARLOS: Hey. We're just going for a burger. No meat dresses for me.

MONA: And I don't kiss on the first date.

CARLOS: Old-fashioned, huh?

MONA: I was brought up right. Can you really teach me how to moonwalk?

CARLOS: Sure, *no te preocupes*, I'll take you to a club. Tonight.

MONA: Show me now.

CARLOS: Okay.

(He starts to dance, a moonwalk, and sings to sing the Lady Gaga song.)

"Baby, I was born this way, I was boo-o-r-n this way."

MONA: *(Standing, she tries to copy his dance moves.)* I can't do it.

CARLOS: Sure you can. Just put one foot in back of the other, then slide.

(He dances some more.)

MONA: You're good!

CARLOS: I'll show you more tonight.

MONA: Just so long as you don't try to snog me on the dance floor.

CARLOS: "Snog?"

MONA: You know – put the moves on me.

CARLOS: Snog, huh? You think you're so English.

MONA: I don't mess around. And get me home by eleven o'clock. My parents look out for me.

CARLOS: *I'm* lookin' out for you!

MONA: This is just one date, understand?

CARLOS: Awesome. You know, you could come to my game after the burger. And before the club.

MONA: They have Wendy's in England.

CARLOS: You ever been there? England?

MONA: No. But I'll go someday.

CARLOS: Just don't be drinking tea with your pinky raised and acting snobby with me.

MONA: *(laughing)* I'm going out with you. What're you complaining about?

CARLOS: Nothing, *mi amor*, nothing.

MONA: Ta very much.

CARLOS: *Chevere!*

(He lets her proceed ahead of him and they exit together.)

THE END

A TALE OF TWO IN ONE

F. Lynne Bachleda

F. Lynne Bachleda produced "A Tale of Two in One" on August 4-5, 2016 in Nashville, Tennessee as a part of Actors Bridge Side Show Fringe Festival at Darkhorse Theater. Rachel Hamilton directed Lee Daniel as HE and Meredith Daniel as SHE. Annie Freeman designed and fabricated the costumes.

Music rights information:

"Happy Together" performed by The Nylons for Windham Hill Records. Music by Gary Bonner and lyrics by Alan Gordon. Originally recorded by The Turtles.

"Maybe This Time" from the stage and film MUSICAL *CABARET*, 1972 film soundtrack on HIP-O label. Music by John Kander, Lyrics by Fred Ebb

NOTE: permission to produce this play does not include the rights to use the above music in production.

CHARACTER

HE: Embryo who wears a blue t-shirt 6 weeks male
SHE: Embryo who wears a pink t-shirt 6 weeks female

The play takes place inside a human uterus.

Actors are barefoot and wear tan-brown body suit tights, plus appropriate blue or pink T-shirts that are able to be easily torn in half vertically while being worn. Red silk sashes or stuffed cord ties 1-3 inches wide and 72-plus inches in length are tied at the waist to represent umbilical cords. Easy to break away/tear abruptly is essential for dramatic effect. Flesh-colored head covers with prominent red veins painted on both sides hide hair and complete the actor's costumes. Contact the playwright (bachleda@bellsouth.net) for images of one production's costume solutions.

The cast should be age 18-20. Most important is that the actors must be very close in age.

AT RISE: He and She enter "dog paddle-dancing" in loopy, dreamy arcs as the music of The Turtles' "Happy Together" begins. They use their hands like flippers and are oblivious to each other.

Imagine me and you, I do. I think about you day and night. It's only right to think about . . . .

Music stops and She begins to sing the same lyric acapella, stopping at the same lyric place as above when She and He come face to face equally abruptly. After peering closely at each other, She twirls around, and flirtatiously begins.

SHE: Does this amniotic fluid make my butt look big?

HE: God.

SHE: Well, does it? I just asked you a simple question.

HE: It's you. I know it's you. I remember your boundless vanity. *(Beat)* For God's sake, why do I have *another* incarnation with you?

SHE: Who were you expecting? Obviously, we have unfinished business, bubba. *(Beat)* And so what if it is me, wonderful me? I'm not terribly thrilled to share a womb with no view with you either, Buster or whatever he-rah, who-rah macho-man-mangler thing you want to be called. Or, shall I refer to you this time as "Mr. Missing Y"?

HE: Listen to you! Is it any wonder I'm not overjoyed to be here? Last time it ended poorly between us. How and who is it gonna be this time, little sinister sister? You, us, me, nada, zipville? *(Beat)* Can a fella get a drink around here?

SHE: Yeah. Still needing a coping crutch. Can't quite make it on your own, can you? Never could. Never can. Never will.

HE: Hey, hey, twin bitch baby! Watch it!

(He faces her nose- to-nose with malice. She looks at him her mouth open a little. For a moment she is lost.)

A SILENCE.

SHE: Okay! Ratchet down, Buster! *(Beat.)* She can already feel us, I think of the damn responsibility of it all, so no fetal alcohol this time. Bar for unborn babies closed, I'm thinkin'.

HE: Months of runny poop in pampers! That'll be my thanks to her for cutting me off when I get out of here.

SHE: IF you get out of here. The odds are against it *(Beat)* Why so angry, Buster? Gonna make a play to really be the Marlborough man this time?

HE: Maybe.

SHE: *A PAUSE as she sizes him up.* That'll be the day. Jeesuz. I'm almost always and every time more butch than you'll ever be.

HE: And so, girly girl, you wanna give me some testosterone? Just this once? Just for old time's sake? It seems you've always got so, so, so much to spare.

SHE: *(coquettishly)* Wait. Wait. We're off on the wrong flipper. Haven't you noticed? I've changed.

HE: *Turning his back to her.* God. I think it must be our forty-seventh time together in this cramped, airless organ.

Turning to face her with competing emotions.

I love you, but remember, "Each man kills the thing he loves."

SHE: And Oscar Wilde continued, "Yet each man does not die."

HE: So, this over-juiced jock-to-be remembers a little poetry from a past incarnation. Hmmm? Nice, eh?

SHE: Oh, brother, part of me truly has missed you.

HE: *Stepping as far away from She as possible.* I want my own life, just this once. Not with some part of you. My own! Not some half-breed, blurry diptych version of us.

SHE: *(laughing)* Oh, fancy words, we have now, do we? "Diptych"? Facing pages of the same book? This book, this time, is yet to be written.

HE: So, yeah, right, half-breed. Who's your daddy, anyway? Huh? Same as mine?

SHE: Yes, fool, the same as yours! It's not about multiple maybe-daddies. It's all about what happens right here, and soon, with you and me. We're not identical twins this time, but we could be. We're still twins. You die, or I die, and things change. Maybe somebody survives to solo, and maybe they incorporate the dead one, the vanished one. Poof! No trace. Wanna come be the real and invisible part of me? *(Beat.)* Spooky, but that's the science, skin head! Got it?

HE: Yeah, right. Sure. Whatever. *(Beat.)* But, really, she can't keep it together. Her knees, I mean. Right?

SHE: I ought to slap you, but these damn flippers don't nearly do you justice, lucky for you, haploid, half-life, that you are. Don't you dare talk about our mother that way! Don't you dare!

She takes a swing at He, but misses.

HE: *(softening)* Hey. Hey. Until we come out of this alive, we're in this together.

SHE: Respect her!

HE: Okay. Okay. *(Beat)* Dance with me, then.

HE begins to sing a capella and, as he does, HE and SHE dance a soft-shoe routine, at which they are well-practiced from having done this many, many times before.

Imagine me and you, I do I think about you day and night. It's only right to think about the one you love and hold them tight, so happy together. . . .

The SFX of banging noises and groans in a sexual rhythm interrupts their simpatico interlude.

HE: Yeah, I remember this. Flat on her back again, except for the occasional top-heavy cat-fight rollover move.

SHE: Show a little respect. She's probably lonely.

HE: God. I hear hollow promises. Do you? Put your ear nub to the wall.

More and louder rhythmic sexual banging SFX into climax.

SHE: It makes we wonder, do you think she knows we're here yet?

HE: If they're not more careful, his bangs will boost us from her rafter and out into the void. I can live with the void, but how can it be so lonely, so lonely with you and me crammed in here?

SHE: It's existential. We know the odds, don't we? What's the latest on conceived twins? Are both of us going to make it out of here alive?

HE: Umm, I'm a little behind in my medical research. It's a bit dim in here. Maybe you've noticed. Last count it was about 15% of the time we both live to tell the tales.

SHE: Are you saying what I think you're saying? *(Beat.)* Speak up! Are you? In more than eight out of ten twins sets, one twin dies in here, inside her, never to experience the flash bang dazzle of the delivery room and all that comes later?

He throws She an arch, sly, and slightly menacing smile.

SHE: Are you threatening me?

HE: Maybe. You could call it foreshadowing.

SHE: Coming from you, I know a threat when I hear one.

HE: Maybe. *(Beat)* Look, I don't necessarily want to or even have to kill you this time. Maybe we could change the script? Something less drastic?

SHE: How? Why?

HE: Well, what if we merged fifty-fifty, for example? Just for something different. You know, spice it up a bit.

She throws He an arch, sly, and slightly menacing smile.

HE: Well, aren't you curious about what would happen if we did?

SHE: You mean you want to be bi-curious? That is so, so retro. Can't you keep up? If we combine into one person, the Facebook gods give us more choices than ever before, at least 56 gender orientations and counting: Agender, androgenous, bigender, cis female, FTM, gender fluid, genderqueer—

HE: God! Enough! I don't care about the blended labels. I just want to be on my own.

SHE: Slimmest of slim chances of that, bubba.

HE: You're making my testosterone boil, and you know what happens then! I'm a heterosexual man this time, and don't make me prove it!

SHE: (*MOCKING HIM*) What would that even look like?

She turns from him and resumes reciting her list.

MFT, neither, pangender, transgender male, transgender female, transmasculine, transfeminine, two-spirit.

HE: *Moving upstage and behind her.* Are you, are you finished yet? Are you? Do you ever, ever, ever stop talking?

SHE: No. And, last, but not least, "Other." There are more on the list, but you get the gist, don't you?

He sensuously takes her red umbilical cord and begins to loop it loosely around her neck

HE: Isn't this a beautiful idea? You always did shine in red, little one.

SHE: Vamping a little, are we? Again? Nothing new under the sun? You bore me. Again.

HE: Continuing to fondle the red silk and tightening it slightly.It's a long red road, the good road.

SHE: It's not a road! It's an umbilical cord, you imbecile. Now stop fooling around!

HE: Where there's a will, there's a possibility. Right, sister?

He pulls the silk very snugly around her neck and give a little tug to accentuate his anger.

SHE: You don't have a will, for Chrissakes. You're a fetus, remember?

She stomps on his arch in the classic self-defense move when being attacked and held from behind. He reacts by letting go of the silk.

HE: Ouch! Why are you always so mean? I was just kidding around. What else is there to do in here.

She steps clear of him.

SHE: Knock it off, dipstick! *(Beat)* What a lousy excuse for a human. You don't deserve—

She unwraps the silk from her neck.

HE: Okay, okay, I'm sorry. I'M SORRY!

SHE: The thought of going through life with you makes me grow horns and a tail!

HE: I SAID, 'I'M SORRY." *(Beat)* I know you're touchy about that sort of thing. Really.

SHE: Really? Then show some respect.

HE: Really. *(Beat)* Come closer. I want to show you the part of me you *can* have. Not this time, maybe next time. Maybe next time.

SHE: Why should I trust you? Why should you trust me?

HE: Because we have the same parents, and at heart we are human, and I want—

SHE: I want, too.

She moves slowly and cautiously toward He. Suddenly, She grabs He's umbilical cord and rips it apart. He gasps for air.

HE: *Falling and dying.* Maybe next time.

She stands over him, and then rips his blue t-shirt lengthwise. Flipping him over, she rips the remainder of one-half of the shirt off his body. Slowly, she stands and pulls the blue half shirt onto her body. She sings a capella.

Imagine you in me. I do. I think about you day and night. It's only right.

Segueing into "maybe this time" (From cabaret)

Maybe this time, I'll be lucky. Maybe this time, I'll stay.
Maybe this time, for the first time, love won't hurry away. . .
All the odds are in my favor. Something's bound to begin. It's
got to happen, happen sometime. Maybe this time I'll win.

Lights out.
End of play.

THE TANGO

Elayne Heilveil

The Original Production was at Theatre West, Los Angeles CA. on Oct. 4, 2016. It was directed by Elayne Heilveil.

THE CAST:
SHEILAH: Sheila Shaw
MANNY: Anibal Silveyra

CHARACTERS:

MANNY (Emmanuel): Late 30's – 50. Latino. A fiery and aging Latin lover. A dancer past his prime.

SHEILAH: Late 30's – 50. A bit insecure, but with a self-depricating charm.

SETTING: Manny's Tango Studio. Night.

We hear TANGO MUSIC as the lights come up. A desk and chair is off to the side in an otherwise bare stage. MANNY is poised center stage staring out as if into a mirror. His head is high, arms extended, as if holding a partner, in the regal dancers pose. He moves gracefully, marking steps to the music. After a moment Sheilah ENTERS. She stands in the doorway, unseen, watching in awe his masculiine grace. Manny does a slow turn and spots Sheila. She shrinks back, embarrassed.

SHEILAH: Oh, I'm sorry. So..soooo sorry. I didn't mean to interrupt. I was just…

MANNY: No, no, please, come in. Come in. (*Shuts music off.*)

SHEILAH: Am I…too early? Too late? I mean, I… can go.

MANNY: No, no. You are…(*checks her out*) perfect.

SHEILAH: Really?

MANNY: Your time is my time, Senora. (*He bows gracefully.*)

SHEILAH: Oh my. Well, actually, I turned around twice and started back home. But then I thought, No Sheilah, you promised yourself you would do this. Something that… (*Deep breath*) scares you.

MANNY: Ah, but to dance, is a fearful thing? (*Sad face.*) No.

SHEILAH: Well, I mean, it's the *tango*. And, well, (*Looks down at her imperfect body.*)…look at me.

MANNY: I see… an exquisite woman.

SHEILAH: Oh, no, no. It was silly. I just…dared myself, and well, I'm here. Sort of. (*Looks around.*) Like an out of body experience.

MANNY: So we must get you back to the feeling *in* the body, no?

SHEILAH: No, please. I just thought it would be… more practical than sky diving.

MANNY: Well, I am glad you have not fallen from the sky, Senora. But have landed here, yes? But if you will, (*He crosses to the table and gallantly pulls out the chair for her to sit.*) we shall compose ourselves, with the papers?

SHEILAH: Oh, sure. Of course. (*She sits. He hands her a stack of papers.*) Just as long as I'm not signing my life away. I have (*Jokingly.*) 'commitment' issues.

MANNY: A mere f*ormalidad*. Nothing more.

He stands behind her, closely, as she skims the stack of papers. He leans down. She can feel his breathing.

SHEILAH: Oh, I see. Uh huh. Uh huh. All these paragraphs, like boiler plates…

MANNY: You see a plate, I see a dish, no?…who sizzles?

SHEILAH: A dish? Hardly. No. I just read all kinds of things. It's a legal term they use in contracts. It means it's just the standard stuff. But, no worries, I'm just here for the complimentary class. It is…complimentary?

MANNY: I assure you, it is quite…(*Seductive.*) complimentary.

SHEILAH: Yes, well. It's just that I sit all day. As you might have noticed, and just… need to stretch. Once. Or twice. Every… now…and then.

MANNY: We cannot have Emmanuel responsible for the possibilty of, how you say, stretching too far the limits?

He reaches over her shoulder to move the papers closer to her. His face is by her neck.

SHEILAH: Oh no, of course not. (*Glances back through the papers.*) Uh huh. I see. If someone slips, or pulls their back out… dipping. I suppose. (*Making light.*) As long as there are no missing floor-boards…or… anything.

MANNY: I will assure you it is very smoothe. The floor. There is no… how you say, slippage?

SHEILAH: Oh, of course, of course. (*Waves papers in front of her like a fan.*)

MANNY: But, I must be honest. Because if we do not have the hon-esty, the truth between us, there is no trust. With the beginners, once or twice or… maybe more, they have… um…*han caido*… ah…fallen? .

SHEILAH: Oh, dear, they have?

MANNY: *Enamorado*…in love.

SHEILAH: Ah.

MANNY: With the power, the intention, of the dance of course. (*He extends his muscular arm, to demonstrate.*)

SHEILAH: Oh, of course. The dance. Is it hot in here?

MANNY: It can get quite…steamy. With the dance, of course.

SHEILAH: Right. It could be me. With the change. I mean I am… changing. Maybe. Soon. You know, I…I thought there would be other people…. in the class I mean.

MANNY: Ah, but registration has been … *lento*. Because…we are…

select. Yes? But, no worries, please, I charge you the same for the one to one.

SHEILAH: I see. But it says here it's a *series*… Six or…eight…

MANNY: People who take the dance, they come sometimes, in love, to learn the ways to be, to feel   each other. Together. But you, you have come alone? A woman such as you? It can be a bit more…(*Shrugs*.) costly?

SHEILAH: Oh, it's not that I have no one. Or, or nobody. No. There is a Steve. But he's, well…just another Steve. There was Steve one. Ten years ago. Steve two. Two years after that. And now, Steve three. I know it's strange. But always, there is something… wrong…with Steves.

MANNY: They are not…Stephanos?

SHEILAH: Just plain old Steves. I mean, they're very nice. But it could be just be a little thing, like the way a piece of lettuce gets stuck in a tooth. Or the way their hands lay limp in mine. I find… something. And year after year, I just sit there, and watch them snore away on my couch on New Year's eve and watch that ball drop. Five, four, three, two…to what? Another year of wrong words, wrong Steves, wrong…me's. And I think, is this it? Is this all? Is this what my life is?

MANNY: Your life will be forever changed… with the tango. And I will…charge you the same for the one to one. You and Emmanuel will be…very private.

SHEILAH: Uh huh. It's just that I…

MANNY: …do not trust Emmanuel?

SHEILAH: No, no.

MANNY: No, no, no. Then you will not sign a thing! No, no. I will not let you. (*He sweeps the papers from her.*)

SHEILAH: But…

MANNY: I can see you have attention to detail. Which is very, very good. In the work. In the life. And in the tango. But you need… how you say…reassurance? To 'commit'. So, you will see first. I will show you. And you… tell me. (*He backs away to the center space anddemonstrates.*) Fast, fast. Stop! Fast, fast…Slow. (*Then does the steps in   time, to match.*) T…A…NG…Oooo.

SHEILAH: Ohhhhhh. Uh huh. Very nice.

He extends his arm for her to join him. She slowly crosses to him.

MANNY: Come, come.

(She stands beside him.)

What beauty do *I* see in the light. In the hair this way?

SHEILAH: Oh, this? No. It's just my…head. (*Fluffs her hair.*) I must have slept on it wrong.

MANNY: Her hair was full, in waves, thick and wild down her lean, long back, with streaks of tarnished gold.

SHEILAH: I…I was just trying some highlights.

MANNY: You must forgive me. It brings a memory of the flames. With the eyes that smolder with   the sizzling coals.

SHEILAH: Actually, they've been quite…well, puffy and red. From all the strain.

MANNY: Lift the arm, up, up, please. Ready.

SHEILAH: It's just a little…flabby.

MANNY: In here, we are FIRM. (*He straightens*). Now tell me, who you are. Who is… the Senora now?

SHEILAH: Who… am I? (*She tries to keep her arm up, tightens muscle.*) Ummm…Sheilah?

MANNY: Firm!

SHEILAH (*Straighter; firm.*) SHEILAH?!

MANNY: And why have you come… to Emmanuel, Senora Sheilah?

He moves his arm to another position. She tries to mimick.

SHEILAH: Sorry. I feel like I'm applying for a job.

MANNY (*Circles around her.*) We apply, to dance, no? And to be…a partner, yes? A partner in dance, is like a partner in life. One must try different ones to see the fit. Who feels the music, the rhythm, the feel of each other's pulse. Who will lead. Who will follow. Who will feel…the feeling. Tell me of yourself, please. *(He raises her arm again. And faces her towards the downstage 'mirror'.)* Who are you? In the mirror. Who do you see?

SHEILAH: (*Faces herself in 'mirror'.*) Oh God, no.

MANNY: Now, now.

SHEILAH: Okay. Well…I am… Sheilah.

(He stands more firmly to show her. She straightens taller.)

Sheilah!

MANNY: And how have you come to me... Sheilah.

SHEILAH: Well, I came here...by train. I mean, it started on the train. The...the thoughts, I mean.

MANNY: The feeling of the rocking. The rumble. The quiver of the rhythm, as it fills the body?

SHEILAH: Actually, it was just the thoughts.

MANNY: Tell me, Ms. Sheilah, what you are thinking? (*Crosses around behind her; runs his fingers up her spine to straighten.*)

SHEILAH: Well, I, ah, was thinking... You know, coming home at night. I'm up at six, feed the cats...

MANNY: The cats know of the stretch, yes? (*He stretches to show her.*) Ahhhhhh.

SHEILAH: Yes, well, (*Imitates.*) Ahhhh. Then I water the plants, (*Stretches.*) ahhh...eat of course, something simple, clearly not simple enough...

MANNY: (*Continues to circle.*) Not simple at all. But full, and lush...

SHEILAH: Uh huh. And then, the...the bus to the train and into a little cubicle all day long where I proof read books, mostly texts to find mistakes.

MANNY: You are looking, always, for what is wrong then? When there is so much...of Sheilah to be discovered. A shame, a shame.

SHEILAH: That's me. The Shame Buster. Always looking, looking, for mistakes. No matter how much someone thinks it's perfect, there is ALWAYS something.

(*He continues to circle around her and adjust. She chatters nervously.*)

An excessive verb, a misplaced noun, non sequiturs that lead absolutely nowhere. Even if it's just a little comma, an extra elipses, an apostrophe gone wrong, a whole world of meaning can just... fall apart. Right before your eyes. When you are... (*Notices him staring with fascination.*)...looking...

MANNY: Yes?

SHEILAH: Yes, and well, by the end of the day, you can imagine, I get back on the train and just... stare. Please don't stare at me like that.

MANNY: Stare at who? The woman who shuts her eyes and whispers the verbs, the nouns, the non *equadors* of the mind. This woman who is the wonder with the words?

SHEILAH: (*Politely.*) I think you meant non *sec..*quiturs?

MANNY: (*Insulted.*) You must forgive me my words. I am from Argentina and I speak Spanish! (*He turns away, "hurt".*)

SHEILAH: No, no, wait. Please. Uhh… (*With american accent*). "Donde es biblioteca?"

MANNY: (*Offended*) What? You think Emmanuel needs the book to speak?

SHEILAH: Oh, no, no. 'Where is the library?' is the only thing I re-memember from high school spanish.

MANNY: Ah, but Argentinian Spanish is different of course from the Spanish spoken in Spain. Or in the high schools of…wherever.

SHEILAH: (*Appeasing him.*) Oh, of course. Of course.

MANNY: There are many other languages we speak as well. Like Italian, and French. Many more. All mixed up. *Vos Sabes'?* You know? Do *you* understand?

SHEILAH: I…I just know those are the romance languages. And look at me? I can't even speak….

MANNY: The language of love? (*A challenge.*) My language?

SHEILAH: (*Threatened; backs away.*) You…you know, actually, to tell the truth, to be honest, like you said, I…I had considered… taking tap. They have classes right near me at a senior center. Not that I'm quite there yet. But (*Checks watch.*) it's getting closer every minute. And, well, since it seems a little…quiet here, with… without any… others… I mean, I   wouldn't want to…

MANNY: …tell me? From the heart? Why you have come? The truth. You fear to tell me?

SHEILAH: Oh, no. I'm not…feared. At all. Really.

MANNY: *(A challenge.)* So…there is nothing more? Inside this… ' Sheilah'?

SHEILAH: Okay, fine. (*Summing up the courage.*) Every day I come home on the train, and when   it gets dark, I see the sign, MANNY'S TANGO, on the second floor. And well, sometimes, I can see someone up here, dancing. And it's like I'm peeking in…inside, the window of… I don't know, it's silly. I just see somebody. Dancing. Alone.

MANNY: One can dance by themselves. One can feel the feel within them. And when the time is right, when they hear the music, *feel* the music in the body, they are ready, and the partner will find them. And not someone who wants to tap, tap, tap away a life in a…how you say, senior center?

SHEILAH: No. I didn't mean, I mean, when I look up, I imagine…
I'm sorry. It really *is* silly.

MANNY: To imagine…?

SHEILAH: … that… it could be me. That they are waiting for…me.
I said it was silly but I think, Sheilah, get off the train. Go, now!
Dance! Live! Do…*something.*

MANNY: And you have come to Emmanuel? To Emmanuel Ricado
Stefano Piazelli. *(Proudly.)* Third time runner-up in the Argentinian
world cup Tango finals, to find what?

SHEILAH: …I don't know. The…someone. Dancing. In the window?
(Beat.) Is it you?

MANNY: Manny Piazelli? Who has loved and lost. Too many times.
Who has felt the twists and the turns, and the rips and the tears
and the stabbing pain *(Holds his shoulder.)* in the pectoralis
muscle. Is that who you want to see? Is that who you want to
know? No, no.   It is quite dangerous to dance this dance.
It can take a lifetime to heal. To learn to love again…the real
tango. And this night, this class, you are here, I can see, for only
the complimentary time. And I have no more time… no more,
for the… complimentaries!

(Starts off in huff, as if he's going.)

SHEILAH: Wait. I'm sorry. I don't know what I was thinking. It was
just… a dream. I know nothing of…this world. YOUR world. And
I have come…I just came…to see…*(Starts crying.)* Forgive me.
(Fumbles for a tissue in her bag, then embarrassed, turns to leave.)

MANNY: I come here, every night, to this empty room. And I practice,
and practice to see if one day, one day, I could feel again the blood
that rushes through the veins. The mirror in each other's eyes,
how their arms, their embrace, loose but firm, hold each other.
How their chests swell with rage and pleasure. No. The tango is
something you do not *do*. You do not speak to find the wrong in
the words. You feel! You *feel* it! So NO. The tango is not a dance
for one who has… *commitment* issues!

(He packs up the papers as if he's finished with her.)

SHEILAH: *(Turns to him.)* Once, I saw someone on the train. A
stranger. We never spoke. He would look at me…and I would
feel… without the words, that feeling. But then I'd look away. I

couldn't look him in the eyes. I was afraid. And then, years later, I saw someone else…in a window…

MANNY: …Who scared you? Well, I am not a stranger on a train! And I am not a Steve. I am…a Stephano!

SHEILAH: Yes.

MANNY: (*He straighten, head high.*) I am…Emmanuel. Ricado. Stefano. A beast. A human… person. Who will not fear! Who… feels! And you…? (*A challenge.*) You are…?

SHEILAH: I am…(*Takes a breath. Stands taller.*) a Sheilah!

They stare at each other with blazing intent. A standoff. After a moment we hear the Tango MUSIC. And with his eyes locked on hers…

MANNY: Shall I sign you up for the six class special?

SHEILAH: No. (*Holding the stare.*) Eight will be better.

He raises his arms in the dancer's pose. She raises hers. And as the MUSIC begins to swell we FADE OUT.

THE END

Lawrence Harbison

YOU AGAIN

Katherine H. Burkman

YOU AGAIN was produced by WILD WOMEN WRITING and SHORT NORTH STAGE, July 21-30, 2016 at The Garden Theatre, 1187 N. High St., Columbus, OH 43201

CAST:
ELSIE: Acacia Duncan
GERALD: David Fawcett
One performance: Chad Hewitt

Director: Katherine H. Burkman
Stage Manager/Lighting Designer: Geoff McTurner
Choreographer: Melissa Gould

The song, "Come Again, sweet love doth now invite," is by John Dowland, lyrics anonymous. First published in Dowland's First Booke of Songes or Ayres, 1517

CHARACTERS

DEATH or GERALD: is a dapper man of any age from 30-60

ELSIE: is a lovely young woman at the outset, 18-30, but she ages as
life goes on. She moves more slowly, age being mostly an attitude

SETTING: An empty stage with a black curtain as background. Place is
only suggested by the words of the play, as we move from library,
to mountains, to lakes, to bedroom and home

TIME: Today

ELSIE: *(Schubert's quartet No. 14, "Death and the Maiden," plays quietly. ELSIE is looking for a book in the stacks of an imaginary library. Music fades. She speaks to man who is following her.)* Are you following me? I find the stacks of this library scarey enough without somebody looking over my shoulder.

GERALD: As a matter of fact, I was looking over your shoulder to see what interested you. One can get lost in the stacks in this library, don't you think? But I am here to find you.

ELSIE: I venture into the stacks quite a bit. Think of all the lifetimes it would take to read all these books.

GERALD: I know. I've been working at it forever. Quite endless.

ELSIE: I'm just looking for some escape reading. I have to read mysteries between serious books so I can keep going.

GERALD: But you can't escape me.

ELSIE: I don't recall seeing you at the library before. Are you a professor or a student?

GERALD: Neither, though I am a student of life. You may call me Gerald if you like.

ELSIE: I'm Elsie. I think I've seen you before. Are you spying? Where have you seen me?

GERALD: Oh, the likely places. On the pond. On the Pier. In the park. In. . . the dark. But you move so quickly. I no sooner see you at the lake, then you are off to your classes. I stop in at your class and you are off to the movies. I see you at a movie and you are off to. . .

ELSIE: You seem awfully nice for a stalker. You remind me of some of those old actors from long ago. Cary Grant, maybe. With a little of Fred Astaire. At any rate, I'm sure I've seen you often from the corner of my eye.

(Pulls out an imaginary book)

You won't catch me though. I do move fast. I used to run track. And I'm off. Please don't follow me.

GERALD: I just want you to know something, Elsie.

ELSIE: And what's that, Gerald?

GERALD: If you fall, I'll be there to catch you.

ELSIE: Sounds more ominous than comforting. But thanks, I suppose. Goodbye.

(GERALD moves upstage and hums the tune of "Sweet Love Doth Now Invite." ELSIE moves to another area of the stage,

disposes of her imaginary book and handbag and arrives at an imaginary mountain, which she begins to climb)

GERALD: *(Appears behind her climbing and is out of breath)* You do move fast, Elsie. I can hardly keep up with you.

ELSIE: Gerald! You again. I honestly like to be alone when I climb mountains. I do my best thinking up here in the heights.

GERALD: Sorry about that. But I did promise to be there should you fall. You seem to me to be taking an awful lot of chances in life. Aren't you the least bit attracted to me?

ELSIE: We've barely met. You're plenty good looking if that's what you're asking. Of course I'm attracted to you. You have an engaging. . . smile. But I don't fancy being caught. Look out there at the world, Gerald. The blues, the yellows, the flowers, the hotels, the fields, the cattle, the clowns, the. . .

GERALD: Please stop climbing for a minute so I can catch my breath. You don't need to fall for me, you know. You could just, uh, succumb. Here, slow down, take my hand.

ELSIE: You make that sound like a marriage proposal. Take your hand? I don't think so, Gerald. We haven't known each other that long. Sorry if you're out of breath, but I'm not, so goodbye again.

(She climbs faster and GERALD gives in, turns back and shrugs. ELSIE jumps off the mountain, moves to another area of the stage and pretends to take off her climbing clothes and shoes. She sits by an invisible lake and draws her hand through the water. GERALD lurks)

GERALD: I don't know if you know how beauteous you look sitting by this lake. Would I were the water that you caress so lovingly. Would I could take that lovely body into my arms and hold you forever.

ELSIE: Gerald! You again. Beauteous? I think you'd better drop the literary words thing. Forever is a hell of a long time.

GERALD: I have all the time in the world. "We are such stuff as dreams are made on, and our little life is rounded with a sleep." Shakespeare.

ELSIE: Oh, you think you can get to me through Shakespeare, do you? Don't you do anything? You don't go to college. You dress like, like a playboy. Are you the playboy of the American World?

GERALD: Well, not of the Irish world alone.

ELSIE: Ah, well read, are you?

GERALD: I study to read you, my dear.

ELSIE: I'm not your dear, Gerald. And I'm on the move.

(She wades into an imaginary lake and begins to swim, slowly at first but then more quickly. We hear a bit of Shubert in the background)

GERALD: *(Shouting)* Well, you're dear to me, Elsie. If I were able to swim I would follow you in.

ELSIE: *(Floating on her back)*I'm too fast for you, Gerald. You need a less active, less athletic type. Go find her.

GERALD: Been there. Done that. It's you I need . . . to be mine.

ELSIE: That will be the day.

GERALD: Yes, my darling, there will be a day. Or perhaps a night.

ELSIE: Dream on. I'm not just playing hard to get. Despite your attractions, I have miles to go before I'll fall. Too bad you can't swim. The water is divine.

GERALD: You like the divine? Perhaps one day, Elsie, you will come to me. You will be on the brink. And though you are cruel to me now, I'll be kind. Au Revoir.

(GERALD goes upstage and waits)

ELSIE: *(She climbs out of the imaginary water and pretends to get back into her clothes: As she gets her pretend dress back on, GERALD comes behind her and pulls up and imaginary zipper, then moves away. ELSIE speaks to the audience)*To be absolutely honest with you, I find Gerald somewhat breathtakingly attractive. I am ever so sorely tempted. Did you see his forehead? And his blue, blue, blue eyes. But he could be dangerous. He is an admitted stalker. And what does he do when he isn't following me about? I think, perhaps, it is time. . . to age.

(She goes and stands in front of a pretend mirror and begins to put on lipstick.. She is now in her bedroom)

Are those lines next to my eyes? Am I grown middle-aged?

(She looks at her nails)

I need a manicure, that's for sure. I do love Philip. I guess I'll say yes when I see him tonight.

ELSIE: *(Continued)* After all, if we are to have children, I can't wait

---

too much longer. I wonder what Gerald will have to say.

(She turns to audience)

He's still lurking, you know. Always about, especially when I think I'm alone—he turns up. All sorts of offers. Always tempting. But somehow I feel, how shall I put this, as if he exists somewhere beyond the pleasure principle. Maybe I'm just not mature enough for somebody so. . . haunting.

(She sits on floor and brushes her hair with imaginary brush)

GERALD: *(He crawls into her room through an imaginary window, takes the imaginary brush from her and begins to brush her hair, singing as he does so)* Come again! sweet love doth now invite
Thy graces that refrain
To do me due delight,
To see, to hear, to touch, to kiss, to die,
With thee again in sweetest sympathy.

ELSIE: Gerald. You again! You are incorrigible. How did you get into my bedroom? Where did you learn to sing like that? Do you think I don't know what that song means? Because I do. To die? I know full well that is a euphemism for to fuck. You are just getting more forward as we age. I'll have you know I'm going to get married. I'll be engaged the next time you see me and before you know it, I'll be the mother of three.

GERALD: *(He continues to brush her hair and to sing the verse)* To see, to hear, to touch, to kiss, to die, With thee again in sweetest sympathy. Mother of three? A dangerous business, motherhood. Childbirth, not an easy matter. What would you do if you lost one? Down to two? And another? Down to one? And yourself? Down to. . . But I'll be there, to catch you should you fall.

ELSIE: Gerald! Look in the mirror. See me. I am young and strong and on the run. Childbirth will be a breeze. I love children. I can live with a little croup if they must scare me. Look out the window I gather you climbed in. There is a world of people out there. Somebody gave birth to them. Many of them will give birth. Life is a dangerous business. Has it ever occurred to you that you're a bit over-protective? Don't get me wrong. I appreciate your concern. But I've got to run. Please close the window when you leave.

GERALD: *(Leaves by the pretend window, still singing his verse. Closes the pretend window. Retires upstage)*

ELSIE: *(She has aged considerably. She stands center stage holding a pretend handkerchief to her eyes. She is waving with the other hand)*Goodbye my love. Drive carefully. Oh that your father had lived to see the day when his third child left for college.

(She waves some more)

Don't get lost in the stacks darling. Oh, you probably won't even go to a library, will you? Just to google. Well, at least you won't meet any tall, dark strangers who will threaten to catch you when you fall. Although, I guess I wish you could meet Gerald. He's the middle-aged man who you've seen lurking from time to time. If you met him, he might offer to catch you if you fall. But you won't fall, my dear, will you? The first year away is the most difficult, but you'll sail on.

(Pause)

It's me who might fall. I'm afraid of this empty nest. I'm. . . alone.

GERALD: *(Moves forward from upstage to join her)* You're not alone, Elsie. I'm here.

ELSIE: Oh Gerald. You again.

GERALD: Be honest. What would you say if it were not me, again, and again, and again.

ELSIE: Hard to explain, Gerald, but even though I would miss you, you do continue to scare me. I never fell down when I was young, but now I sometimes feel unstable on my feet. I haven't decided yet if I want you to catch me should I fall.

GERALD: I notice you take a little drink before dinner each night.

ELSIE: *(Laughs)* Do you think that's why I feel I might fall? Surely you wouldn't feel like the grand conquering hero should I fall down dead drunk. Why would you even want me?

GERALD: I will always want you, Elsie, drunk or sober, steady or shaky, young or old, happy or sad. You can't possibly understand the longing I feel, or the length of time I have longed. I entertain myself by reading the books you have written. The last one was a gem. It seemed, what shall I say, to complete you.

ELSIE: I'm glad you're a fan, Gerald. Perhaps I'll dedicate the next one to you. If I write a next one that is.

(Pause)

Do you hear that music? It's Schubert. *Death and the Maiden.*

GERALD: Medieval, you know. It means the dance of death.

ELSIE: Do you dance, oh learned one?

GERALD: Yes.

(He takes Elsie in his arms and they waltz to the Shubert quartet music for a bit. ELSIE breaks away)

ELSIE: I finally know who you remind me of, Gerald. My father. He was the anxious type. Always afraid my brother and I would fall down, or get hit by a car, or fail our exams. I sometimes wondered if he wanted us to fall, so he could catch us, to fail, so he could comfort us, to die, so he wouldn't have to worry about us.

(Pause. She looks at him closely)

Do you want me to die?

(GERALD smiles and reaches out a hand, which she does not take)

I must see to dinner. And my drink, of course. I'd ask you to join me, but I don't want you to. . .

(ELSIE waves at GERALD as he goes upstage and she goes into an imaginary house. When she emerges, she is stooped over with age. She picks up an imaginary phone and speaks into it)

Grandma loves you little pumpkin face. I'm so excited that you are bringing your mommy and daddy to visit next week. Yes, I still have your doll house waiting. And a surprise too, sweetie. Yes, of course I'll tell you a Pegasus story. Nothing like a ride on a flying horse. We'll scare mommy and daddy. Give them my love. Bye.

(She walks a bit and stumbles, but she is caught by GERALD before she can fall)

Gerald. You again.

GERALD: I caught you, Elsie.

ELSIE: Yes, you did. You kept your promise.

GERALD: Let's go into the bedroom. Lie down with me, my beloved. Lie down with me and I will promise such delights that will make you wish to fall and fall and fall again. I have waited so long.

ELSIE: *(As she accompanies GERALD into an imaginary bedroom)* Yes, my dear. You have been faithful. Far be it for me to make you wait too long.

(He offers his hand)

I'll take your hand now, to steady me.

(She does so and as he takes her stage left, she begins to sing "Come Again," and he hums as he leads her. They stop at the edge of the stage and as sHE: leans her head back on his shoulder, he kisses her neck. Lights dim slowly to black)

The End

3 Or More Actors

BABY GAY A Politically Incorrect Comedy in Ten Minutes

Wayne Paul Mattingly

Originally produced by Shades Repertory Theatre, Haverstraw, NY, March, 2017. Directed by Samuel Harps.

CHARACTERS:

ABBY: 20's-30's, a fashionably dressed young mother; old money

ELECKTRA: 20's-30's, old money young mother whose fashionable attire suggests pulp fiction villainess

GENDRA: 20's-30's, large, well-dressed, German-Irish young mother; new money, suppressed accent

TAWNY: 20's-30's, naïve young mother; new money, well dressed

SETTING: Central Park, NYC

TIME: Present, late Spring

A fashionably dressed young mother, ABBY. sits on a bench in Central Park with a baby carriage in front of her. Gurgling sounds are emitted from the carriage from time to time to which ABBY responds.

ABBY: Gay? What's that? Gay? That's my little gay baby, yes. Who's Gay? Hmn? Who's my little gay baby?

ABBY stands, looks out at a field perhaps, gently rocking carriage.

ABBY: Who's Momma's little baby Gay? You are! That's right! You are!

Another fashionably dressed, but suspiciously punk young mother arrives with her baby carriage. She bears no tattoos— but that's the anomaly. Her clothes and demeanor somehow suggest a Pulp Fiction villainess.

ELECTRA: Hi. Do you mind if I join you?

ABBY: Oh, not at all. Do we, Gay?

ELECTRA: That's your son? *(she looks in)* He's special. What's his name?

ABBY: He's Gay. I named him Gay. Well, he named himself.

ELECTRA: Like Gaylord? Or…?

ABBY: No no no. That's his name. I mean, he told me that.

ELECTRA: He told you that?

ABBY: Oh yeah. Listen. You might hear him. He proclaims himself all the time.

A moment waiting.

ABBY: Wait a sec. He'll say it. That's all he says. Gaygaygaygaygay-gaygaygaygay..

ELECTRA: Hmn.

ABBY: It was his first word. Gay! Gay! And then he pointed to himself. I mean, what more proof does one need? I say to him, Who's Gay? Who's Gay? He points to himself. Say, Who are you? Who are you? He says, Gay! Gay! Nothing else. That's all he says.

ELECKTRA leans into Gay's carriage.

ELECTRA: What are you? Hmn? What are you?

Indistinct gurgles come from carriage.

ELECKTRA: *(terrifically excited)* Oh my god! He said it! He said it! I heard him clear as a bell!

ABBY: I told you, didn't I?

ELECTRA: Yeah, but, you know.

ABBY: Yeah, I know. You know what else?

ELECTRA: No, what?

ABBY: I can tell your baby is not a boy. Because whenever Gay is around another baby boy, he pulls on his peepee. He gets very excited. And look, he's not doing a thing.

ELECTRA: Well, that's because he's probably a little confused.

ABBY: Confused? What are you saying? Do you know how intelligent this baby is? Do you realize how few babies self-identify at six weeks? Much less speak.

ELECTRA: No-no, you're mistaking me here. My baby—

ABBY: What's her name. She's got to be a girl.

ELECTRA: No, listen, uh…oh, I'm sorry, I didn't introduce myself. I'm Elecktra.

ABBY: Abby. Pleased, I'm sure.

ELECTRA: So, Abby, here's the thing. My baby isn't a boy or girl. The whole gender-polarization thing, that is, lines between true and false and shit, are imaginary. I mean…as in, socially, in the big picture, they're, yeah, powerful, but still just collective fantasies. We wanted to overcome that.

ABBY: I'm trying to follow you…but what's the baby's name?

ELECTRA: Well, we haven't figured it out yet. We're like you. That is, the individual should choose its own name.

ABBY: So what's the big confusion for Gay? I mean…

ELECTRA: Well, Elecktra's spawn, mine…is a eunuch!

ABBY: Get out of here! No kidding! That's so cool! I wish I had thought of that!

ELECTRA: Yeah, so you see, Gay may sense something, but it may seem confusing if it's his first time coming across a eunuch.

ABBY: \ *(goes to Gay's carriage)* You may be right. He's pulling on his belly button now. How'd you…do it? I mean, you know, who went along with that?

ELECTRA: I know an over-zealous moil who does anything for money.

ABBY: A Jew?

ELECTRA: No-no, he's a Christian who pretends to be a Jew to get the moil work, but I know him, so…

ABBY: He knew how to do that?

ELECTRA: Well no…he sort of screwed it up—he was well-intentioned, but couldn't perform more than a bris—

ABBY: You're Jewish?

ELECTRA: Oh, no, but Melvin—the moil—since he pretends to be…well, he came very highly recommended—when he flubbed the job, we had to fly to Mexico—quick—I mean, the kid was castrated anyhow.

ABBY: Wow. That is so progressive.

ELECKTRA: Yes, well, we almost lost the baby. But that's why doctors exist in Mexico, isn't it?

Two well-dressed, new money New York women roll up with their baby carriages. They try to raise their speech above their middle class breeding, but New York accents slip through. GENDRA, German-Irish, is the larger and more forceful of the two women.

GENDRA: Good afternoon, ladies. Care if we make it a foursome?

ABBY: *(whispering, as if to get the last of private conversation in)* How does it pee?

TAWNY: Eightsome.

GENDRA: Octet. You mean octet.

ELECKTRA: *(whispers)* It's like a trans-gender.

ABBY: Ohhh! Huh?

TAWNY: Yes, eight! Four adults and four babies!

TAWNY'S baby begins to cry. ABBY quickly checks her carriage. GAY sings out—his name, naturally.

ABBY: You've got a boy in there. I can tell. Gay is getting excited and pulling on his pee pee.

TAWNY: How did you know?

GENDRA: He's always crying. No wonder Athena has no respect for him. Besides the fact that he doesn't speak yet—at three months!. Athena is already speaking French. We sound waved French conversation into my womb as soon as I discovered I was pregnant. Plus: mathematical problems by binary numeric sound impulses. She can solve algebraic problems in binary numeric vocal responses.

ABBY: How do you know…you know, how to know if she's correct or…

GENDRA: She gurgles. Our German nanny translates. She's indispensable.

TAWNY: *(to ELECKTRA)* What's your baby's name?

ELECTRA: It hasn't decided yet—that is, we decided to let it make up its own mind. But lately it's been saying, "me llamo! Me llamo," or something like that. We have a Spanish housekeeper. From Columbia or Ecuador—I can't remember.

ABBY: It's a eunuch!

GENDRA: Really?! Horrific!

TAWNY: What's a eunuch?

GENDRA: She had its genitals removed.

TAWNY: Really?

ELECTRA: We felt gender specificity needed to be avoided. All its parts, that is—including reproductive organs—aren't entirely necessary. It's all about "this dog don't hunt." Besides, it was really its idea.

GENDRA: How's that?

ELECTRA: Well, it kept stabbing itself—*(she points to her crotch)*—with diaper pins.

TAWNY: Well, I think that's terrible.

ELECTRA: Well, there was certainly no mistaking that message.

ABBY: No, no. Absolutely not.

TAWNY: Terrrible. What about disposables?

ELECKTRA/ABBY/GENDRA: No way/What?!/Disgraceful!

ELECTRA: What kind of mother do you think I am?

GAY'S carriage may be shaking fairly strenuously at this point.

GENDRA: *(looks into Gay's carriage)* He's naked and abusing himself! Would you please control that little fiend of yours

ABBY: Gay. His name is Gay.

GENDRA: Well, you're his mother. Can you keep him from exercising his abominable acts—And subjecting my Athena to his vile bestiality!?

All the women's heads follow some air bound sputum from GAY'S carriage to TAWNY'S baby.

GENDRA: Oh my god, your little porn star ejaculated on that poor baby! Why IS his penis exposed? It should be covered at all times! Thank god he didn't strike my genius Athena. The last thing she needs is to become pregnant while still in diapers.

ABBY: Ha! For all you know. My Gay has no interest in propagating with your Athena: he's gay! He pronounced his identity at five weeks. Ask Elecktra, she's heard him. She'll tell you as well as he.

ELECTRA: The baby's queer. Heard him say so. No doubt about it.

TAWNY: How can that be? How could the good Lord allow that in a baby? Oh my god! He's licking that stuff off his fingers. He likes it.

ELECTRA: The Good Lord? The Good Lord hung out with twelve dudes and a prostitute. I'm sure He did His share of licking.

GENDRA: Nonetheless, I would appreciate it if you'd place something over his bestial appendage. Here, take my coffee cup.

ABBY: Are you suggesting my baby Gay should...excuse me, ejaculate into a Starbuck's cup for your satisfaction?

GENDRA: I'm just trying to protect my innocent baby from unwholesome and unhealthy behavior. —She is unbesmirched by sociopathic problems at this point!

ABBY: Did you just call my kid a sociopath?

GENDRA: If the Pampers fit.

ABBY: You know, your brain brat is a pre-lesbian. Guaranteed. All her bodily functions are being processed through her brain because they're suppressed by data. It's like squeezing a pig through a watermelon.

GENDRA: Nice try. Athena never touches herself. Unless she has her gloves on, of course. She knows her hygiene.

TAWNY: Wow, my little guy has his fingers everywhere and he never makes any distinction travelling from here to there. He really likes that white stuff.

ABBY: Gay is very tasteful.

ELECTRA: Listen. He's saying it again, "Me llamo, me llamo."

TAWNY: I wonder if you lose your peepee if it's like losing an arm. As if, you have the memory of it sometimes, but...then you don't.

ELECTRA: "Me llamo, me llamo."

ABBY: I don't think so. They lose their umbilical cords and—

GENDRA: Precisely. Seek that connection to their mothers for the balance of their lives.

ABBY: Well, that's true enough.

ELECTRA: I think I'll name him, Mellamo, then.

ABBY: That's...like, so perfect. Specially for a eunuch.

TAWNY: That's a sweet name for a baby without anything, you know, down there.

GENDRA: Well, ladies, it appears we've named a child today. No small accomplishment.

GENDRA leans into her carriage.

GENDRA: "Merde?" Excuse me, ladies. Would any one of you happen to have an extra diaper?

ELECTRA: Mellamo? Mellamo?

ABBY: Gendra? Did that baby of yours just use profanity?

GENDRA: I have no idea where she picked it up.

They all begin sniffing, reacting to the stink.

GENDRA: However, I do believe my Athena just communicated an action. In French.

TAWNY: Pee Wee? Do we have an extra diaper for Athena? Hmn? His fingers are sticky.

ABBY: Gay? Gay? Who's Gay?

END OF PLAY

BRIDE OF GODZILLA

Felix Racelis

Bride of Godzilla was performed September 22, 23 and 24, 2016 at the Stella Adler Theatre in Hollywood as part of the inaugural Short+Sweet Hollywood Festival. John Fingal O'Donnell directed:

SHELLEY: Mara New
DAVID: Damian Kerr
JESSICA: Maithy Vu
STANLEY: Sunil Vernekar

Producer was Kaz Matamura.

For permission to use "Love Me Tender" and "Hound Dog" please contact Broadcast Music, Incorporated (BMI).

Special thanks to Lawrence Nash for his editing skills and support.

CAST OF CHARACTERS

SHELLEY: Driven, ballsy female studio executive, sporadically insecure, 40s.

DAVID: Shelley's secretary, quick-witted, sharp, gay male, late 20s.

Wife/husband writing team of:

JESSICA: Asian American female, bright, energetic, late 20s.

STANLEY: Asian American male, eager, enthusiastic, late 20s.

SCENE: Shelley's office.

TIME: The present.

SYNOPSIS: Jessica and Stanley have a final chance to pitch a film project to a no-nonsense female producer.

Scene

SETTING: *SHELLEY's office furnished with a large desk cluttered with files and scripts. To one side of Shelley's desk, stage left, are two chairs hugging a small end table. To the other side of Shelley's desk, stage right, is a single chair. The furniture is stylish and uncomfortable. A map of the world, indicating the movie studio's worldwide offices, hangs behind Shelley's desk. A box of tissue sits on a corner of the desk.*

AT RISE: *An exit interview/pitch session is in progress. SHELLEY sits behind her desk, reviews a file. DAVID sits in the single chair. JESSICA and STANLEY sit in the two chairs to the opposite side of SHELLEY.*

SHELLEY: …no plane movies, no President movies, no Kung Fu movies, no high concept thrillers that a thirteen-year-old can deduce by the top of Act II. My office is looking for a movie that's gigantic YET unique. I need to make a statement.

(beat)

Have you got anything else?

(JESSICA turns to STANLEY, both at their wits' end. STANLEY motions for JESSICA to proceed.)

JESSICA: How about a Godzilla-like creature?

SHELLEY: Godzilla!? GODZILLA!? I can't believe you're using your final opportunity to pitch a project on that.

(beat)

You're joking, of course.

(rising from her desk and extending her hand)

Still, I'd like to thank you both for participating in our studio's Cultural and Ethnic Diversity Awareness and Integration Project, which, as you know, is being phased out next month.

JESSICA: *(adamant)* It's not Godzilla. It's a Godzilla-like being. It isn't a remake or sequel.

STANLEY: It's a fresh take on Godzilla as…

(stumbling)

a…three-dimensional creature.

(SHELLEY checks her iPhone.)

SHELLEY: No.

(to DAVID)

When's our next meeting?

DAVID: Ten minutes, but he's already in the waiting room tearing through the cross-word puzzles.

(JESSICA and STANLEY exchange desperate glances.)

JESSICA: *(blurting)* It's a musical!

SHELLEY: A Godzilla musical? I don't think so. Now, if you'd kindly gather up your things...

STANLEY: Actually, it's a romance.

SHELLEY: My, my, who's talking here?

STANLEY: *(seizing his chance)*Big, bulky mass of a monster, feared by all around him, he yearns to be understood...and loved. It's the romance angle that was totally missed in the remake.

(As STANLEY talks, he extracts two Godzilla toys from a black bag. STANLEY and JESSICA each take a toy to illustrate their story. They both lean close to Shelley's desk to peer at her map.)

JESSICA: The Godzilla-like creature travels back to the jungles of Japan to find his mate...his Bride.

(STANLEY plucks a tissue from the desk and wraps it over the head of one of the toys to create the Bride.)

STANLEY: He doesn't find her in Japan. He searches high and low, but...nothing. So he walks across the...the...

JESSICA: ...Pacific to the shores of China. Perhaps she might be found in the sweltering, sultry streets of Shanghai.

SHELLEY: *(astounded)* You're putting me on, right? You've got to be putting me on. David, what do you make of this?

DAVID: It's the freshest thing I've heard all week. I'm dying to find out what happens next.

JESSICA: But she's not in China either.

STANLEY: So the Godzilla-like being treks on, through the great...

JESSICA: Himalayas, across the...the...

STANLEY: ...the Black Sea...

JESSICA: ...through the Swiss Alps until...

STANLEY: ...he spots...something tall...

JESSICA: glimmering in the distance. It's...it's...

> *(JESSICA looks at STANLEY for help. DAVID leans in to catch JESSICA's revelation.)*

SHELLEY: *(impatient, to DAVID)* Go offer this next guy some coffee!

DAVID: This is the good part!

(SHELLEY shoots DAVID a hard expression.

DAVID exits.

JESSICA and STANLEY exchange a look of desperation, having lost their champion.)

SHELLEY: Wrap it up, OK? I have another interview.

JESSICA: He spots...the Eiffel Tower...he falls in love...he breaks out into...into...

STANLEY: *(desperate)* ...an Elvis Presley song. "Love Me Tender, Love Me Sweet..."

SHELLEY: *(reverie)* Presley. Mmm...Elvis. The King.

> *(motioning with her arms)*

His Fall. His Rise. His Fall. His Donuts.

(The writers follow SHELLEY's rising and falling motion. They look at each other with a glimmer of hope. DAVID returns.)

SHELLEY: Didn't we just acquire the Presley rights?

DAVID: You've been sitting on 'em for a long time, among other things.

> *(beat)*

But why Presley? He's done to death.

SHELLEY: No, wait, there's got to be a hook. Elvis...Elvis...Elvis, the King, idolized and ravaged by millions of women, yet deeply insecure and troubled. Loved but misunderstood.

> *(to DAVID)*

What do you think?

DAVID: *(to JESSICA)* Are you going for some David Lynch kind of thing?

JESSICA: More of a Tarantino kind of thing.

DAVID: Tarantino?

SHELLEY: *(coming to her senses)* Sorry, I don't know what I was thinking. It's not big enough. I need something colossal, something really big.

STANLEY: *(under breath)* Ball breaker.

SHELLEY: You are two very talented young people and I want to thank you both for participating and sharing...

(JESSICA rummages desperately in the black bag.)

JESSICA: *(interrupting)* A dinosaur!

(JESSICA extracts a stuffed Barney.)

SHELLEY: Read my lips! No dinosaurs!

(JESSICA searches madly in the bag.)

JESSICA: *(to STANLEY)* I can't find it. Did you let the baby play with the bag again?

STANLEY: No, these are our toys!

SHELLEY: *(loudly clearing her throat)* Ahem! Thank you, but I must...

JESSICA: *(interrupting)* A dog!

(JESSICA pulls out a stuffed toy dog.)

SHELLEY: *(mystified)* A dog?

JESSICA: It would cut down on royalty payments. And dogs are BIG! Sixty million American households own at least one dog.

SHELLEY: A dog...

STANLEY: ...musical!

SHELLEY & STANLEY: *(turning to each other)* A dog musical!

STANLEY: Seventy-six percent of Americans have a positive impression of musicals and want them back.

DAVID: Look, if we could get Elton John...

SHELLEY: I can get Elton John.

DAVID: Animated feature?

SHELLEY: A dog?

JESSICA: Live action adventure musical. Americans have a love affair with dogs and musicals.

(STANLEY holds his head in his hands, makes a prayer gesture.)

JESSICA: *(Cont'd)* The public would eat it up. Think of the merchan-
dising, the stuffed toys, video games...a chance to cash in big!
DAVID: If you could pull it off...

*(SHELLEY stares at the air above her, pondering what she's
just heard.)*

SHELLEY: A dog...a dog...

(starts crying)

...oh PUMPKIN!
DAVID: Boss lady, are you okay?
SHELLEY: *(beat)* I had to...

(straining)

put...put Pumpkin to sleep last year!
DAVID: Oh, God, not this again! Lord deliver us!
SHELLEY: Mommie couldn't be with you all the time, Pumpkin,
because Mommie had very important staff meetings she couldn't
miss!! But you forgave her, didn't you, Pumpkin? I know you
forgive Mommie!

*(SHELLEY sobs uncontrollably. JESSICA offers SHELLEY a
tissue, which she accepts. SHELLEY wipes her eyes.*

SHELLEY opens a locket on her necklace and shows it to JESSICA.)
JESSICA: Hair? A lock of Pumpkin's hair?

*(Grief stricken and speechless, SHELLEY nods in the af-
firmative.)*

JESSICA: I'm so sorry. Was she...?
SHELLEY: *(regaining her composure)* Old age. Fifteen good years.
She was my...best friend.

(SHELLEY weeps again.)

JESSICA: This will be her tribute, then. To Pumpkin! To every dog
who's ever lived in the shadow of a human, loyally at their side,

(directly to SHELLEY)

enduring years of neglect...
STANLEY: *(echo)* Neglect.
JESSICA: and abandonment.
STANLEY: *(echo)* Abandonment.

(SHELLEY wails.)

STANLEY: Pumpkin's last days: It's DRIVING MISS DAISY meets OLD YELLER!

DAVID: Can't I get the new guy now? Please?

SHELLEY: NO!! Let them finish! Go on!

(STANLEY and JESSICA turn to each other in astonishment, do an air fist bump behind SHELLEY's back.)

JESSICA: ...ahh...But that's rushing to the end! We open with Pumpkin's early days as an adorable puppy...No puppy was cuter!

SHELLEY: Yes, yes!!

STANLEY: The apple of her mother's eye.

JESSICA: Her first puppy steps, the inevitable house training. Great comedic potential.

SHELLEY: Oh, Pumpkin!

DAVID: Oh, God Yuck!

STANLEY: *(triumphant, singing)* "You ain't nothin' but a hound dog..."

(DAVID shakes his head.)

BLACKOUT

END

BRINE SHRIMP GANGSTERS

Bryan Stubbles

Art Emia: Earl L. Burnett III
Anthro Pod: Jacom Clarkson
Nau Plii: Abbey Wood

Directed by Ardon Smith
Written by Bryan Stubbles

Presented by Utah Theatre Kopanang at The Great Salt Lake Fringe Festival. July 29, 2016.

CHARACTERS

ART EMIA: (50s) overweight, male. Boss of brine shrimp bosses.
ANTHRO POD: (20s-30s) in shape, male. New to the game.
NAU PLII: (20s-50s) slinky femme fatale. Foreign.
SETTING: The Great Salt Lake, Utah, USA. Now.

LIGHTS UP:

The Great Salt Lake. Empty stage, save for a lone chair. The boss of brine shrimp bosses, ART EMIA sits on this chair. Ill-fitting suit. Note: all characters are anamorphic brine shrimp.

ENTER younger ANTHRO POD. He kisses the hand of EMIA.

EMIA: Anthro....Pod. Stop watching gangster movies. That's not how the families of the Great Salt Lake operate. Not these days.

ANTHRO: Boss Art Emia, we are but brine shrimp in the ecosystem of a giant salt lake. What do we know?

EMIA: And stop reading Kierkegaard! You existential punk! Stand up!

ANTHRO stands up straight.

EMIA: We need men-shrimp in these waters. Real men-shrimp. Like in the olden days. Not these   metro shrimp with their pampered exoskeletons. We're losing ground to tougher foreign groups.

ANTHRO: The Turkmen?

EMIA: Yes, the Turkmen! We need to stop these guys from invading Farmington Bay.

ANTHRO: You can't blame them.

EMIA: *(incensed)* What? They're our enemies. We blame them for everything. And they're foreign.

ANTHRO: Please. Understand. They probably came with some weird mineralogist who had visited the Kara-Bogaz-Gol in Turkmenistan and then came here.

EMIA: We are The Great Salt Lake Brine Shrimp we don't understand our enemy. We dip them in freshwater.

EMIA laughs maniacally.

ANTHRO: That's cruel.

EMIA: So are turf wars. The gills on our feet will flow with blood!

ANTHRO: We can avoid it.

EMIA: Avoid violence? This is the sodium hydroxide trade.

ANTHRO: The kids call it "drox."

EMIA: We can throw them back into the Kara-Bogaz-Gol. From whence they came.

ANTHRO: Let me talk to them.

EMIA: You are young.

ANTHRO: We can win this without violence.

EMIA: The young ones are so weak. But I hate losing soldiers. Talk to her.

ANTHRO: Her?

EMIA: And bring this.

EMIA hands ANTHRO a *[squirt]* gun wrapped in a towel.

EMIA: Just in case. Now get out of my sight.

EXIT ANTHRO. EMIA sits back in the chair.

EMIA: Schmuck.

Lights down.

When lights go back up the chair is moved around with the back facing the audience. No EMIA.

ANTHRO checks his cell phone. The towel wrapped around a pistol lays on the chair.

OS A KNOCK then a woman ENTERS.

She is NAU PLII, (20s-50s), slinky, nice evening dress. Foreign.

NAU: You wanted me?

ANTHRO: If you're Nau Plii, yeah.

NAU: What's a big boy-brine shrimp like you want with a little girl-brine shrimp like me?

ANTHRO: It's what the boss wants.

NAU: Art Emia is a fool. And you're a fool for taking orders from a 300 day-old fat brine shrimp.

ANTHRO: I follow my job through. He wants Farmington Bay back.

NAU laughs in his face.

NAU: I don't have any claim over Farmington Bay. I just came to diversify the market. Great Salt Lake customers deserve competitive prices.

ANTHRO: These are our drox waters.

NAU: Stupid Utah brine shrimp. Did you just come out of a brackish well? You get your own kids hooked on drox. At least we come here from Kara-Bogaz-Gol in Turkmenistan and get your Utah brine kids high. Our kids are clean.

ANTHRO approaches her.

ANTHRO: It's a dangerous game, Nau.

NAU: You crave it.

ANTHRO: How can I get you to leave Farmington Bay?

NAU: You can't. We are here. Just like Antelope Island. Accept it.

ANTHRO picks up his towel.

NAU: What a big man-shrimp you are. I know that's a gun.

ANTHRO upset.

ANTHRO: You're right. We can -

NAU takes the towel from him.

NAU: Sucker's play!

NAU unfolds the towel, revealing a brightly colored water pistol.

She holds it up using the towel.

ANTHRO: Don't! Careful.

NAU laughs.

NAU: Freshwater. Nice. You really know how to hurt a brine shrimp, don't you?

ANTHRO: It was Art Emia.

NAU: Sure. At least in Turkmenistan, brine shrimp have morals. You sick, sick shrimp.

NAU aims gun.

NAU: Do you want to suffer or meet your maker in an instant?

ANTHRO: That's a choice?

ANTHRO gets antsy.

ANTHRO: Hey, um, Nau.

NAU: Anthro dear.

ANTHRO: Maybe we can work out a deal.

NAU: I have a deal for you.

NAU squirts ANTHRO's foot with the squirt gun. Also, NAU squirts the audience, so they can get in on the action.

WHAM! ANTHRO drops to the floor screaming and convulsing in pain. Very guttural sounds.

ANTHRO: Oh! It hurts! No! I'll never crawl on algae again. You evil shrimp-woman. AHHHH!

Gutteral screams. Grabs his foot and sputters about the stage on his back.

NAU stoops next to ANTHRO.

NAU points the pistol up ANTHRO's nose.

NAU: Tell me about that deal, honey.

ANTHRO: Uh - I can help you.

NAU: You? You can't even help yourself shed your own exoskeleton.

ANTHRO: Shoot me, you evil, evil woman-shrimp from Kara-Bogaz-Gol.

NAU: Now you're a tough little briny.

ANTHRO: No I'm not.

ANTHRO starts to cry. NAU pulls him up and holds him close to her.

NAU: Be an adult brine shrimp for once in your life.

NAU holds him in her arms.

NAU: You know, the brine shrimp gene pool in Turkmenistan shrinks with the lake.

NAU feels his shoulders.

NAU: A good man-shrimp is hard to find.

ANTHRO: We have that problem, too. After you turn 21 days old, it's impossible to find any eggs to fertilize.

NAU: But it is possible. Think of the possibilities.

NAU kisses him.

NAU: We can work together. You can be a strong brine shrimp for me, can't you?

NAU hugs him.

LIGHTS DOWN QUICK.

When they come up, ART EMIA back in his chair. No NAU. OS KNOCK.

ENTER ANTHRO, with towel.

EMIA: I hope you bring me good news.

ANTHRO limps, due to his foot being shot with freshwater.

EMIA: You've earned a promotion.
ANTHRO: You don't have to worry about Nau again.
EMIA: Beautiful.

EMIA hands ANTHRO a bag of epsom salt.

EMIA: You did a good job for me.

ANTHRO admires the bag before dropping it.

EMIA: What?

ANTHRO points his squirt gun at EMIA.

EMIA: You're in big trouble, crustacea.
ANTHRO: Stand up, shut up.

EMIA stands up.

ANTHRO: Farmington Bay is mine.
EMIA: Under my dead exoskeleton it is.
ANTHRO: I get tired saying the same question twice.

From USL a stream of water hits EMIA in the back. He falls on his stomach.

NAU ENTERS from USL carrying a super-soaker. She also squirts the audience.

EMIA: I treated you like a son. You freshwatered me in the back. Cough. Cough.
ANTHRO: Hashtag "first-world problems."

ANTHRO shoots EMIA in the head with the squirt gun. EMIA dead. ANTHRO squirts the audience, too.

ANTHRO looks up. NAU has the super soaker aimed on him.

ANTHRO: Come on. You wouldn't do a fellow brine shrimp gangster like that, would you?
NAU: I wouldn't? I want the whole bay.
ANTHRO: I thought you loved me.
NAU: Nice thought.

ANTHRO points his gun at her. NAU walks closer.

NAU kicks him in the chest with her sole. ANTHRO drops his gun. Momentarily shocked, ANTHRO staggers and NAU unleashes the super soaker on him (and the audience).

ANTHRO crumples into a ball on the floor. Insane laugh from NAU as she stands over EMIA and ANTHRO's bodies.

LIGHTS DOWN.

CARLA

Chip Bolcik

"Carla" was originally produced as part of the L.A. Cafe Plays at the Ruskin Group Theater in Santa Monica, CA in October 2017, with the following cast and crew:

CAST:
Nina Brissey as NINA: Shayne Anderson as ROCCO: Julia Mc-Ilvaine as CARLA: Directed by Cloe Kromwell

Producer Michael J. Myers
Artistic Director John Ruskin

CAST OF CHARACTERS

NINA - A waitress. Funny, thoughtful, attractive. Likes ROCCO.
ROCCO - Over the top New Yorker, handsome, dresses like a biker.
    Fun, determined, frustrated.
CARLA - Biker chick, pretty, strong, absolutely sure of who she is.

TIME: The present.
PLACE: Coffee shop in Brooklyn.

NINA makes ROCCO a coffee drink. ROCCO looks at his phone. He has a toothpick in his mouth. He always has a toothpick in his mouth.

NINA: So, this is it, huh? You think this girl's the one?

ROCCO: I don't know yet. I gotta meet her first.

NINA: You sounded like you were ready to marry her a few minutes ago.

ROCCO: Yeah, but a few minutes ago she wasn't texting to say she'd be right in.

NINA: Gettin' cold feet?

ROCCO: I don't know, maybe.

NINA: What's this one's name?

ROCCO: Carla.

NINA: Again? That's, like, five Carla's in a row.

ROCCO: What can I say? I like the name. What's wrong with that?

NINA: It's shallow. That's what's wrong with that.

ROCCO: It's not shallow. It shows I got discriminating taste.

NINA: How is it that only dating girls named Carla is discriminating?

ROCCO: When a woman notices you're looking for a specific characteristic, she digs that.

NINA: First of all, the name Carla isn't a characteristic. It's a name.

ROCCO: Your opinion.

NINA: And secondly, women like it when a man pays attention to them for who they are, not for their name.

ROCCO: How do you know?

NINA: 'Cause I'm a woman, in case you didn't notice.

ROCCO: I noticed.

NINA: Then you must notice that I like the way you say hi when you come in for coffee. Or the way you always ask about my dog. Or the way you compliment my eyes. That's the stuff women like.

ROCCO: How is Brucie, by the way?

NINA: See? That's what I'm talking about. You remember details like his name because you pay attention. That's what impresses me. I mean, that's what impresses a woman.

ROCCO: Too bad your name's not Carla.

NINA: Why?

ROCCO: I'd ask you out if it was.

NINA: Rocco!

CARLA enters.

CARLA: Rocco?
ROCCO: Yeah?
CARLA: I'm Carla.
ROCCO: Carla! How you doin'?
CARLA: I'm doin' good. How you doin'?
ROCCO: Yeah, real good, real good.

NINA comes over with ROCCO's drink.

NINA: Oh, brother. Can I get you anything?
CARLA: I take it you're not a Carla?
NINA: No, my name's Nina.
CARLA: Too bad. You look like a Carla.
NINA: I'm not. What can I get you?
CARLA: Could I get a Danish?
ROCCO: Seriously? You like Danish?
CARLA: Only the best food in the world, right?
ROCCO: Absolutely.
NINA: *(not impressed)* Be right back.

NINA exits.

CARLA: You got a thing for her?
ROCCO: I don't know. Why you say that?
CARLA: I got a sense about these things.
ROCCO: What, like a sixth sense or something?
CARLA: Yeah, it's a gift. So what's the story with her?
ROCCO: I don't know. I like her okay, but her name's Nina. I gotta
  have a Carla.
CARLA: I like that. Tell me more. You got a job?
ROCCO: What kind of question is that, do I got a job?
CARLA: If I'm gonna marry you, it's a legitimate question. I gotta
  know if my future husband is gonna take care of me.
ROCCO: Shouldn't we date a little before we talk about marriage?

NINA enters.

NINA: You're talking about marriage?
CARLA: Why not? Carpe diem. Seize the day. Know what I mean?
NINA: You just met him.
CARLA: So what? He's clean, he speaks English and he's got his teeth.

ROCCO: Every one of 'em.

NINA: You're going to marry a man for his teeth?

ROCCO: They happen to be very good teeth.

NINA: *(to CARLA)* What about his personality? The things he likes and dislikes? What he cares about? Aren't those important to you?

CARLA: Hey, most men don't even don't even care what your name is. Rocco here wants me.

NINA: No he doesn't. He wants someone named Carla.

CARLA: And I'm someone named Carla. Most guys just wanna go to bed with you. At least he wants to go to bed with Carla.

(to ROCCO)

You do want to go to bed with me, right?

ROCCO: Absolutely.

NINA: No, Rocco. You're better than that. He was in a four-year relationship with a woman.

CARLA: What happened there?

ROCCO: She ended it. Didn't see a future with a guy named Rocco.

CARLA: Why not? It's a good name.

ROCCO: Thank you. She didn't like it though. I don't want to talk about her no more.

NINA: He never talks about her.

ROCCO: It's a sensitive subject.

CARLA: Sensitive, with good teeth. What's not to love?
(she turns to ROCCO)

Rocco?

ROCCO: Yeah?

CARLA: I do.

ROCCO: You do what?

CARLA: I'll marry you.

NINA: Oh, come on. You just met.

CARLA: Yeah? And I see the thing you got for him. If he's good enough for you, he's good enough for me.

ROCCO: Whoa, who said I got a thing for somebody.

CARLA: Not somebody, her. It's as clear as the teeth in your mouth. You like her.

NINA: We're just friends. He comes in here for coffee, that's all.

CARLA: Yeah?

(to ROCCO)

How long you been coming in here?

ROCCO: I don't know, couple months.

CARLA: And you live in the neighborhood?

ROCCO: Neighborhood adjacent.

CARLA: How adjacent?

ROCCO: Twenty six blocks.

CARLA: That's what I thought.

(to NINA)

See? Nobody comes twenty six blocks just for a cup of coffee. He likes you.

NINA: *(to ROCCO)* Then how come you've never asked me out?

CARLA: Your name's not Carla.

NINA: Alright, Rocco, what is the deal with this Carla thing?

CARLA: Yeah, why you gotta be with someone with my name? Not that I'm complaining, mind you.

ROCCO: I don't wanna discuss it.

NINA: Why not? I mean, how are you ever going to find real happiness if you limit yourself?

CARLA: Hey! Real happiness is standing right here with the right name.

NINA: I'm sorry, Carla, but I know this man. He deserves a woman who's thoughtful and sensitive. Not someone who says I do just because he likes her name.

CARLA: *(to ROCCO)* You gonna let her talk to your fiancee like that?

NINA: Fiancee?

CARLA: That's right. This is the man I'm marrying.

ROCCO: Hold on, hold on. Carla, I like you just fine, but this is goin' a little fast here. We gotta take it slower.

CARLA: For what? I know what I want...

(she waits for him to respond. He doesn't.)

I thought you did, too. If you don't, then I withdraw my acceptance of your proposal, and I'm out.

She gets up to leave.

ROCCO: Hold on, I didn't say I don't know what I want.

CARLA: You didn't have to. It's clear you want her. The sooner you admit it, the better off you'll be.

CARLA: *(CARLA moves to ROCCO, rubs his body with her hands)* Good bye Rocco. You missed out on the Carla of your life.

CARLA takes the toothpick out of his mouth with her mouth. She exits with it still in her mouth.

NINA: You didn't miss anything.

ROCCO: I liked her.

NINA: Then why didn't you stop her?

ROCCO: I don't know.

NINA: Is she right about you and me?

ROCCO: No, I can't go out with you, Nina.

NINA: Why not?

ROCCO: Because of your name.

NINA: Stop it, Rocco. Why is that name so important to you?

ROCCO: I can't say.

NINA: Just tell me.

ROCCO: No, it's embarrassing.

NINA: I won't embarrass you. Just tell me why it has to be a Carla.

ROCCO: If I tell you, you promise you won't judge?

NINA: Yes.

ROCCO: Alright. You know how I don't talk about my old girlfriend?

NINA: Yeah.

ROCCO: Her name was Carla.

NINA: Seriously? You want to go out with someone just because she has the same name as your old girlfriend? That's sick, Rocco. You know that, right?

ROCCO: You said you wouldn't judge.

NINA: You're right, sorry. But why would you date women with the same name?

ROCCO: I got my reasons.

NINA: What are they?

ROCCO: I don't want to tell you. It's embarrassing!

NINA: I still won't judge.

ROCCO: Yes you will.

NINA: I swear!

ROCCO: Fine. I have to date a Carla because of this!

He lifts his tee shirt. The name CARLA is tattooed across his chest.

NINA: Holy shit. That's a big tattoo.

ROCCO: I know.

NINA: Wait a minute. That's why you want someone named Carla? Just because of a tattoo? That's sick, Rocco. Really sick.

ROCCO: You said you wouldn't judge.

NINA: I was wrong. Who dates a woman just so he can keep a tattoo?

ROCCO: It's very painful to have them removed. They have to use lasers and burn them off. It hurts and it smells

NINA: How do you know?

ROCCO: Because before Carla, I dated a girl named Constantine.

He turns, shows her the remnants of a tattoo on his back. It's red, like it's recently been removed, but it's clear that it said Constantine.

BLACKOUT

CATATONIC

Nedra Pezold Roberts

Premiere presented by The Group Rep at the Lonny Chapman Theatre, Hollywood, CA., July 2-August 7, 2016. Patrick Skelton (Tom), J. Christopher Sloan (Rick), Patrick Burke (Harry), Paul Cady (Tom understudy), Larry Margo (Director), Troy Whitaker and Kevin Dobson (producers).

CHARACTERS

TOM: Male, 20-something. Harry's former partner, now with Rick.
RICK: Male, 20-something. Now with Tom, caught between Tom and
Harry in a tug of war over a pet.
HARRY: Male, 20-something. Tom's former partner.

PLACE: Tom and Rick's apartment. A black-box stage can also be used.
TIME: The present.

AUTHOR'S NOTE: When HARRY is on stage, he stays stage left.
TOM stays stage right. RICK is caught between the two, moving in a kind of helpless tug-of-war. When TOM speaks to the
audience, he moves downstage center. For dialogue, TOM and/
or HARRY join him.

The stage is bare. In the darkness, a spotlight captures RICK as he enters, frustration vibrating off his aggressive stride. He suddenly notices the audience and halts in his tracks, then moves DC to confront the audience.

RICK: We've got this situation. Tom, Rick, and Harry. I'm Rick, so I'm in the middle, being used as a scratching post. The kind cats sharpen their claws on. Well, not a literal post but . . . oh, you know what I mean. It's true that when I hooked up with Tom, I realized he had some baggage from his previous relationship. I was ready to accept that, you know. Help him work through it. But in no way was I prepared for Harry. I mean, who could be?

The doorbell rings. To the audience as lights come up and he heads for the door, SL.

Don't move. Wait right there and see for yourself.

RICK opens the door. HARRY is a bit furtive and holds a cat-carrier.

HARRY: Are you sure he's not here?

RICK: I told you it was safe when you called, didn't I?

HARRY: Yes, but Tom can hold a grudge.

RICK: It's not a grudge; it's a restraining order. And he's not here, so you can give me Tucker and go.

HARRY: His name is Sophie, not Tucker.

RICK: Harry. Just give me the cat.

HARRY: If you call him by the wrong name, you'll warp his psyche.

RICK: The cat, Harry.

HARRY: In a minute. I've got something to say first.

RICK: Give me the damn cat.

HARRY: I've got something to say!

RICK: *(he shares a look with the audience, then grabs the carrier, and the cat makes an angry noise)* Quiet, Tucker. Your jailer will be gone in a minute, and I'll let you out of your prison.

HARRY: Don't call it a prison. He'll hear you.

RICK: You're nuts, you know that?

He moves upstage to open the carrier and let TUCKER out. Both men turn their heads suddenly as if watching the cat run swiftly out of the room.

HARRY: See? You've upset him. Sophie is very sensitive. And you're confusing his identity when you call him by the wrong name.

RICK: By what stretch of the imagination is Tucker the wrong name?

HARRY: Tom and I named him Sophie Tucker when he was a kitten. He knows that name, responds to it. It's who he is.

RICK: It's who he was until the vet pointed out that Sophie was a boy. Then Tom declared the cat was now Tucker. Not Sophie. Just plain Tucker.

HARRY: Tucker sends the wrong signal. It's homophobic.

RICK: Listen carefully, you lunatic. You're gay, I'm gay, Tom is gay. Tucker is not. He's a cat.

HARRY: How do you know he's not gay?

RICK: Jesus.

(RICK moves closer towards the front door)

Thank you for returning Tucker. I'll bring him to your place at the regular time next week.

HARRY: *(removes a folded paper from his pocket)* I have a few concerns you should share with Tom.

RICK: This isn't recess in junior high, Harry. And I'm not passing your notes to Tom.

HARRY: Then I'll have my lawyer contact his lawyer, and Tom won't be happy if we go back to court.

RICK: Over a cat?

HARRY: Sophie isn't just a cat, he's a family member. A product of my union with Tom.

RICK: Harry. I'm being patient here.

HARRY: Sophie wouldn't eat his gourmet cat food. And he refused his organic treats. I think Tom's frequent absences are affecting Sophie's appetite. He misses Tom.

RICK: Tom's an airline pilot with an irregular schedule. You know that. If the cat lived here full time, he wouldn't have to adjust to a different house every other week. You're the one who sued for joint custody.

HARRY: And Tom's the one who took out a restraining order. He doesn't want me to see Sophie.

RICK: Tom doesn't care if you see Tucker. Tom just doesn't want to see you.

HARRY turns away and moves UL, stopping with his back to the audience. RICK moves DC.

RICK: Tom came home that night, and against my better judgment, I shared Harry's list of gripes. Tom was not . . . happy. And the beat goes on.

TOM enters SR.

TOM: He looks fine to me. He ate his food and chased the laser light like he was still a kitten, full of energy. Harry's imagining things.

RICK: He seemed genuinely concerned.

TOM: Yeah, seemed. What he's really after is sole custody of Tucker. No way am I gonna allow that.

RICK: Oh, I don't think—

TOM: He figures if he complains enough, I'll give in and let him keep Tucker. That's the kind of passive-aggressive stunt he used to pull when we were together. Complain, wait, complain, wait. Hoping to wear me down. Tucker is fine with the present arrangements. End of discussion.

RICK: He pees in the bedroom closet when you're gone.

TOM: Harry?

RICK: Tucker!

TOM: Since when?

RICK: Since you and Harry started this joint custody mess.

TOM: I've never noticed a problem with the closet.

RICK: That's because I clean it up right away. But I have to keep checking, because he likes to do it all over again after I've cleaned up. And he freaks when I try to put him in the cat carrier to do the hand-off to Harry. He runs away or tries to climb up the curtains. He's like the devil on speed.

TOM: He's just playing with you, Rick.

TOM moves UR, stopping with his back to the audience. RICK moves downstage to the audience.

RICK: This is my life. I'm the rope in a tug-of-war between Tom and Harry. Meanwhile, that cat is laughing his furry ass off at me. This can't go on. I never signed up for divorce counseling.

HARRY moves to meet RICK, DL.

HARRY: I realize I complain a lot.

RICK: Really? What was your first clue?

HARRY: It's my job to look out for Sophie's best interests if Tom is going to callously ignore them.

RICK: Tom loves Tucker. He takes good care of him.

HARRY: He's not feeding Sophie the organic treats we agreed on. Sophie has a very delicate stomach.

RICK: Delicate stomach? That cat eats olives, string, and pizza crust.

He even eats paper!

HARRY: I knew it! This proves Tom is unfit to raise Sophie. Tell him he'll be hearing from my lawyer.

HARRY returns UL, his back to the audience. TOM meets RICK DR.

TOM: *(agitated and waving a paper at RICK)* He's riding the crazy train again. This is beyond vindictive. It's . . . it's—

RICK: What's that?

TOM: A letter from Harry's lawyer.

RICK: Wow. I know he threatened to have his lawyer contact you, but I thought he was just blowing smoke. I mean, are cat treats really such a big deal?

TOM: Treats? Is this about those damn organic pellets? The man's insane. Tucker hates those pellets. And I refuse to spend twenty dollars a bag for grass clippings held together with glue.

RICK: Is that what they are?

TOM: Might as well be. They're hard as rocks and smell like dead fish.

RICK: Maybe if you talked to Harry, the two of you could reach some kind of compromise.

TOM: Whose side are you on anyway?

RICK: Tucker's, I think.

TOM moves UR, turning his back to the audience. RICK moves DC.

RICK: So I finally got sick of this insanity and told Harry to get his butt over for a summit meeting. No lawyers. Just us. Tom pitched a fit, but I was unilaterally voiding the restraining order.

The three men are all DC with RICK in the middle. TOM and HARRY have their backs to each other, at first, arms folded across their chests.

RICK: Gentlemen, we're here to find a mutually agreeable solution to our problem, and we're going to resolve it quickly. Because right now Tucker is probably peeing in our closet.

HARRY: For the record, I'm here against my will.

TOM: Same here.

RICK: Tough. We're settling this now. Harry, I mean this seriously. What do you really want?

HARRY: I want Tom to agree to let me take Sophie to see a therapist.

RICK: A therapist?

HARRY: Yes. I think he's been traumatized by our break up.

TOM: There's nothing wrong with Tucker. He's fine. If anyone needs to see a therapist, it's Harry.

HARRY: Every time Sophie comes to my apartment he hides. For at least two days. He won't come out from under the bed. Not even to eat. I have to push his food under the dust ruffle.

TOM: He eats fine here. You give him that organic crap and he hates it. Get a clue. Feed him cat food.

HARRY: The stuff you give Sophie is terrible for his digestion. It gives him gas.

TOM: It doesn't.

RICK: Actually, it does.

TOM: I've never noticed that.

RICK: Because I put deodorizers in every rom. That cat's farts are almost as lethal as tear gas.

HARRY: Tom, you don't really care about his digestion. You're a terrible parent!

TOM: And you're—

RICK: Guys! This sniping isn't getting us anywhere. Focus, Harry. What do you actually want?

HARRY: I want him to admit that he's a terrible parent and that he doesn't love Sophie as much as I do.

TOM: Not gonna happen.

RICK: Your turn, Tom. What do you want?

TOM: I want Harry to admit I'm better with Tucker than he is, and that that's the real reason our relationship imploded.

HARRY: You never put in the effort I did. And you were never home!

RICK: Ah, truth at last. Okay, enough about the two of you. Here's what's going to happen. From now on, that cat is mine, not yours. And neither of you has any say in how he and I partner up.

HARRY: You can't do that! I have rights.

RICK: The cat has rights, too. And they don't include being used as the ball in a ping pong tournament. Tom? Forget the restraining order. And Harry? You can visit the cat whenever you want. He hates that damn cat carrier and getting shuffled back and forth every week.

HARRY: You can't just claim Sophie.

RICK: Pay attention. I just did. That cat and I get along. I ignore him and he ignores me.

TOM: Actually, that's true. Tucker's calm around Rick. More like he allows Rick to inhabit his space.

HARRY: We'll need to write up a whole new agreement. But you'll have to call Sophie by his name, and stop referring to him as "the cat."

RICK: You can write up any agreement you want, but the cat and I are going to ignore it. And as of now, his name is no longer Sophie Tucker. It's Cat. That's what he is, so that's the name.

TOM: He won't respond to that. It'll just confuse him.

HARRY: Tom's right.

RICK: It figures. The one thing you agree on is your hypocrisy. You each call him by a different name and you think that doesn't confuse him? If all three of us call him Cat, he'll adapt quickly.

TOM: Actually, you might be right about that.

HARRY: Yeah, it's a point.

RICK: So it's Cat from now on?

TOM: I can accept that if you do, Harry.

HARRY: Oh, all right.

RICK: Okay. Done. Time to go check where Cat's been pissing.

The three men move upstage together. Blackout

COFFEE BREAK

Tasha Gordon-Solmon

Actors Theater of Louisville, Humana Festival
April 9-10, 2016
Directed by Meredith McDonough, featuring

WOMAN 1 - Brenda Withers
WOMAN 2 - Deonna Bouye
1 - Barney O'Hanlon
2 - Nate Miller

CHARACTERS
WOMAN 1 – 20s – 30s
WOMAN 2 – 20s – 30s
1 – 20s – 40s, any gender
2 – 20s – 40s, any gender

SETTING
TIME – always 4 o'clock
PLACE – a coffee shop

A coffee shop. Two women sit down at a table, each a carrying a coffee cup.

WOMAN 2: Apparently they could restructure the entire department.

WOMAN 1: Really?

WOMAN 2: That's what Karen said. But you know Karen

WOMAN 1 & WOMAN 2: She'd say anything

WOMAN 2: The way I see it, they would have to
What?

WOMAN 1: Do you have anything… in your cup?

WOMAN 2: Decaf

WOMAN 1: In the foam

WOMAN 2: It's a regular coffee

WOMAN 1: I have something
In my foam

WOMAN 2: Oh

WOMAN 1: It's a heart

WOMAN 2: I see that

WOMAN 1: He made me a heart
Do you think it's like
A move?

WOMAN 2: A…

WOMAN 1: He's cute right?
Do you think he's cute?

WOMAN 2: I think that's just what they do

WOMAN 1: Boys that like you but don't know how to say it?

WOMAN 2: Baristas

WOMAN 1: You didn't get one

WOMAN 2: It's a regular coffee

WOMAN 1: You said decaf

WOMAN 2: That's the same thing

WOMAN 1: You don't think he likes me?

WOMAN 2: I don't know if he does

WOMAN 1: Why wouldn't he like me?
What about me is there to not like?

WOMAN 2: I'm saying it might be standard coffee art
And not a confession of love

WOMAN 1: We come here every day
I've never had a heart before
And suddenly I do

WOMAN 2: From the new guy who's proba-
WOMAN 1: Should I go talk to him?
    I'll wait for him to come to me
    Will he come to the table?
    I'll stay in my chair
1 & 2: The table and the chair
1: The chair thinks:
    Isn't it amazing we were paired up
    Like we fit
    Like we match
    Like somehow we came from the same place, and were made for each other
2: The Table thinks:
    These chairs are fine
    We were in the factory together
    So now we're here together
    Makes sense
1: The chair thinks:
    Look at those legs
    All four of them
2: The table thinks:
    I wonder if someone will fix my wobble today
    I don't like it when they start stuffing napkins underneath
    You need firm elevation with an injury
    Cardboard
    Or a wood chip
1: The chair thinks:
    Sometimes
    When table and I touch
    I catch it wobble a little
    I think I make it nervous
2: The table thinks:
2: *(cont'd)*
    This wobble is a pain my oak
    And it gets worse every time a damn chair bangs against me
    1: The chair thinks:
    I think this is love

The next day. Women 1 & 2 go to sit at their table, as before, with their coffees.

        Lawrence Harbison

WOMAN 2: So I asked Dan if he thought there would be lay offs and
    he said no. But you know Dan, he's…
    Are you okay?
WOMAN 1: Sure
    You were saying
    About
WOMAN 2: Potential layoffs
WOMAN 1: Uh huh
WOMAN 2: Well when I spoke to Dan, unreliable source that he is
    You seem a little on edge
WOMAN 1: I'm fine

    beat

    I'm afraid of love
    Not afraid excited
    Afraid of being excited
    Afraid if I'm excited, I'll be disappointed
    But why would he disappoint me now, if he hasn't yet, right?
WOMAN 2: What are you…?
WOMAN 1: Andrew
WOMAN 2: Who?
WOMAN 1: It says his name on his nametag
WOMAN 2: The foam guy?
WOMAN 1: re: cup
    I need to know but
    You do it
    What do you see?
WOMAN 2: A cappuccino
WOMAN 1: In the foam
WOMAN 2: A squiggle of chocolate syrup maybe
WOMAN 1: What kind of squiggle
WOMAN 2: It could be… a messy cloud?
WOMAN 1: Let me
    She looks, gasps
WOMAN 2: What
    What
WOMAN 1: It's a
    (vagina)
WOMAN 2: Pardon?
WOMAN 1: See how there's the loop on that side and…

WOMAN 2: I can see how it kind of looks like petals, maybe a flower
WOMAN 1: My flower
  Oh Jesus

She picks up a scone from her saucer, that was hidden on the other side of her cup.

  He gave me a scone
  On my saucer
  He gave me a free scone
  And drew a you-know-what in my foam
  And gave me a scone
  This is getting so intense
1 & 2: The saucer and the scone
1: The scone thinks:
  I can't wait for my dip in the coffee
  To get warm
  And wet
  To sink into the murky deep
2: The saucer thinks:
  Oh scone
  I feel the vibrations as you languidly move in the coffee
  Then lie back on me
  Softened, spent, dripping, crumbling
  To pieces on my surface
1: The scone thinks:
  If only there was someone to hold all my pieces
2: The saucer thinks:
  I could hold the pieces
1: The scone thinks:
  Oh that saucer below me
2: The saucer thinks:
  Oh that scone above
  That unbleached, gluten free, cranberries and traces of nuts
1: The scone thinks:
1: *(cont'd)* That porcelain, dishwasher safe, made in China, do not
  microwave
  I'd microwave
  If I could
  The scone thinks:
  If only

2: If only

Same as last time, the women sit, coffees, table.

WOMAN 1: He was being weird

WOMAN 2: He seemed normal

WOMAN 1: It's because I wasn't here yesterday

WOMAN 2: I don't think he's disappointed after two days of serving
you coffee

WOMAN 1: That's not all he—

WOMAN 2: Maybe he'd be disappointed after coffees with his friend
every single day

And then being ditched out of the blue

WOMAN 1: I'm sorry were you waiting for me yesterday?

WOMAN 2: Where were you?

WOMAN 1: I took a sick day

WOMAN 2: Are you alright?

WOMAN 1: I needed some space

Things were starting to move so fast

I couldn't see him

WOMAN 1: *(cont'd)* And I couldn't go into the office because that
would make me think of getting coffee, which would inevitably
lead back to him

So I called in sick

WOMAN 2: That's um

WOMAN 1: But when four o'clock came along, I realized

I need him

And I miss him

And now it's too late

He was so cold when I ordered

WOMAN 2: I don't think he was cold

WOMAN 1: He asked if I wanted my latte iced

WOMAN 2: It's hot out

WOMAN 1: There's no foam in an iced latte

It was his passive aggressive way of questioning whether I'm in
this for real

Which is a valid question because I didn't know yesterday

But I do today and it's too late

She looks into her cup, decomposes a little.

Yup

WOMAN 2: What is it

WOMAN 1: Nothing

WOMAN 2: I'm sure it's not that bad

WOMAN 1: Fighting tears
It's nothing
There's nothing in the foam
Excuse me I need a napkin

1 & 2: The napkins
They think:

1: We were altogether

2: One package
One set

1 & 2: Layer
upon Layer
upon and upon and upon
endless infinite togetherness

1: And then one day

2: One goes away

1: And another

2: And other

1: Upon layer Upon layer

1 & 2: upon and upon and upon

2: endless

1: infinite

2: aloneness

A week later. The women sit at the table, with their coffees.

WOMAN 2: It's good to see you

WOMAN 1: I missed our coffee breaks

WOMAN 2: Me too

WOMAN 1: It was too hard to be around....
I've been using the instant in the employee kitchen

WOMAN 2: The one on the sixth floor?

WOMAN 1: Seventh

WOMAN 2: Aren't you going to look?

WOMAN 1: It didn't even cross my mind

WOMAN 2: You're only going to be thinking about it the whole time
Well

WOMAN 1: A smiley

WOMAN 2: That is definitely two eyes and a happy mouth

WOMAN 1: That's nice
    Even though it's over
    It feels good knowing you meant something you know?
    That it wasn't all me
    That he wishes me the best
    I wish him the best I do even though it's hard
    I think this is the closure I needed.
WOMAN 2: That's good
WOMAN 1: We should find a new place
    Maybe with tea
WOMAN 2: I got laid off
WOMAN 1: When?
WOMAN 2: Last week
WOMAN 1: You met me in the lobby
WOMAN 2: I wanted to say goodbye
WOMAN 1: I'm so sorry was it the
WOMAN 2: Restructuring
WOMAN 1: What are you gonna do?
WOMAN 2: I have some interviews
WOMAN 1: We should still keep in touch
WOMAN 2: Definitely
WOMAN 1: You live downtown right
WOMAN 2: Uptown
WOMAN 1: We can meet in the middle
    For coffee
    Or tea
WOMAN 2: That sounds nice
WOMAN 1: lightly
    Yeah, we're more than coworkers

Woman 1 sips her coffee.

2: The coworker
    The coworker thinks:
    Of Her
    Drinking her coffee
    The way she holds the cup
    The way she takes a sip
    With an ease that is disarming
    A grace that is alarming
    Never noticing

Who buys her coffee every day
Who pulls out her seat
Slips a scone onto her plate
The coworker thinks:
I wonder what She thinks
This colleague this acquaintance this friend
I wonder if she'll ever think of me
The way I think
The way so many things think
But are rarely thought of
WOMAN 1: Hey
It's gonna get cold
WOMAN 2: Thanks.

She takes a sip from her cup.

CRAM SCHOOL SNOW DAY

Reina Hardy

Original production: The first version of "Cram School Snow Day" was created as part of Live Art DC's Live Art in a Day 2015, (a 24-hour play festival), directed by Anna Lathrop and starring Erik Harrison, Elizabeth Hansen, Genevieve James, Reginald Richard and Jon Jon Johnson.

The play was first produced as part of Landing Theater Company's Redemption Series, 9/22-10/1 2015 in Houston, TX, directed by Rob Kimbro.

The cast was:

ANDREA - Laura Moreno
KAMI - Alli Villines
JASON - Andrew Garrett
RICHARD - Harold Trotter
MISS LENA - Rachel Dickinson

SETTING: Cram school teacher's lounge, an America city. The near future.

CHARACTERS
JASON: male, 20s
ANDREA: female, 20s
MISS LENA: female, 50s
RICHARD: male, 20s
KAMI: female, 20s or 30s

SYNOPSIS: In the near and dangerous future, a group of cram school teachers wait for the kids to show up or for the city to explode into violence… whichever comes first.

BIO: Reina Hardy is a playwright from Chicago. Her plays, which usually contain magic and sometimes contain science, have been produced in Chicago, NYC, Austin and DC. They include "Glass-heart" (Rorsharch Theater and the Shrewds), "Changelings", (The Vortex), "A Map to Somewhere Else" (Everyday Inferno, NYC) and "Annie Jump and the Library of Heaven (KCACTF TYA Prize.) Honors include: Michener Fellowship, National New Play Network New Play Showcase, Kennedy Center MFA Playwrights Workshop, Interact 20/20 Commission, 2015-16 Pipeline Playlab, Jerome Fellowship Finalist, Collider Commission, Terrence Mcnally Prize finalist, GPTC Holland New Voices Award, KCACTF Mark Twain Prize Runner up. Publications include: "Best American Short Plays, 2012-2013," and "Best Scenes for Two Actors," Applause, "Best Stage Monologs for Men," "60 Seconds to Shine," and the upcoming "105 5-Minute Plays for Study and Performance," from Smith and Kraus. She is currently developing "Fanatical: The Musical" with the Stable in the U.K. for a 2017 production.

Five cram school teachers are sitting around the lounge on a Saturday, somewhere between anxious and bored out of their skulls. We are in the future, but not too far. There are chairs, but not enough chairs.

Miss Lena is trying to make a call. It isn't going very well. Everyone else has given up on work completely.

JASON: I think we'd be totally justified in leaving.

RICHARD: You wanna give up the hours, I'm not gonna stop you.

JASON: I mean if we ALL left...

ANDREA: Then the kids would come, and there'd be no-one here and something terrible would happen and ABC Test Prep School gets sued out of existence.

JASON: Are the kids even showing up?

KAMI: Well, we're not gonna know for an hour... so...

JASON: What kind of school program doesn't have a snow day policy?

KAMI: We do have a snow day policy. When the public schools declare a snow day, we declare a snow day.

JASON: BUT IT'S SATURDAY.

RICHARD: Sometimes, Jake, it's real obvious you haven't been working here long.

JASON: It's Jason.

RICHARD: Uh-huh.

JASON: I just think John could have officially cancelled if he wasn't going to come.

ANDREA: But that would entail thinking of his employees as human beings whose time is finite and has value.

KAMI: He doesn't always come on Saturdays. We're still expected to teach.

ANDREA: Yeah, what are we expected to do when we can't log into any of the computers? What does he think we'll do if we know the network password? Look at porn.

RICHARD: I would for sure look at porn.

ANDREA: I would too, at this point. I would look at anything. I'm SO BORED.

KAMI: I brought my ukulele.

VARIOUS: NOOOOOOO

ANDREA: Sorry, Kami. You guys remember when you could get the internet on a phone?

RICHARD: That was a year ago.

KAMI: You hear on the radio about the snipers?

ANDREA: What? No.

RICHARD: It's true. Great Nation got a snipers corps.

ANDREA: That's ridiculous, you need years of training.

RICHARD: Nu-uh. Gun has a computer that aims for you.

MISS LENA: *(Eastern European accent- whatever the performer is comfortable with)* Hello?

Everyone is suddenly paying attention.

MISS LENA: Ok, yes. I will call back.

(to the crowd)

Miss Kim says she isn't sure. She hasn't heard from him either.

ANDREA: Fuuuuuck.

KAMI: Andrea has a point- we should think of what we can do if the kids show up and we can't access the class material.

ANDREA: I printed out the tests on Friday.

VARIOUS: Thanks, Andrea,/ Thanks, print bitch.

KAMI: Still leaves us with two hours of time to fill.

RICHARD: I vote we wait till the kids don't show up. Who's with me?

Richard and Andrea raise their hands.

JASON: If we ALL left, and just told John that we demanded the full shift pay-

ANDREA: *(interrupting him with an old union song, sung to "The Battle Hymn of the Republic")* SOLIDARITY FOREVER!

ANDREA/RICHARD: SOLIDARITY FOREVER!

RICHARD: Hallelujah!

ANDREA/RICHARD: SOLIDARITY FOREVER!

ANDREA: Get your ukulele, Kami!

ANDREA/RICHARD/KAMI: THE UNION MAKES US STRONG!

JASON: Ok, ok. god.

KAMI: *(with ukulele, suddenly alone)* THE STARS ABOVE IN HEAVEN NOW ARE LOOKING KINDLY DOWN THE STARS ABOVE IN HEAVEN NOW ARE LOOKING KINDLY…. oh sorry.

ANDREA: I'm gonna go check on the weather.

She exits.

RICHARD: Don't pout, Jake. I'm like 70% sure we're gonna get paid.

JASON: It's not about the money. I'm here to help kids, not waste my time.

RICHARD: Ha ha ha ha ha ha ha HA HA HA. Shut up.

KAMI: They go to school eight hours and sit down and take tests, they come here and do it for another three hours, and five on Saturday. There are better ways to help kids than working here.

JASON: The scores matter. We're talking about their future. Some of them barely speak English and they're supposed to take a test- in English- that determines the trajectory of their future? They need something to make up that gap.

RICHARD: And that's why their parents pony up their hard-earned under the table cash so that John can hand it over to your Ivy League ass.

JASON: I went to UCLA

KAMI: Don't let Richard give you a hard time. *(pointing at Richard and whispering)* U Penn.

RICHARD: That's right. I'm just disappointed in myself. I got nothing better to do then aid the immigrant menace.

Andrea re-enters.

ANDREA: Shit, it's really coming down now. Buses are going to be a nightmare.

JASON: I left home just in time to get trapped here all weekend. So quiet.

KAMI: That's one good thing about snow. Nobody makes trouble in the snow. Kids are happy, but everyone else just wants to sleep.

RICHARD: You're right. It hasn't been this quiet all year.

KAMI: Not on Saturday. We've had Great Nation marchers every Saturday since Christmas. I kept track.

RICHARD: I can't believe the shit those assholes chant in public, like kids couldn't possibly be listening. Kids are always asking me what this or that means, and I gotta be like "don't ever say that word."

KAMI: I always tell them it's a parade. Just a parade. I hope by the time they understand what's going on, it's over.

MS. LENA: They understand.
They may not know every word, but kids know when they are being talked about. When their parents are being talked about. They always know when they're not wanted.

ANDREA: She's right. I was working here during the election. During the primaries, even. How does an eight year old know the name of a Republican presidential nominee? But they all knew. Everyone stiffens. They hear something outside. This probably shouldn't be a sound effect that we create- but from their reactions we know it's bad.

KAMI: Do you hear that?

ANDREA: Goddammit. Spoke too soon.

Everyone listens for a second.

ANDREA: Wow. Those are some words I haven't heard in a while…. bringing back the classics.

JASON: I hope those fuckers get mowed down by the Chinese mafia.

KAMI: Jason!

RICHARD: No, he's right. Coming into THIS neighborhood, saying immigrant this and immigrant go home like this isn't Chinatown. They are asking for trouble. Someday they'll get it.

Pause

ANDREA: It seem like there's a lot more of them then usual?
I hope the kids don't come today.

Everyone starts- HARD. Like they've heard a gunshot or an explosion.

VARIOUS: *(except Miss Lena)* What was that? /Shit! / What was that?

KAMI: Was that a gunshot?

RICHARD: How the fuck would I know?

Another loud noise. Everyone starts again.

ANDREA: Oh god, oh god oh god oh god…..

Miss Lena, with great purpose, puts one hand to her lips and strides out of the room.

ANDREA: *(trying to go after her)* Where is she going- where are you going?

KAMI: Stay here Andrea, stay here!

They all wait. After a moment, the lights go out. The teachers strangle-scream. Miss Lena re-enters with a flashlight.

MISS LENA: We are closed. For the snow day.

ANDREA: You locked the doors?

MISS LENA: We'll stay here, for now.

RICHARD: *(shaking)* Ukelele jam times, right?

KAMI: Are you ok?

RICHARD: I'm fine, I'm just a literal fish in a literal fucking barrel.

Everyone starts again.

RICHARD: What was that?

ANDREA: They're breaking glass.

KAMI: What if this is why John didn't come in? What if they DID something to him?

RICHARD: I had a dream, and this was the actual way I was going to die in the dream...

JASON: No-one is going to die. We don't have to stay here. We can slip out the back door and blend in with the crowd...

RICHARD: Not all of us can blend in with the crowd, Jason!

JASON: I mean, none of look like immigrants. Not even Miss Lena and... she is one.

Everyone looks at Miss Lena.

MISS LENA: These things never last for that long. If they break the glass doors, they will take the computer in reception, and when they see how many doors there are, they will get bored. At any rate, we need to be here in case the children come.

Everyone sits. After a moment.

ANDREA: Miss Lena... you've been through some shit, right? Like, back where you... Like, at what point do you say... enough is enough. I'm not doing this anymore. I gotta find somewhere else to go?

pause

KAMI: Andrea. Shut up.

They sit for a moment. Kami takes out her ukulele, and plays the battle Hymn of the Republic, humming the tune. When the song is over, they pause. They listen.

ANDREA: Is it over?

JASON: What is that noise?

KAMI: When children are playing... a couple blocks away... and it sounds like screaming... like something terrible is happening to them, like they're all being murdered... but when you get close, they really are just playing…. You know what that sounds like? Do you know if it sounds any different…. when something terrible really is happening?

No-one knows. After a moment Miss Lena gets up and leaves the room. Everyone watches her go.

Then there is a muffled yelp- a jump scare from off stage. The teachers strangle scream and clutch each other.

Miss Lena enters. She is dusted with snow. She's carrying something.

MISS LENA: No school today.

She throws a snowball at the teachers.

MISS LENA: The children are having a snowball fight.

END OF PLAY

THE CUT OF MEMORY

David Strauss

The Cut of Memory originally premiered at the Lowndes Shakespeare Center in Orlando, Florida on July 15-31, 2016 as part of an evening of short plays entitled "Summer Shorts." It was directed by Chuck Dent and produced by Playwrights' Round Table.

The cast was as follows:

Daniel - Mark Davids

Melanie - Brienna Killgallon

Peter - Anthony Marando

DJ - Joshua Ryan Roller

SYNOPSIS: The darker side of virtual reality is explored as a son finds his father lost in his own memories of his ex-wife.

SETTING: A dingy and messy living room, no specific location. Sometime in the near future.

CHARACTERS:

DANIEL: Male, late 40s

DJ: male, 20s, younger version of DANIEL: Peter - male, 20s, Daniel's son

MELANIE: female, 20s, DJ's girlfriend

Lawrence Harbison

LIGHTS UP.

(A man, late 40s, is sitting in a chair. This is DANIEL. He has on some type of VR goggles, the design of which I'll leave up to the production. Around his chair are the detritus of someone who has not been very active - candy wrappers, water bottles, beer cans, newspapers, etc. He is dressed raggedly, in sweats or a beat-up bathrobe. He should be lit dimly if possible.

Also onstage, not next to him, are a younger couple, early 20s, DJ and MELINDA, at a table, and in much better light. They are dressed well, holding hands, making eyes at each other, smiling. This is a first date but it's going really well. They are not aware of DANIEL in any way.)

DJ: Oh My God, you too?

MELINDA: I totally did!

DJ: I thought I was the only one who loved that movie!

MELINDA: Are you kidding? I saw it like ten times. I mean, in the theater. I would buy a ticket, watch it through, go to the bathroom when they were cleaning and then sneak back in and see it again!

DJ: Oh, you criminal.

MELINDA: Yup, I was once asked to describe myself in three words. I said "I am a rebel."

DJ: Get down with your bad self. (beat) Okay, I apologize, that was a very white thing to say.

MELINDA: That's okay. I myself come from a long line of white people. *(If not applicable to the actor, use "I'll let it go.")*

DJ: I just never met anyone who was that into it. I usually kind of pretend I've never seen it. Oh my God, the bit with the raisinettes!

MELINDA: "Excuse me, sir, can I have my raisinette back?"

DJ: "Excuse me, sir, can I have my raisinette back?"

(They collapse in hysterics.)

MELINDA: The part at the end, where they kiss, so roman-- I mean, yeah, I like it. As first kisses go.

DJ: Uh oh, that's a lot of pressure on me now.

MELINDA: That's assuming I want a first kiss.

DJ: Spoiler alert: I was kind of hoping there would be.

MELINDA: Spoilers back: I'd be okay with one.

(DJ leans in to kiss her, puts his hands on her face, very softly,

and starts a very passionate kiss. Right in the middle of it:)

DANIEL: Freeze.

(DJ and MELINDA freeze. A couple seconds. They do not move.)

DANIEL: Rewind, ten seconds.

(DJ and MELINDA step back from each other and replay the last ten seconds.)

DJ: Uh oh, that's a lot of pressure on me now.

(Another man, early 20s, PETER, enters. He is well dressed, perhaps a suit. He does not see DJ and MELINDA at this time or any other. PETER heads right to DANIEL.)

MELINDA: That's assuming I want a first kiss.
DJ: Spoiler alert: I was kind of hoping there would be.
MELINDA: Spoilers back: I'd be okay with one.

(He leans in to kiss her, puts his hands on her face, very softly, and starts a very passionate kiss. Right in the middle of it:)

DANIEL: Forward six minutes.

(DJ and MELINDA are now caressing each other's faces. Making out. In between kisses:)

MELINDA: You know, I don't live too far from here.
PETER: Dad?
DJ: And?
MELINDA: We could go back there. Put on our movie. Maybe share some raisinettes.
DJ: Okay.
PETER: Dad?
MELINDA: Or, you know, just go to bed.
DJ: I think I'm okay with that.
PETER: Dad!
DANIEL: Freeze.

(DJ and MELINDA freeze instantly.)

PETER: Dad! Take off the headset now.
DANIEL: Forward. Six months, four days later. 10:15 pm.
PETER: Dad! I know you can hear me.

(DJ and MELINDA have moved away from the table. It's six months later, and one of their first fights.)

DJ: Look, I told you I'd be back after we were done!

MELINDA: You knew I needed your car, mine is still at the dealership. I have to go shopping and it's after ten and the damned place closed fifteen minutes ago!

DJ: It's not a big deal, you can buy your stupid crap tomorrow.

MELINDA: Stupid?!

PETER: DAD!

DANIEL: Freeze.

(DANIEL removes the glasses. DJ and MELINDA exit.)

PETER: Dad.

DANIEL: Oh. Peter.

PETER: I went by your office to see if you wanted to get lunch and they told me you weren't in today. That you hadn't been in all week.

DANIEL: I was... *(looks around at his mess)* cleaning.

PETER: Bullshit. You've been replaying all morning, haven't you?

DANIEL: No. Just for a little bit.

PETER: Oh yeah, what time is it?

DANIEL: I...I dunno. I don't have any clocks in here.

PETER: It's 11:00.

DANIEL: Sure, about 11.

PETER: No, it's actually 3:30. How long were you in there?

DANIEL: I don't have to answer to you. You're not my boss.

PETER: No, and I have no idea how you still have a job. Your assistant told me you haven't been to the office more than once or twice this month. Is this what you've been doing, sitting here and replaying all day long, day after day, instead of living in the real world? Why the hell haven't they fired you?

DANIEL: Because Edgar...appreciates the value of self reflection.

PETER: Great euphemism. So he's addicted too? More and more of—I wonder how long it takes before the economy falls off a cliff. Three guys and two women in my office stopped showing up this week.

DANIEL: You wouldn't understand.

PETER: No, I don't. *(beat)* Okay, that's not true. I do, a little. It's not like I haven't tried, once or twice.

DANIEL: Not so mighty on your high horse, are you?

PETER: I never claimed to be. But there's a difference between looking at the past and wallowing in it. I...miss her too.

DANIEL: That's not it.

PETER: It's not? I mean, I assumed...I mean, after mom...I mean, I can understand why you'd want to relive the good memories. The end...I know it was hard, but—

DANIEL: You don't understand.

PETER: Then tell me, dad. I'm trying to understand. What do you replay, the first time you met, the first date, your wedding?

DANIEL: Sometimes.

PETER: I can get that. You try and replay the good times, it helps deal with the pain of losing her.

DANIEL: I lost her a long time before she died.

PETER: Well, I know, but...you know Roger would have let you come to the funeral. I get that you and he can never be friends, after what happened. With mom. But he's not an ogre. He would have let you come.

DANIEL: She didn't want me in her life anymore. She made that clear.

PETER: You were her first husband. She loved you at some time. And you're my father. You had a right to be there. I told you this.

DANIEL: It's really 3:30?

PETER: Yeah. I told the office I'd come back in tonight and finish the Grimwood project. Look, have you eaten at all?

DANIEL: I'm not hungry.

PETER: I'll go make you something. I'm guessing you have some of those frozen burritos in the freezer?

DANIEL: And bring me a scotch.

PETER: Maybe. Give me a couple minutes.

(PETER exits. DANIEL looks around at the mess around him and puts the glasses back on.)

DANIEL: Date: December 3, 1992. 11:15 pm.

(DJ and MELINDA are again onstage. MELINDA is holding a baby in her arms, swaddled up tight, and is rocking back and forth. She is angry and hurt. DJ has had a few drinks.)

MELINDA: I asked you to come home right after work.

DJ: I went out with the office. It was an office...thing. C'mon, relax. *(Trying to amuse her, break the tension)* "Excuse me, can I have my raisinette back?"

MELINDA: Don't joke with me. I'm not in the mood. I'm guessing you don't actually have the credit card receipt, right? You lost it. And when the bill comes in it will say "Highway Steakhouse" or something instead of the damned strip club, to make it sound classy.

DJ: Yes, I went out with the guys from the office. What do you want me to do, be the one loser who has to run home and bail out? This is the important networking part of it. If you want me to end up as a partner someday, I have to do this part now.

MELINDA: You know he's colicky. I haven't been able to stop moving for...all day. Every time I stop moving he starts crying. I can't even put him down to sleep, he has to keep moving or he cries. I just...need a break. Please, it's really hard.

DJ: Well, I'm here now. Just give him to me.

MELINDA: Not with that attitude.

DJ: Look, I'm here. I'm his father.

MELINDA: Then start acting like one!

DJ: I...I don't know what to do.

MELINDA: I need you here! Not staring at a pair of boobs or partying with your idiot single office mates. I need your help, and you're NOT here!

DJ: I'm sorry. I'll...I'm sorry.

MELINDA: I don't know if you can do this, Daniel. I really don't. Maybe you're just not cut out for being a dad.

DANIEL: Rewind, five seconds. *(He has begun to cry.)*

MELINDA: I don't know if you can do this, Daniel. I really don't. Maybe you're just not cut out for being a dad.

(PETER walks back on stage carrying a soda.)

PETER: Dad, I threw one of the cheddar cheese ones in the microwave. Give it a few minutes. And here's a Coke—

(PETER sees his father with the glasses on. He walks over and rips them off, almost throwing them down.)

PETER: *(Continued)* God damn it, Dad!

(He sees his father is crying. A long pause.)

PETER: *(Continued)* You're not replaying the first date, are you?

DANIEL: No.

PETER: Then what?

DANIEL: I...don't wanna talk about it.

PETER: Dad, I'm here. I know this has something to do with mom.

DANIEL: The fights. I...replay the fights. Melinda and I—your mom, we—

PETER: I don't understand.

DANIEL: Our first fight. When I left her without a car when she needed to go grocery shopping. The first time I came home drunk when you were a baby. The time we argued over her going back to stay with her family with a one year old. The time she told me she was leaving me for him. I know the exact dates and times. Of all the big ones. I've replayed them all many, many times. I try and watch the good times, but they...they don't mean anything anymore.

PETER: But why? Why focus on the pain? If you're going to lock yourself in your own memories, why not at least remember the good times?

DANIEL: Because I don't deserve the good ones! I don't deserve them! I screwed up everything. We could have been happy. I just...I don't know why, but replaying the good stuff doesn't mean anything. I can't feel anything from it. Like it's not even happening to me. I'm...empty. I don't know how else to deal with all this. Replaying the pain...is the only way I feel anything.

PETER: Dad, you know there are...support groups. In the real world. To help deal with the... losing mom. So you can do it without getting lost in your own mind.

DANIEL: Don't want them. I don't want them to take away my pain. Right now it's the only thing I feel. *(pause)* Thanks for the burrito. You can leave it on the table when you leave.

PETER: But dad—

DANIEL: Go back to work son. You've done your good deed for today, but I'm not your problem to fix.

PETER: I can help you.

DANIEL: I don't want it.

(DANIEL puts the glasses back on. PETER stands there, unable to help his father.)

PETER: Dad, please, don't.

DANIEL: March 3, 1994. 3:15 am.

(MELINDA walks on carrying a suitcase and whatever else indicates she's leaving, DJ trailing after her, desperate.)

DJ: So, that's it? You're leaving? In the middle of the night.

MELINDA: Whatever we had once, Daniel, we don't have it anymore. I can't raise Peter by myself.

DJ: You're not by yourself.

MELINDA: I feel like I am.

DJ: Where will you go? Your parents?

MELINDA: For now. Peter is with my folks tonight while I packed.

DJ: And after that?

MELINDA: I don't think you need to know that.

DJ: You're making a mistake. C'mon, "Excuse me, sir, can I—"

MELINDA: No. No raisinettes. No silly stories. I've been thinking about this for a long time. Daniel, I want you to understand, we could have made this work, but you didn't want to try. I want you to think about that. You could have made this work if you'd wanted to.

DJ: That's not true. I did want to.

MELINDA: I don't agree, Daniel. And I hope you don't forget that you could have fixed this.

DANIEL: Rewind, five seconds.

MELINDA: I hope you don't forget that you could have fixed this.

DANIEL: Rewind, five seconds.

MELINDA: I hope you don't forget that you could have fixed this.

DANIEL: Rewind, five seconds.

MELINDA: I hope you don't forget that you could have fixed this.

DANIEL: Rewind, five seconds.

MELINDA: I hope you don't forget that you could have fixed this.

DANIEL: Rewind, five seconds.

(And PETER stands there, helpless, as his father can't stop.)

LIGHTS OUT.

DON'T BLEED ON ME

Andy AA Rassler

'Don't Bleed On Me' was first produced by Lee Street Theatre in Salisbury, NC from June 17-19, 2016 with the following cast:

ATHLETIC: Alex Thompson
ANKLE: Matthew Ensley
COLORED: Chuck Riordan

Directed by: Andy AA Rassler
Lights/Sound Operator: Lisa Perone
Costumes: Linda Hughes
Lights: Chaz Cable
Set: Summer Eubanks
Office Manager: Christina Banner Pettus
Production Manager: Justin Dionne

CHARACTERS (All are socks)
ATHLETIC: The 'dumb jock' type. Slow to understanding. Anything.
ANKLE: Sharp, caustic, rude.
COLORED: An innocent victim.

SETTING: The inside of a washing machine.
TIME: Present

Note to director: The characters may suggest male actors, but this
piece was written with universal actors in mind: any gender,
ethnicity, age. The joy in this piece is in the creativity it lends to
space, costuming and characterization.

AT RISE: ATHLETIC and ANKLE are 'swimming' around the space, clearly having an incredible time. *Note: In the original production, the socks had specific places they were blocked to change directions as the load agitated in the other direction. This can be very effective in showing actor intention if you time it with precision and thought.

ANKLE: I thought we'd be in that smelly, disgusting hamper forever! Clean! Clean! I feel so clean!! (sings a note(s), happily)

ATHLETIC: *(starts coughing, spitting, choking)* I...I'm...I think I'm drowning! Help! Heeeeeeeeeeeeeeeeeelp!!

ANKLE: Why can't you ever just enjoy things?

ATHLETIC: I...can't...breathe!

ANKLE: You really think you're drowning, don't you?

ATHLETIC: This is it! This is it! Is that a light? Do I see a light?!?

ANKLE: Fluorescent light, yes. On the ceiling. In the laundry room.

ATHLETIC: I can't breathe! I. Can't. Breathe!

ANKLE: Of course you can't breathe. We don't breathe. Socks don't breathe. *(slaps his/her face)* Snap out of it!

ATHLETIC: Wh—what?

ANKLE: Every time wash day comes around we go through this, you cotton-brained idiot. We can live in the air. We can live in the water. You're not drowning.

ATHLETIC: Oh, thank God. That was a close one—

As ATHLETIC finishes this thought, COLORED drops into the scene, face first and stays there for a few beats while ATHLETIC and ANKLE stare at him, then take to each other. COLORED sits up, and ATHLETIC, ANKLE, and COLORED all stare at each other for a brief beat or two, then ANKLE begins screaming and runs as far away as s/he can. When ANKLE screams, so do the other two, and for a few beats they are all screaming and yelling—total chaos for three socks. ANKLE is the first to stop running, screaming and yelling, looking with disdain at the other two. ATHLETIC and COLORED have transitioned from running and yelling in fear, to chasing each other in fun. ANKLE/he grabs ATHLETIC as s/he runs by.

ANKLE: What are you doing?

ATHLETIC: I'm...I'm...I'm running around with him/her. You started it!

ANKLE: Just calm down and move over here with me.

ATHLETIC: I'm calm.

ANKLE leads ATHLETIC as far away on the stage as he can from COLORED.

COLORED: What is that? What are you doing?

ANKLE: Look, no offense or anything, but we can't get too close to your…to…can't get too close to…well, to you.

COLORED: You can't get too close to me? You can't, huh?

COLORED approaches and the other two *(lead by ANKLE)* back away, trying to keep the same space between them.

ANKLE: Just keep your distance, okay? This is a white load and you're not supposed to be here.

COLORED: I'm not supposed to be here? Do you think I want to be here?! I didn't ask to be here, okay? Home girl just saw me on the floor, panicked, and threw me in.

ANKLE: Yeah, well, home girl made a mistake and now you just have to stay away from us.

ATHLETIC: Yeah, stay away from us.

COLORED: I don't have to stay away. This place belongs to me, too. It's not just yours.

ANKLE: We were here first.

ATHLETIC: Yeah, we were here first.

COLORED: You were here first? First before who? You think there weren't other loads in here before you?

ANKLE: Well, we got here before you did and we were having a great swim around before you came.

ATHLETIC: I thought I was drowning, but I wasn't. I guess.

COLORED: I'm not bothering you! You want to swim? Go ahead and swim! Go enjoy your stupid white bubbles and swim.

ATHLETIC: Yay! I'm swimming again!

COLORED: That's right! That's right! Swim! Get clean and white again!

ATHLETIC: I even smell better! I love laundry day!

ATHLETIC 'swims' away, making happy sounds and/or singing as s/he 'swims.'

COLORED: Why aren't you swimming?

ANKLE: I don't think this is going to work.

COLORED: What? That we just leave each other alone?

ANKLE: Stupid over there can swim around and we can keep our distance, but it doesn't make any difference. We're all in the same water.

COLORED: And?

ANKLE: And, if we're all in the same water, then it doesn't matter how far away you are—

COLORED: I'm still going to color the load? Is that what you're trying to say? Well, no matter how far away you are, you're going to fade me! Ever think of that?

ATHLETIC: Woo-hoo!! Oh, Lord, I don't ever want to leave here!

ANKLE: *(grabs ATHLETIC)* Not too close, stupid! You want him/her to bleed on you?

ATHLETIC: *(immediately panicked)* Bleed on me?? Are you bleeding?

COLORED: All this worry because I might bleed on you? You're serious, aren't you?

ANKLE: We're white. You're not. The water mixes us together and your color bleeds on us. Then we're not so white anymore. Nobody wants that.

COLORED: Oh, no! Nobody wants that! What's going to happen to our world if the lilly-whites don't stay that lilly-white? How will the humans organize their sock drawers?? How will we know one sock from another? How will we label socks and know which outfits to wear with them? How will we know how to pair them together or where they belong? Tragedy in here! Tragedy up in here! Tragedy in the washing machine!!! Help!! Help!!

ANKLE: Hey, make fun of me all you want, but if we're not white anymore,—

ATHLETIC: *(sputters)* I don't care if we can breathe down here, it still feels weird to get those bubbles up my nose.

COLORED: You prejudiced, jacked-up, son-of-a-bitch. I'm not so bad you know. Why do you hate me? You don't even know me!

ANKLE: This isn't about you! I'm fighting for me! You get that?

COLORED: No, I don't get that!

ANKLE: You bleed on us, we change.

COLORED: I change, too.

ANKLE: Okay, you change, too. We're different. And she doesn't like that so much because she likes her whites white, you know? So you bleed on us, and we—

ATHLETIC: I can't wait for the rinse cycle. I love the rinse cycle.

COLORED: We what? I bleed on you and you what?

ANKLE: She makes us into rags. I've seen it happen.

Let this somber moment sit for a moment, then ATHLETIC accidentally collides with ANKLE, sending him/her right into COLORED's arms. ANKLE tries to fight COLORED off and it ends up in a scuffle with all three of them, on the floor, rolling over and over. Dialogue below happens during the scuffle. During this scuffle, all will also pull off their shirts to reveal a color underneath that is all the same—a shade somewhere between COLORED's color and white. [This seems the best way to handle this, but if the director sees some other clever way of handling this color change, the answer is: yes!]

ANKLE: Off! Off! Get off!

COLORED: I'm not on! I'm trying to—

ATHLETIC: I'm stuck. I think I'm stuck!

ANKLE: Get away!

COLORED: I'm trying to get away!!

ANKLE: What the hell—

ATHLETIC: We're…it's…

ALL: Get away from me!!

They all break apart from each other and are all their new color.

ATHLETIC: Oh, snap dragons. Look at me!

ANKLE: Oh, my God. My God! It happened. You bled all over us.

COLORED: Hey, I'm not too excited about my color fading, you know. It's not all about you.

ATHLETIC: I'm totally not white anymore.

ANKLE: It's over. I'm a rag now.

COLORED: What about me, huh? My match didn't get in this load. I'm a different color now and we don't even go together anymore. I'm probably a rag, too.

ANKLE: *(anger rising)* Why did you come in here? I told you to stay away from us! I told you to stay away!!

ANKLE attacks and they roll around, COLORED just defending him/herself. ATHLETIC sees this and hurries over to tear them apart.

ATHLETIC: Stop it, Anks! Stop it!

ANKLE: S/he's sent us to the rag pile, Crew! The rag pile! I'm not white anymore!

ATHLETIC: I know that!

ANKLE: You aren't either! It's over, do you get that? That stupid sock plopped in here and bled all over us and now it's all over.

ATHLETIC: I don't think it's over, Ankle.

ANKLE: She hates when her whites aren't white! We'll never get back in her sock drawer!

ATHLETIC: So, right. You're right, that's the end of that. So what? We go to the rag pile and that's just the next thing starting. It's just this thing ending and the next thing starting. That's not so bad, right?

ANKLE: But we don't know what the rag pile is like. It could be horrible.

COLORED: Could be.

ATHLETIC: But the drawer wasn't a picnic, either, was it?

ANKLE: It was kind of cramped.

COLORED: And dark.

ATHLETIC: You couldn't even see the socks right around you! Rags is better. I betcha rags is better.

Pause on stage where ANKLE and COLORED think over what ATHLETIC said.

COLORED: I kind of like this color, you know? I don't know that I've seen this exact shade before.

ANKLE: It's definitely different.

ATHLETIC: Like a blob fish. Those are different.

ANKLE: Blob fish?

ATHLETIC: Blob fish. *(Does a blob fish impression.)* Different.

ANKLE: *(to COLORED)* I guess this isn't so bad. You're not so bad.

COLORED: I told you that before. *(pause)* White isn't really even a color. Did you know that?

ATHLETIC: What? Mind. Blown.

ANKLE: Well, the rinse cycle is about over. Nothing we can do now but go with the flow.

COLORED: I don't know about you, but I think the rag pile sounds like fun!

ATHLETIC: A lot more fun than that stupid, stuffy drawer.

ANKLE: We're slowing down...

ATHLETIC: It's almost time...

COLORED: Come on, y'all...

ALL: To the rag pile!!!

BLACKOUT

EVOLUTION

Peter M. Floyd

Originally produced at the Boston Theater Marathon XVIII, May 8, 2016, by imaginary beasts. Directed by Matthew Woods

CAST:
FRID: Noah Simes
NELLA: Joy P. Campbell
OTTO: Joey C. Pelletier

CHARACTERS:
FRID, male mammal
NELLA, female mammal
OTTO, male reptile

NOTE: The sexes given above for the three characters are only suggestions; in a production each can be portrayed as any gender.

Scene: A jungle, sometime in the early Paleocene Epoch

At lights up, FRID sits on a tree branch (which may simply be implied) looking ahead thoughtfully. NELLA enters. Both of them are small furry tree-dwelling creatures, but this too may be implied.

NELLA: Frid! What are you doing?

FRID: Thinking.

NELLA: What? There's no time for thinking. We've got stuff to do.

FRID: Like what?

NELLA: Like hunting, killing and eating.

FRID: I don't feel like doing that just now.

NELLA: Don't feel like doing that? Frid, we're warm-blooded. Do you know what that means? We have to maintain a body temperature that's considerably warmer than that of our environment in order to stay alive. This means that we must eat a much larger amount of food than cold-blooded animals of a similar body size.

FRID: I know that, Nella.

NELLA: Then stop lying around, and join me in getting some food! Rumor has it that there are some tasty grubs in the big lumpy tree by the river. We should get there before everyone else does.

FRID: It's just— Do you ever think, Is this all there is to life? Chasing down food and eating it?

NELLA: Yes. I think about that a lot, actually. I think, Thank God *(whatever that is)* there's nothing more to life than getting and eating food.

FRID: It just seems to me that there should be more.

NELLA: Oh, and sex, of course, but only in season. Can you imagine being sexually active all through the year? It would be so distracting!

FRID: But don't you have any kind of ambition?

NELLA: What do you mean?

FRID: Well, remember the dinosaurs?

NELLA: The what?

FRID: Dinosaurs. You know, those titanic creatures who used to walk the earth, keeping us in constant mortal terror, and forcing us to retreat into the trees for our own safety, leaving them undisputed masters of the earth.

NELLA: Oh, those dinosaurs!

FRID: Remember? There was this big explosion, and then the sky turned gray with ash, and all the dinosaurs died, just like that. *(Snaps his fingers.)*

NELLA: Actually, I think it took a couple of centuries.

FRID: Well, in geological terms...

NELLA: So, what's your point?

FRID: My point is that with the dinosaurs gone, there's a power vacuum. Right now, no one is master of the Earth. Well, why not us?

NELLA: Um. 'Cause we're tiny insect-eating tree dwellers?

FRID: Well, who says we have to be like that forever? We could grow big.

NELLA: We could? How?

FRID: We could evolve.

NELLA: What does that mean?

FRID: It means to change. You know, the dinosaurs weren't always giants. At first, they were no bigger than a housecat.

NELLA: What's a housecat?

FRID: I have no idea.

NELLA: You're saying we could grow up to be as big as the dinosaurs were?

FRID: That's right!

NELLA: *(looking at herself)* That's a little hard to believe.

FRID: It's the laws of nature, kiddo.

NELLA: So, then we'd rule the world?

FRID: Well, if we got bigger before anyone else does, we would.

NELLA: Just like the dinosaurs?

FRID: Uh-huh.

NELLA: Until they all got killed 'cause they got too big.

FRID: Uh-huh. Wait, what?

NELLA: Well, when the sky got all dusty, it was the big creatures that all got killed off, right? Little creatures like you and me survived.

FRID: What's your point?

NELLA: Maybe size isn't everything.

FRID: That statement does not compute.

NELLA: Shh. Otto's coming.

FRID: Should we hide?

NELLA: Too late. He's seen us.

OTTO enters. He is some kind of reptile, but again this can be implied rather than explicit. He should be much larger than NEELA and FRID.

OTTO: Hey, Frid. Hey, Nella.

FRID and NELLA: Hey, Otto.

OTTO: What's up?

FRID: Not much.

NELLA: You're not going to eat us, are you?

OTTO: ...Maybe.

FRID: Please don't.

OTTO: Well, look: I ate the day before yesterday, so I'm good for the rest of the week. I can just sit in the sun for the next few days.

FRID: Good to know.

OTTO: Yeah, that's right, you guys are warm-blooded, aren't you? Gotta be eating all the time. Man, that must be rough.

NELLA: It's who we are.

OTTO: *(realizing he committed a faux pas)* Oh, hey, I don't mean anything bad by that. You know, whatever works for you. I'm not judgmental.

FRID: Good.

OTTO: Warm-blooded, cold-blooded, everyone tastes the same.

FRID: Otto, I've got a question for you.

OTTO: Shoot.

FRID: Why do you eat us?

OTTO: It's the law of nature, isn't it? Things eat other things.

FRID: But why do you eat us? Why don't we eat you?

OTTO: What? That's crazy.

FRID: It's cause you're bigger than us, right?

OTTO: Well, that's a factor, I guess... But it's not everything.

NELLA: No, it's not! Remember when Greta got eaten last spring? She was pretty big, but six or seven of those ugly guys with the big teeth and long, hairy legs jumped her. They were smaller than her, but there were more of them, and they could go faster.

FRID: She wasn't that much bigger than they were. If she was like ten times their size, they wouldn't have gone near her.

OTTO: Hey — You guys aren't thinking of evolving, are you?

FRID: ...Maybe.

OTTO: Why? What's the point?

NELLA: Somebody wants to become the dominant life form.

OTTO: Ah, you don't want that. Take it from someone who's further up the food chain: it's a lot of responsibility having to keep the ecosystem balanced by making sure populations are kept in check. Much easier to be the chasee than the chaser.

FRID: You're just afraid that if we evolve, we might start to bite back.

OTTO: I just don't want to rock the boat.

NELLA: What's a boat?

FRID: *(ignoring her, to OTTO)* I think maybe it would be interesting if we got big, and started chasing you around.

OTTO: Well... I could get bigger, too.

FRID: I'd get bigger. And, if I got big, I could eat you any day of the week. I wouldn't be taking time off between meals.

OTTO: Well, what if I got fast?

FRID: Fast?

OTTO: Yeah, I actually have been doing some serious thinking about evolving. I'm gonna lose the legs. All of 'em.

FRID: Get rid of your legs? That's crazy; you won't be able to move at all.

OTTO: Sure I will. Worms move, don't they? If I get lean and long, I can whip along fast as a wet sneeze.

FRID: Ridiculous.

OTTO: And then, when I'm hungry, I can catch you and wrap my whole body around and squeeze...

FRID: Say what?

OTTO: ... and basically crush you. Then I can eat you.

FRID: That's sick.

OTTO: It's an idea. I might just go for poison fangs instead.

FRID: Oh, yeah? Well, if I get big I can just step on you.

NELLA: Oh, come on, Frid, this is stupid. Being big isn't everything.

FRID: Oh, yeah? You got a better idea?

NELLA: I was thinking we could get smart, instead.

FRID: Smart?

OTTO: Smart?

NELLA: Yeah. I think we could increase our brain power. So we're more clever.

FRID: What good would that do?

NELLA: Well, we could—

FRID: I mean, look at the dinosaurs. They ruled the planet for 150 million years, and they were as dumb as an old stump. Brains the size of walnuts!

OTTO: Actually, that's just a myth.

NELLA: And what about our paws?

FRID: What about 'em?

NELLA: Have you noticed how hard it is to hold onto anything? Well, if one of our claws was kind of opposite the other ones, we could really get a grip on things. It would be easier to hang onto trees. Or we could pick up rocks and throw them at someone like Otto, when he's trying to eat us.

OTTO: Whoa! What's with this rock-throwing?

FRID: *(condescendingly)* Nella, I don't think you really get what evolution is about. If you want to dominate the world, you have to be bigger or stronger or faster than everyone else. Being smart, or having weird opposable claws isn't going to make any kind of difference. *(sarcastically)* Hey, how 'bout this? I'll evolve my nose so it'll get really long and can pluck fruit off trees and squirt water.

NELLA: You don't have to be rude.

FRID: Actually, now that I've said it, it's kind of a neat idea.

OTTO: How 'bout this? I'm gonna have a tongue that looks like a fork, and that I can use to smell!

FRID: Well, I'll grow a pair of massive teeth that curve out of my mouth, and that I can use to spear things!

NELLA: All right then. You know what I'm going to do? I'll develop the ability to construct my own environment. I'll use my brain to harvest the resources of the earth to gain the energy needed to power the devices I create. As the years pass, I'll hack down the forests, dig up the ground, and drain the oceans, transforming more and more of the planet into my own playing ground and leaving all you other creatures to inhabit whatever blasted wastelands I leave behind. I'll change the very nature of the earth, sky and water, and make them all poison to you. Your teeth and claws will mean nothing to me, as I'll create ways to bring death from afar, death by the thousands, by the millions. You'll cry out in pain, fear and anguish, but I'll show no mercy. By the time I'm done, I'll have torched this planet completely, leaving nothing behind but your burnt bodies and evaporating tears. That's how I'll rule the world.

Pause.

NELLA: I'm totally kidding.

FRID: Whew!

OTTO: You scared me there, Nella!

FRID: Okay, what do you guys think about ears? I think if I had a pair of massive ears, that would be just the awesomest thing.

END OF PLAY

FIRST DAY IN TRADE

Jennifer O'Grady

First Day in Trade was first produced by Rover Dramawerks as part of its 365 Women a Year Festival from May 5-14, 2016 in Plano, Texas. The cast was as follows:

KRISTEN: Taylor Davis
LAURIE: Christian Hopson
DENNIS: Chance Gibbs
JACKIE: Suzy Dotson

Director: Kayla Freeman
Artistic Director: Carol M. Rice

CHARACTERS
KRISTEN: 22. An editorial assistant
LAURIE: 24. An editorial assistant
DENNIS: 24. An editorial assistant
JACKIE: 56. An editor

TIME AND PLACE: 1985. The editorial offices of Doubleday Books in New York.

This play requires:
    A desk or small table
    An office chair
    A circa 1980s phone
    A typewriter
    Two circa 1980s shoulder bags
    A file folder or two
    Two disposable coffee cups
    A bagel
    A pack of cigarettes

Monday morning, a little before 9 A.M. KRISTEN sits at her new desk. She wears a skirt and a pink blouse. A phone, a typewriter, an uneaten bagel, a coffee cup, and a folder are on the desk. Her shoulder bag is visible. LAURIE stands next to her, wearing a shoulder bag and holding a coffee cup. KRISTEN is staring open-mouthed at LAURIE. A beat.

KRISTEN: You're kidding me, right?

LAURIE: Where are you from?

KRISTEN: You're not kidding?

LAURIE: Don't you read?

KRISTEN: No!

LAURIE: You're in publishing and you don't read?

KRISTEN: I don't read tabloids!

LAURIE: She's a former First Lady. Widow of a gazillionaire.

KRISTEN: I know…

LAURIE: How could not know about her? All of New York knows.

KRISTEN: Why does she want to work?

LAURIE: Why not? She has a brain.

KRISTEN: Do they pay her?

LAURIE: Presumably.

KRISTEN: Why?

LAURIE: Uh, becomes it's a company and they pay people?

KRISTEN: She doesn't need money!

LAURIE: Shh!

KRISTEN: *(quietly; looking around)* Where's her office?

LAURIE: Around that corner. I don't think she's in yet.

KRISTEN: Why didn't Marty tell me?

LAURIE: Sometimes when he interviews new assistants, they ask too many questions. I gather you didn't ask any.

(Beat)

KRISTEN: Jesus…

LAURIE: It isn't a big deal. She's really nice.

KRISTEN: She lived in the White House!

LAURIE: So?

KRISTEN: So? The pink suit?

(LAURIE looks blank.)

The pink suit! She was wearing it that day.

LAURIE: What day? *(Beat)* Oh.

KRISTEN: And she didn't take it off. Not until the next day.

LAURIE: Ew.

KRISTEN: *(Nods)* I bet she hates that color now. I would.

(LAURIE looks at KRISTEN's blouse. KRISTEN looks too.)

Oh shit.

LAURIE: It's just a blouse. That was a long time ago.

KRISTEN: Twenty-two years. My parents remember that day.

LAURIE: My mom remembers too. Everyone older than us remembers exactly what they were doing when they heard about it.

KRISTEN: I can't imagine living through anything that makes me remember what I was doing when it happened.

LAURIE: And what if you were doing something you don't want to remember? Like … having sex with someone disgusting, or …

KRISTEN: Or getting fired.

LAURIE: I remember that.

KRISTEN: You got fired?

LAURIE: "Laid off." You know what publishing is like right now.

KRISTEN: *(Shakes head)* This is my first job.

(Pause)

LAURIE: Well, welcome to Doubleday.

(She starts to go.)

KRISTEN: Laurie?

(LAURIE turns.)

Who's her assistant?

LAURIE: Jeannette. She's older. She's more like a secretary.

KRISTEN: So she's friendly?

LAURIE: She's a bitch.

KRISTEN: You said she's really nice.

LAURIE: Who? *(Beat)* Oh. Yeah. Be careful, okay? She doesn't like being stared at.

KRISTEN: What if I have to go over there?

LAURIE: Better bring a weapon.

(KRISTEN stares at her.)

I'm kidding.

KRISTEN: That was in poor taste, don't you think?

LAURIE: Don't worry. She's really nice.

KRISTEN: Does she talk to you?

LAURIE: Not really.

KRISTEN: But she's friendly?

LAURIE: I don't really know her but she's really nice. *(Beat)* Do you smoke?

KRISTEN: *(reaching for her bag)* I have some …

LAURIE: No, not for me. For her.

KRISTEN: *(Looks at her)* What?

LAURIE: She bums.

> *(KRISTEN stares at her.)*

She bums.

KRISTEN: What do you mean?

LAURIE: I mean she goes around looking for cigarettes.

KRISTEN: Why?

LAURIE: She used to smoke. She doesn't want to start up again, so she doesn't buy any cigarettes.

KRISTEN: Are you telling me one of the world's richest women might ask me to give her cigarettes?

LAURIE: Well. . .

KRISTEN: For free? And expect me to give them to her?

LAURIE: She's really nice.

KRISTEN: I can barely afford my rent!

LAURIE: Maybe you shouldn't be buying cigarettes.

KRISTEN: That's not the point! She can buy her own damn cigarettes.

LAURIE: It's not like she can just walk into a cigarette store.

KRISTEN: She must have a staff of fifty. Let the Kennedys buy her cigarettes.

LAURIE: Think of it this way: It'll be a story you can tell your kids someday.

KRISTEN: I can't afford any kids!

LAURIE: *(hearing something:)* Shh.

> *(LAURIE picks up a folder and studies at it. KRISTEN fiddles with her typewriter. An elegant, dark-haired, middle-aged woman—unmistakably JACKIE—walks quickly past. KRISTEN tries to look without staring. JACKIE exits. Beat.)*

KRISTEN: *(silently)* Oh my God…!

LAURIE: Don't stare like that, okay?

KRISTEN: *(whispering)* Holy shit!

LAURIE: I'd better get to work. Marty should be here soon.

KRISTEN: Don't tell her I smoke.

(Beat)

LAURIE: Really?

KRISTEN: Yes! I can barely afford to eat.

LAURIE: Maybe you shouldn't buy cigarettes.

KRISTEN: Don't tell her, okay?

(Pause)

LAURIE: Welcome to Doubleday.

(LAURIE exits. A pause, then DENNIS enters.)

DENNIS: Oh, hey, hi. I'm Dennis. I work for Barbara. You must be Kristen.

KRISTEN: Nice to meet you.

DENNIS: Marty in yet?

(KRISTEN shakes her head. Quietly:)

Do you know about...?

(He gestures toward JACKIE's office.)

KRISTEN: *(Nods)* Laurie just told me.

DENNIS: You didn't know?

(KRISTEN shakes her head no.)

Oh. Well, she's really nice.

KRISTEN: Do you smoke?

(Beat)

DENNIS: Not often. Do you?

KRISTEN: Not really.

(Pause)

DENNIS: I'd better go do some work. Ask Marty to call Barbara when he gets in, okay?

(DENNIS exits. KRISTEN looks around, then picks up the phone and dials.)

KRISTEN: *(on the phone)* It's Kristen. Do you know who works here?

… What? Why didn't you tell me?! … No I didn't know! I read novels!...I just caught a glimpse of her. She takes people's cigarettes.

(JACKIE enters. KRISTEN looks at her. Beat. JACKIE smiles and waves her hand, as if to say, "Don't rush, I'll wait." A beat.)

KRISTEN: *(on the phone)* I have to go.

(She hangs up quickly. Beat. JACKIE smiles. She has a lovely smile.)

JACKIE: Is it true that you might have a cigarette?

(KRISTEN nods.)

Would you be able to spare one, do you think?

(KRISTEN takes out her pack and offers it to JACKIE.)

Just one, please.

KRISTEN: Take two.

(Beat)

JACKIE: Thank you.

(She takes the pack and shakes out two, then puts it down.)

KRISTEN: Do you need a light?

JACKIE: *(Shakes head.)* That's a beautiful blouse.

(A beat)

KRISTEN: Thank you.

JACKIE: *(Looks at blouse a moment, then:)* Thank you.

(JACKIE exits. KRISTEN doesn't move. LAURIE enters and looks at her.)

LAURIE: You gave her cigarettes, didn't you?

KRISTEN: How did you know?

LAURIE: Everyone does, once they find out she's a real person.

KRISTEN: She is real! Jackie Kennedy Onassis is a real person!

LAURIE: Just don't stare at her, okay?

(LAURIE goes. KRISTEN picks up the cigarette pack and looks at it.)

(Lights down)

END OF PLAY

I DON'T KNOW

James McLindon

Original Production by Company One, Boston Theater Marathon
May 8, 2016

Director: Phaedra Scott
Sergeant: Robert Cope
Recruit 1: Matt Feldman
Recruit 2: Brenna Sweet
Recruit 3: Tonasia Summer Jones
Recruit 4: Kai Tshikosi

Second Production by Source Festival, Washington, DC
June 8- July 3, 2016

Director: Anne Donnelly
Sergeant: Kevin McGuiness
Recruit 1: David Johnson
Recruit 2: Rebecca Ballinger
Recruit 3: Emily Gibson
Recruit 4: Nate Shelton

CAST OF CHARACTERS
(In Order Of Appearance)

SERGEANT: MALE, FORTY TO FIFTY, MADE OF GRANITE
SOLDIER 1: MALE, AROUND 18-20
SOLDIER 2: FEMALE, AROUND 18-20
SOLDIER 3: FEMALE, AROUND 18-20
SOLDIER 4: MALE, AROUND 18-20

Race blind/Diverse casting is encouraged.

SETTING: The play takes place entirely on the roads of a military
    base. The time is the present.

Young SOLDIERS running, men and women, green army fatigues. Their older male drill sergeant runs alongside them singing a marching cadence, to which they give the response. All running should probably be done in place. Generally, everyone yells at the top of their lungs, although some quiet moments are nice.

SERGEANT: I don't know, but I've been told,
SOLDIERS: I don't know but I've been told.
SERGEANT: Eskimo pussy is mighty cold.
SOLDIERS: Eskimo pussy is mighty cold.
SERGEANT: I don't know but it's been said,
SOLDIERS: I don't know/ but it's been said,
One of the SOLDIERS, PRIVATE 1, a male, interrupts.
PRIVATE 1: /Sir excuse me sir!

The unit grinds to a halt.

SERGEANT: What the goddam hell is so important that you interrupted my cadence, soldier?
PRIVATE 1: Sir this worthless private is concerned that—!
SERGEANT: In cadence, soldier. In cadence.
PRIVATE 1: (Pause) Sir, yes, sir!

ALL start to run. PRIVATE 1 takes a moment to think. He's got it. With his words, all begin running again.

PRIVATE 1: Sir, I think I gotta say,
SOLDIERS: Sir, I think I gotta say,
PRIVATE 1: That last verse was retrograde.
SOLDIERS: That last verse was retrograde.

The SERGEANT stops. His eyes narrow. The unit stops.

SERGEANT: Are you trying to slip a goddam half rhyme past me, private, is that what you think you're doing!?
PRIVATE 1: Sir no sir!
SERGEANT: You know what I call a half rhyme in a cadence, son!? I call it a goddam motherless failure, that's what I call it!
PRIVATE 1: Sir, this worthless private realizes that he has failed, sir!
SERGEANT: Is your concern that this time-honored cadence, which has been recited by generations of soldiers without complaint, mentions the thermal properties of northern lady parts, private?
PRIVATE 1: Sir in part yes sir!

SERGEANT: And what if I told you that this cadence is about the plight of felines left outside on a winter's night in the arctic.

PRIVATE 1: Sir … Alaskan cats sir!?

SERGEANT: On a god dam winter's night, private!

PRIVATE 1: Sir in that case this worthless private would stand corrected sir!

SERGEANT: Good! *(Pause)* Alas, private, I do not believe the verse is about cats found above 66th parallel north. The ribald manner in which it is traditionally chanted suggests to me that, in fact, it takes as its subject and primary concern none other than lady parts … found above 66 degrees of latitude. In that respect it sadly does appear to be retrograde in this man's army.

PRIVATE 2, a female, steps forward.

PRIVATE 2: Sir "this person's army" sir!

SERGEANT: *(Dangerous pause)* Thank. You.

PRIVATE 2: Sir this verse is also offensive to indigenous and first persons hailing from the far north sir! Sir may this worthless private offer a palliative verse sir?

SERGEANT: Oh, words can not convey how eager I am to hear your contribution, private!

PRIVATE 2: Sir yes sir!

The SERGEANT begins to run again. The SOLDIERS follows.

PRIVATE 2: I don't know but I've been told.

SOLDIERS & SERGEANT: I don't know but I've been told.

PRIVATE 2: Northern wieners whether aboriginal or not are mighty cold.

SOLDIERS & SERGEANT: Northern wieners whether aboriginal or not are mighty cold.

PRIVATE 2: I don't know but it's been said—

The SERGEANT stops and again the Unit grinds to a halt.

SERGEANT: Now, your use of wiener, private, does it connote that breed of dog formally known as dachshund? Is the concern with the plight of dogs on a winter's night in the land of the aurora borealis?

PRIVATE 2: Sir no sir! This worthless private uses wiener to invoke the slang term for gentleman parts … found north of 66 degrees of latitude. Thus achieving parity with the prior verse sir!

SERGEANT: But it did not scan for shit, did it!? *(In ear of nearest male soldier)* Now is it all right with you ladies if we continue!?

FEMALE SOLDIERS: Sir yes sir!

NEAREST MALE SOLDIER: Sir did you mean "ladies" as a gendered form of insult sir!?

SERGEANT: *(Pause; under his breath)* God. Damn.

The SERGEANT starts running again. The SOLDIERS follow suit. They run for ten or 15 seconds silence. Then:

SERGEANT: This is my rifle, (grabbing his crotch) this is my gun,

SOLDIERS: This is my rifle, (grabbing their crotches) this is my gun,

SERGEANT: This is for fighting, (grabbing his crotch) this is for fun.

SOLDIERS: This is for fighting, (grabbing their crotches) /this is for fun.

PRIVATE 3: *(Female)* /Sir, excuse me, sir!

The unit grinds to a halt again.

SERGEANT: Might you also have an observation for us, private!?

PRIVATE 3: Sir yes sir!

SERGEANT: Then by all means, if you please!

PRIVATE 3: Sir thank you sir—!

SERGEANT: In cadence.

A pause. They begin to run.

PRIVATE 3: Sir, not trying to be snarky,

SOLDIERS: Sir, not trying to be snarky,

PRIVATE 3: Last verse celebrates patriarchy.

SOLDIERS: Last verse celebrates patriarchy.

SERGEANT: And might you also have a palliative verse to grace us all with?

PRIVATE 3: Sir yes sir!

SERGEANT: Well?

PRIVATE 3: Unit cohesion we must bolster,

SOLDIERS & SERGEANT: Unit cohesion we must bolster,

PRIVATE 3: This is my rifle, *(grabbing her crotch)* this is my holster.

SOLDIERS & SERGEANT: This is my rifle, *(all but SERGEANT grabbing their crotches)* this is my holster.

SERGEANT stops and the Unit grinds to a halt.

SERGEANT: But I don't have a holster, do I, private. I only have a gun!

PRIVATE 3: Sir this worthless private sees her mistake—

SERGEANT: Good.

PRIVATE 3: —although she notes that she does not have a gun sir.

The SERGEANT stares her back into line. He begins running

again and the SOLDIERS follow. PRIVATE 4, male, speaks up.

PRIVATE 4: Sir this worthless private suggests we alternate verses sir!

SERGEANT: How the hell are we building unit cohesion when we're literally not all singing from the same page, private, now how!? Huh!?

PRIVATE 4: Sir if we alternate verses so that we're all singing the same melody albeit with inclusive gender-appropriate terms we will create a unity. E Pluribus Unum. Out of many one sir!

A long pause. The SERGEANT considers if this can stand. It can. But barely. He, then they, run. A pause. He starts to sing, his eyes daring the SOLDIERS to find fault.

SERGEANT: If I die in a combat zone,
SOLDIERS: If I die in a /combat zone,
PRIVATE 2: /Sir excuse me sir!

The SERGEANT stops and the SOLDIERS grind to a halt.

SERGEANT: Dear sweet mewling baby Jesus, you cannot possibly have found anything offensive in that verse!

PRIVATE 2: Sir not that verse sir!

SERGEANT: What then!?

PRIVATE 2: Sir although two gender-specific verses that consider the similarities between weapons and human genitalia seems to provide an inclusive environment to men and women alike sir, this worthless private is concerned that, that…!

SERGEANT: That what, private!?

PRIVATE 2: Sir that treating gender as inherently binary marginalizes genderfluid, pangender, genderfree and otherwise genderqueer military personnel! Sir!

A long pause as the SERGEANT considers this. Then, beaten, he throws his hat down, crumples to the ground, and holds his head.

SERGEANT: Aw, fuck it!

The SOLDIERS look at each other, uncertain how to proceed. PRIVATE 2 kneels beside the SERGEANT. She still yells.

PRIVATE 2: Sir it's all a bit much for you isn't it sir!

SERGEANT: I remember when all I had to do was yell a bunch of obscenity-laced, yet folksy rants at new recruits and they'd all just shit their damn drawers. (Pause) Good times, soldier, good times! But this crazy world, it's just spinning way too fast for me now. They said I had to deal with women, and I dealt with women. They said I had to deal with the gays, and I dealt with the gays. But Jesus Maloney Christ, now you're saying I gotta deal with, with, with … what in the sweet fuck did you even just call them?

ALL but SERGEANT: Sir genderfluid, pangender, genderfree and otherwise genderqueer military personnel sir!

SERGEANT: Yeah, them. I can't do it, private. This just isn't my world any more. I, I can't do it. (Pause; quiet) It used to be so simple.

PRIVATE 2: Sir well but misogynistic, racist, heteronormative—

SERGEANT: Yeah, but goddam simple! I miss that.

As PRIVATE 2 talks, the SERGEANT slowly uncrumples.

PRIVATE 1: Sir when the Germans demanded we surrender at the Battle of the Bulge, did we surrender sir!?

SERGEANT: 'Course not. We told those assholes to go screw themselves.

PRIVATE 3: Sir when they told you to take Fallujah, did you say you couldn't do it sir!?

SERGEANT: We kicked those bastards' asses!

PRIVATE 4: Sir when Truman integrated the army in 1948, did the Army's mostly Southern drill instructors resign en masse sir?

SERGEANT: Hell, no, they didn't!

PRIVATE 2: Sir or did those Southern DI's rise above it, did they suck it up, did they just do their damn jobs sir!?

SERGEANT: They sure as shit did do their damn jobs, soldier!

PRIVATE 1: Sir will you rise above it like they did sir!?

SERGEANT: Damn straight!

PRIVATE 3: Sir will you suck it up sir!?

SERGEANT: Hell, yes!

PRIVATE 4: Sir will you do your damn job sir!?

SERGEANT: You goddam know I will!

The SERGEANT has risen and retrieved his hat. He is revived, saved, whole again.

SERGEANT: Soldiers, form up! We'll figure out all of these verses tomorrow. For now, we're gonna run home and get us some chow!

SOLDIERS: *(Saluting smartly, happily)* Sir yes sir!

> *They begin to run. A few seconds pass.*

SERGEANT: Momma and Papa was laying in bed,
SOLDIERS & SERGEANT: Momma and Papa was laying in bed,
SERGEANT: Momma rolled over, this is what she said.
SOLDIERS: Momma rolled over, this is what she said.
SERGEANT: Uh, give me some
SOLDIERS: Give me some
SERGEANT: Uh, Give me some
SOLDIERS: /Give me some.
PRIVATE 1: /Sir excuse me sir—!

> *The SERGEANT does not stop running.*

SERGEANT: I KNOW, PRIVATE, I KNOW! *(Quietly)* We'll fix that
   one tomorrow, too! *(Pause)*
   I don't know, but I've been told,
SOLDIERS: I don't know, but I've been told,
SERGEANT: Best to die before you're old.
SOLDIERS: Best to die before you're old.
SERGEANT: I don't know but it's been said,
SOLDIERS: I don't know but it's been said,
SERGEANT: Soldier fights until he's dead—

> *Blackout.*

I JUST LOVE THAT KEITH URBAN

Shari D. Frost

'I Just Love That Keith Urban' Was Originally Produced On September 23-24, 2016 By Chameleon's Dish Theatre In Cambridge, Ma,

With The Following Casting:
ILONA - Sheree Galpert
DUDE - Marco Aguirre
DITSY DIVA - Courtney Plati

Producer - Dave Meredith
Kyle Gregory Directed
Lenny Somervell Produced.

CHARACTERS
ILONA: 60s
DUDE: 15
DITSY DIVA: 22
PRODUCER: 20-40s, female

SETTING - The American Idol Audition Line, Any City Usa
TIME - Fall 2015

The American Idol audition line, Any City, USA. DUDE, 15, male, waits in line, a number pinned to his chest, earbuds in his ears. He bops his head to the music. HE's in the zone, preparing. ILONA, 60s, stands behind him, no number. DITSY DIVA, 22, female, stands behind her, also with earbuds and a number. ILONA taps DUDE on the shoulder. HE removes an earbud.

ILONA: *(to DUDE)* Give ya twenty bucks.

DUDE: Huh?

ILONA points to his pinned-on number.

ILONA: Okay, thirty. Thirty bucks?

DUDE: You want my number?

ILONA: If you're not using it?

DUDE: Like, why would I be standing in this long-ass line, if I'm not gonna use my number?

ILONA: It is a really long line. And, geez, this is just one city. I mean, like, what are the odds, right? That you'll get through? To the next round?

DUDE: Oh I'm totally going through to Hollywood.

ILONA: How old are you anyway?

DUDE: And that's your business why?

ILONA: There're rules. You gotta be at least fifteen. You don't look fifteen. Are you fifteen?

DUDE: Can't you not be over 28 either?

ILONA: Forty bucks.

DUDE: I don't think so.

ILONA: You know, you make it through, you're gonna miss most of Algebra, probably have to repeat the year, and baseball practice, or do you run track? And a shot at prom with a cute senior. Some seniors think freshmen boys are veerryy cu-uute...

DUDE: Yeah, okay, so like I'm the next American Idol. Maybe ask someone else.

DUDE puts his earbuds back in. ILONA turns to DITSY DIVA and points to her number.

ILONA: Sixty bucks?

DITSY DIVA: What's your problem?

A PRODUCER enters with a video camera. SHE makes her way down the line, filming. DUDE notices, smiles, waves, tries to make eye contact.

ILONA: I don't have a problem. Ask Simon Cowell! He made the rules. I didn't make the rules. People over twenty-eight have things to say. Simon's over twenty-eight and everyone still listens to him!

DITSY DIVA puts her earbuds in once more. ILONA yanks one back out.

DITSY DIVA: Hey.

PRODUCER notices the commotion.

ILONA: These judges they're...family. For fifteen years we've been hanging out. Fifteen! Every week there they are

(beat)

on my TV. And now, just like that, they're...leaving. Just like that—

DITSY DIVA: *(aware of the approaching camera, behind a fake smile)* —I've auditioned every year for five years and—

ILONA: —Who am I gonna have coffee with?

DITSY DIVA chokes up as PRODUCER approaches, filming. Then, directly into the camera...

DITSY DIVA: *(cont'd)* ...now it's the last-- my last-- Oh my god I can't even say it? Cause, you know, this is totally what I was born to do? And J-Lo personally told me to work hard and come back this year? She said I can sing? And... and, oh my god, my life is so over ? Without this show?

ILONA notices PRODUCER.

ILONA: *(into camera, a sudden realization)* I can sing. I sang at my daughter's wedding. She lives in L.A. now. We Skype.

(beat)

Sometimes.

DITSY DIVA pretends to be enthralled, makes an 'aww how sweet' face at PRODUCER.

ILONA: *(cont'd.)* And I sang at talent night. At the team-building retreat. I was gonna do it again next year, but they laid the whole 'team' off.

PRODUCER starts to move on. ILONA grabs her.

ILONA: *(cont'd.)* I sang for my Dad.

(beat)

May he rest in peace. In the nursing home. Cause I wanted to, but I just couldn't take care of him anymore. At home. And a nurse asked me to sing for the guy in the room next door. He had made a request! He requested me! I did concerts there every other Friday night. After Bingo. Every other Friday. We could shoot the 'hometown visit' there! I got

ILONA: *(CONT'D.)* boatloads of stories I could tell you. You could interview me there. At the nursing home. We could chat all night.

PRODUCER: You still sing there?

ILONA: So, they hired a magician...

The PRODUCER moves on down the line.

ILONA: *(to PRODUCER)* Wait!

PRODUCER points to DITSY DIVA and DUDE'S numbers.

PRODUCER: Sorry, you don't count.

PRODUCER continues on down the line.

ILONA: *(To DUDE and DITSY DIVA)* A hundred bucks. A hundred! Can't you guys use a hundred bucks?

DUDE and DITSY DIVA put their earbuds back in. ILONA keeps talking.

ILONA: But. But, I had so many stories I was gonna tell'em. When I got in there. Cause really it's about the stories, you know? All the people that make it through, they have good stories. And I have good stories. Like this one time, I was singing Sondheim. At the nursing home. And this guy in a wheelchair kept yelling "Anka! Paul Anka!" But I don't know any Paul Anka. So I keep singing Sondheim. And he keeps yelling. So I go home. Do a little googling. And the next week I go back and I sing...

ILONA sings, "...and they called it puppy lo-o-o-ove..." DITSY DIVA pulls out an earbud.

DITSY DIVA: That's what you're gonna sing?

ILONA: No. That's Paul Anka.

DITSY DIVA: I heard of him. Wait did I?

ILONA pulls out one of DUDE'S earbuds.

ILONA: *(to DUDE)* You should've seen his face!

DUDE: Who's face?

DITSY DIVA: Paul Anchor's?

ILONA: *(cont'd.)* My dad, he was all like, "what are you singing that crap for?"—

DUDE: —Old people make me laugh. Say whatever the fuck they want.

ILONA glares.

DUDE: *(sheepish, back-tracking)* I mean...my mom used to sing at my Grandpa's nursing home. On Sundays. It's cool. Like that you did that...

DITSY DIVA: I sang at a nursing home once? With my high school a capella group? It was kind of creepy? All those old people? Drooling?

ILONA: Yeah. Drooling.

DITSY DIVA: I didn't mean...You're not...old...yet...

ILONA: Hundred twenty-five?

DITSY DIVA: No offense? But you should like save your money? That? What you sang? So not what they're looking for?

PRODUCER makes her way back down the line, inching closer with her camera.

ILONA: That was Paul Anka! For the guy. In the wheelchair. I don't like Paul Anka. I like J-Lo--

DITSY DIVA: —I love J-Lo?

DUDE: I'm kinda more 'Young Thug'.

ILONA: Don't say that. I'm sure you're a nice kid.

DITSY DIVA: Like Young Thug's a rapper?

ILONA: Ooh. A rapper. So is that what you're gonna sing? Young Thug? Okay.

PRODUCER: *(filming)* Hey tell me about that Young Thug thing you got going on.

ILONA rips DITSY DIVA's number from her chest, and holds it up to her own.

DITSY DIVA: Hey!

ILONA belts one incredibly long, sustained, impressive note. ALL stop and turn, including PRODUCER. DUDE starts videotaping halfway through the note.

DUDE: *(like "coooool!")* Shi-i-it!

ILONA: *(into the camera, waving)* That was for you Keith!

ILONA: *(CONT'D.)*

(to PRODUCER) That's gonna be on TV, right? So you wanna do my 'profile' interview? Ask me anything. Go ahead. I'll. Tell. You. Anything.

Producer

Sorry.

ILONA: Sorry?

PRODUCER: Sorry.

ILONA charges at PRODUCER.

ILONA: SORRY?!

DITSY DIVA restrains ILONA.

PRODUCER: I'm getting security.

PRODUCER dusts herself off, exits. DUDE stops filming, approaches.

DUDE: Got the whole thing.

ILONA: Delete that right now! You have no right to video tape me! Delete it!

DUDE: I'm uploading it to YouTube. And tweeting it everywhere. Hashtag American Idol. Hashtag older but bolder. Hashtag you should sooo be on The Voice!

ILONA: What, you trying to 'eliminate the competition?' Jesus, I don't even have a number!

DUDE: Bet you get one now.

DITSY DIVA grabs the iPhone, hits 'play,' watches.

ILONA: Yeah?

DITSY DIVA: Helluh yeah!

ILONA: Let me see that.

ILONA yanks DUDE's iPhone out of her hands. SHE hits play, watches, sees a sadly desperate woman on the screen. HER shoulders slump.

ILONA: I'm...'Bikini Girl'.

DITSY DIVA: Oh my god? Like how funny was Bikini Girl?

DUDE: You're not that crazy.

DITSY DIVA: So some people only watch Idol for the crazies?

ILONA: I'm just...I'm gonna miss'em. You know? Harry, and Keith, and Jennifer. I just love that Keith Urban. He is the goofiest judge. I thought we could have so much fun in there. For a few minutes. I could see pictures of their kids. She does that sometimes, J-Lo. She shows pictures. And I got pictures of my daughter. In L.A. We Skype. Sometimes.

Beat.

DUDE takes off his number. Gives it to ILONA.

DUDE: I could use a hundred twenty-five bucks. And a hot senior.

ILONA looks at him like 'eeeewwww.'

DUDE: No I mean for prom! A high school senior. For prom!

ILONA looks at the number in her hands.

ILONA: But, what if you're really the next American Idol?
DUDE: I mean, look at the line. And this is just one city. Like, what are the odds, right? That I'll get through? To the next round?

ILONA struggles with this for a moment.

ILONA: Pin this back on. And when you make it through, I will see you in Hollywood!
DUDE: You're gonna try to meet the judges in Hollywood?
ILONA: No. My daughter.

(beat)

Let me hear you sing. What are you gonna sing?
DUDE: I don't know! I got two songs ready to go. Can't decide which I'm like feeling. You know? Which I can really make my own.

DITSY DIVA puts her earbuds back in, practices.

ILONA: That's important, making 'em your own. They say that all the time. Try 'em out on me.
DUDE: Yeah?
ILONA: I'm a good coach.

SHE smacks DITSY DIVA on the shoulder.

ILONA: You're next. Get ready.

DITSY DIVA smiles, gives a 'thumbs up.' DUDE raps.

End of play

I'M ONLY SLEEPING

Brian James Polak

I'm Only Sleeping was first presented by SHOTZ LA, at The Granada Building, June 6, 2016. Thea Rodgers, Producer. Directed by Alec Engerson.

CAST
FRANKIE: Mia Fraboni
PETE: Langston Brand
RYAN : Andrew Perez

CHARACTERS :
PETE – A former junkie
FRANKIE – Pete's older sister
RYAN – Pete and Frank's younger brother.

SETTING: The inside of a car.

NOTES: // indicates the beginning of the next line but they talk to each other like siblings.
They don't always politely allow the other to finish their sentence.
No pauses or beats are written in the script.
They are present, it is up to you to find them and use them.

Lights rise on a car. It's night.

FRANKIE is snoring in the passenger seat.

RYAN is in the backseat fiddling with his iPhone, but nobody notices.

PETE is humming "I'm Only Sleeping" by The Beatles.

Through the humming maybe some lyrics could slip out.

Pete hums throughout the play whenever he has the opportunity. After a long moment Pete hits Frankie.

PETE: Wake up. You're snoring.

FRANKIE: Sorry.

Frankie realizes something's not right. Pete hums.

FRANKIE: What the...what are you...Where're we going? Where are we going?

PETE: Shut it.

FRANKIE: Why are you driving this car? Hello?

PETE: I said shut it. I can't think with you yacking in my ear like that.

FRANKIE: Excuse me for yacking but I just woke up in the passenger seat of some car with my dead brother behind the wheel. It's not often a guy wakes up in a strange car, you know, when he's not the one driving it. Where are you taking me?

PETE: Nowhere.

FRANKIE: And where are we going?

PETE: Nowhere.

FRANKIE: Yes we are, we obviously are. We're in a car. You're behind the wheel. You're driving the car somewhere and I'm in it. So it's obvious to me that we're going somewhere.

PETE: I'm not driving...

FRANKIE: Yes you are.

PETE: Is the car moving, dummy?

FRANKIE: I don't...it's a car....so probably...

PETE: No...It's not going anywhere.

FRANKIE: Ok. You probably don't know this, but I have a place to be. And I'm ridiculously late. // So if you don't mind.

PETE: This is where you have to be. So sit there and shut up.

FRANKIE: What in the hell is that supposed to mean?

PETE: You're dead, Frankie, ok? You're dead. You died. You're fucking dead.

FRANKIE: Why would you say something like that?

PETE: You. Are. Dead.

FRANKIE: Stop saying that. Do you have any idea how fucked up it is to tell a woman she's dead?

PETE: Frankie, nobody ever tells anybody they're dead unless they are. Nobody told me I was dead until it was true.

RYAN: Would you guys stop arguing? I'm trying to play Candy Crush.

FRANKIE: What is Ryan doing here?

PETE: Dead.

FRANKIE: Ohhhhhhhhh. I'm lucid dreaming.

Pete hits Frankie on the side of the head.

PETE: You're dead, sis. Get used to it. This will be so much easier when you do.

RYAN: That must mean I'm dead too. How did I die?

PETE: I can't tell you that.

RYAN: Did anybody tell you how you died?

PETE: Didn't need to.

FRANKIE: I was just driving up on Mullholland.

PETE: Where were you going?

FRANKIE: It was my weekend to see Katie...
    I was late. So I was really gunning it...

RYAN: Was I with you?

FRANKIE: I don't think so.
    This is...

PETE: It.

FRANKIE: This is it.

RYAN: It's still.

PETE: There's not much surprise in the stillness of death.

FRANKIE: I did nothing wrong. I've been a good mom.
    I tip at the coffee shop. I eat organic food for crying out loud.
    I see my daughter every...every weekend I can.
    I almost never miss a weekend.

RYAN: If you were such a good mom, why didn't you have full custody?

FRANKIE: It's complicated...

PETE: Welcome to hell.

FRANKIE: Was bad enough sharing a bedroom with my little brother and sister.

So. Yes. Eternity in a Honda is hell.

RYAN: It's not so bad.

FRANKIE: I always hated this car.

PETE: You never thought this would be it, did you?

FRANKIE: What are we doing?

PETE: The car overheated. It's gotta cool down before it can go.

RYAN: And then where do we go?

PETE: Couple more passengers to pick up.

RYAN: Mom and Dad?

FRANKIE: Oh dear god.

RYAN: Dad's not going to be happy unless he's driving.

FRANKIE: He'll hate it with you behind the wheel.

PETE: Hell for him will be driving in a car with his kids with no control over where we go.

RYAN: Hell for me is the port-a-potty at a Kenny Chesney concert.

FRANKIE: I'm supposed to be with Katie right now. I never miss a weekend.

Pete hums.

FRANKIE: Stop that. Stop that. STOP THAT. You're driving me crazy with the humming. I hate that song.

RYAN: It's Mom's song.

FRANKIE: I know it's Mom's song. It's annoying. Now that I'm dead I'd really prefer not to spend forever being annoyed.

PETE: Have you ever thought for a moment that maybe this isn't how I wanted to spend eternity? It wasn't so bad when I was alone. But then you appear in the seat next to me, and I'm thinking, Ok, this is what I get for being a junkie.

FRANKIE: This is the car you…

RYAN: When you died I couldn't speak for days. I couldn't get out of bed, but I couldn't sleep.

PETE: Guilty conscience?

RYAN: Maybe. No. A little.

FRANKIE: I wasn't guilty at all. Wasn't my fault you were a junkie.

RYAN: We could have done more, Frankie. We talked about it.

FRANKIE: Am I supposed to apologize? Is that why I'm here? To say sorry Pete, it's my fault you killed yourself? We're all dead. What's the point?

PETE: I needed you. Both of you. And you weren't there.

RYAN: You guys? How did I die?

Nobody knows the answer to this.

They shrug their shoulders…

They give Ryan a sympathetic look.

Pete hums.

FRANKIE: Why do you keep humming Mom's song?

PETE: It's the only song I remember.

RYAN: Ohhhh the thunderstorms…

FRANKIE: You'd beg me to share the bottom bunk with you.

PETE: And Mom would come sing to us.

FRANKIE: It always put you to sleep.

PETE: I remember that.

Pete hums. Frankie joins him.

FRANKIE: This isn't so bad.

RYAN: When I wake up early in the morning

Lift my head

PETE: I'm still yawning

RYAN: When I'm in the middle of a dream
Stay in bed
Float upstream

PETE AND FRANKIE: Float upstream

RYAN AND PETE AND FRANK: Please don't wake me
No don't shake me
Leave me where I am
I'm only sleeping

Perhaps they continue to sing together.

Perhaps they all asleep.

Perhaps the car starts and they drive away.

The lights fade. END OF PLAY

Lawrence Harbison

JUST LIKE THEM

Chris Widney

Produced by Studio CPremiere Date: June 11, 2016 (Hollywood Fringe Festival)

Cast: Anthony Rizzuto, Dominick Vicchiullo, & Julian Zambrano
Director: Edgar Pablos

Characters:

PAULIE THE GIANT PANDA: Roly-poly, playful, bundle of joy. Young, naive, innocent. Loves everyone and everything.

CHUCKY THE CHINESE GIANT SALAMANDER: Suspicious, street-wise, a hustler, an Asian Ratso Rizzo. Absorbs information like a sponge, street smart and book smart as well. Angry.

OWEN: A seemingly nice guy. Place: A basement somewhere in Ohio. Time: Present.

SETTING: A BASEMENT. It is used as a holding area for animals. There are several cages.

PAULIE, a young, cuddly Giant Panda and CHUCKY, a Chinese Giant Salamander, share a large cage. There is sand and rocks, vegetation, perhaps even a small Baobab tree.

AT RISE: OWEN, the owner of the home, cuddles and wrestles with PAULIE while CHUCKY watches suspiciously from the side. OWEN: Yeah, who's my cuddle-bear? Who's my favorite, roly-poly Panda? Is it Paulie?

PAULIE: *(rolling, cuddling)* Yeah!

OWEN: Is it Paulie the Panda? Yes, it is. That's my "bestie." Oo, look at you. Your hair's a little messy, isn't it? Let's brush it out. Whata' ya' say?

PAULIE: Okay!

OWEN: Should we brush it out? Yes, we should.

(As OWEN continues to wrestle and brush PAULIE, CHUCKY sneaks up behind OWEN and, using his sticky, lizard claws, snatches OWEN'S iPhone from his back pocket. CHUCKY slithers to a corner with the phone.)

OWEN: Look at you, much better, now isn't that better? Yes, it is. You're a rock star.

PAULIE: Rock star!

OWEN: Now you two have a great afternoon, I gotta run out for a little bit, okay?

PAULIE: No, no, come on! (an affectionate growl) Ahh-oow.

OWEN: Okay, one more little cuddle for my cuddle bear. *(They wrestle and hug as CHUCKY hides the iPhone.)*

PAULIE: Ahh-oow, that's good.

OWEN: Okay, I gotta go. Bye, Paulie. Bye, Chucky.

(OWEN exits.)

PAULIE: *(rolling around)* I love it when Owen comes to visit.

CHUCKY: *(skeptical)* Uh-huh.

PAULIE: Wrestling, grooming, it's the best!

CHUCKY: `You think?

PAULIE: Yeah!

CHUCKY: He just fed us an hour ago.

PAULIE: Isn't it great?

CHUCKY: So why the second visit?

PAULIE: I dunno. `He wanted to wrestle?

CHUCKY: Right.

PAULIE: Owen's the best.*(CHUCKY pulls out three playing cards and starts playing three-card monte in front of PAULIE.)*

CHUCKY: Here, come on, `wanna play?

PAULIE: Sure!

CHUCKY: *(showing him card)* Here you go, spot the red lady, got her? Sure you do. *(shuffling)* Follow the red lady, easy, you win, right? *(stops)* Which one?

PAULIE: That one.

CHUCKY: *(revealing black card)* No. *(shuffling again)* Remember, Paulie, remember how I told you.*(He stops again, PAULIE points.)*

PAULIE: The middle.

CHUCKY: *(revealing black card)* No. *(shuffling)* I told you. It's never what you think. You got to follow the one you think then pick either of the other two. At least that way you got a shot. *(stops)*

PAULIE: Then that one!

CHUCKY: *(revealing)* Wrong again. See that time I left it where I knew you were following `cause I knew that's the way you'd think.

PAULIE: Oh.

CHUCKY: You're getting hustled, Paulie, understand? Same way you're getting hustled by Owen.

PAULIE: What? No!

CHUCKY: You got dragged outa' China in a net. `Flown to Ohio to live in this guy's basement in a cage. The only sun we get's from that lamp.What do you think's going on down here?

PAULIE: Owen's been nothing but kind. He brings us lettuce, bananas, bugs, we've got our own little Baobab tree - he empties out the dehumidifier twice a day.

CHUCKY: To keep you healthy.

PAULIE: I am healthy. *(tumbling)* Healthier and more flexible than I ever was in China!

CHUCKY: `Cause he's your big pal.

PAULIE: Yeah.

CHUCKY: You're not his friend. You're his commodity. We are commodities, both of us. Valuable commodities.Why? Because we're endangered. We're on "the list." And that makes us special to a very rich, very bored clientele who are really into acquiring things, "What kid doesn't want a Panda for Christmas?" We're party favors to them, freak shows. Something to parade around by the pool after tennis and before croquet.

PAULIE: Owen's not like that.

CHUCKY: The only thing better than "endangered" is "extinct." The Chinese Giant Salamander goes extinct and Owen hits the jackpot. The price for me, the sole survivor when the rest of the species is gone, goes through the roof. That's why he's keeping me around. That's his game, that's the hustle!

PAULIE: No, that's crazy! It doesn't make any sense. Where do you get all this?!

CHUCKY: *(re: iPhone)* Arianna Huffington. See, but you're different. You're the quick money, something to turn over, pay the bills. You know how many of you I've seen come and go?

PAULIE: But Owen and I are "besties."

CHUCKY: Wise up, Paulie! He's hugging you, brushing your "hair" - he calls your fur "hair" - and he just happened to give you a bath last night. What do you wanna' bet at some point in the very near future a truck pulls up and your "bestie's" down here with a couple of goons and crate? And you know where you're going? Maybe some nice, family in Connecticut that's gonna love you for a couple of years while you're still cute. Wait till your claws come in and you scratch one of the "little Angels." You're on-line, on-sale again, probably this time to some crazy, drug lord in Miami who thinks it's hysterical to throw a party and serve Panda chorizos. How about that, Paulie? Do you think that's cute?! (Paulie stops.) … We got one shot. We gotta extinct this guy before he extincts us.

PAULIE: "Extinct him?"

CHUCKY: Any second he's gonna realize he doesn't have his precious iPhone and he's gonna come back down. This is our chance. We take him down then slip out while the cage is still open. If we can make it to the woods, we got a shot. It's still warm out, there's plenty to eat. This, all this is black market. Nobody knows we're down here. Nobody's scouring the woods for a roly-poly Panda and a weird looking Newt. If we can make it to the airport. We make it to Cleveland International, find China Air, all we gotta do is stow away in cargo.

PAULIE: *(rolling around, holding his head)* Geez, I dunno, Chucky. I'm getting a headache.

CHUCKY: We're not extinct yet. That means there's still a few left. And some of them are female. And I'll tell you what; we find 'em, it ain't like there's gonna be a whole lot of competition, if you know what I mean. *(Paulie stares blankly, he's too young)* You will. Trust me. And when you do, it's re-population time and we're the only two bulls at the rodeo. PAULIE: … "Take him down." You mean?

CHUCKY: Come on, Paulie. Don't be as dumb as you look.

PAULIE: It's not my nature, I've never -

CHUCKY: - Blah, blah -

PAULIE: To kill?

CHUCKY: "To kill, to kill." You make it sound like such a big deal. One time, be like them, think like them. They kill each other all the time. At any given moment there is a conflict, a massacre, torture of such magnitude we can't even fathom - *(holds up iPhone)* Watch CNN on-line.

PAULIE: Why do you keep stealing that? It just stresses you out!

CHUCKY: Do we kill each other? I never heard of a white Panda wanting to kill a black Panda 'cause he looks different. Or because he and his buddies choose to believe that something different will happen to them when they die. Or because they believe in a different God. A different God? God at all - I mean, What is God? Some ridiculous man-made construct that has provided thousands of years and thousands of magnificent and noble reasons for them to kill and kill again.

PAULIE: … We have no enemies. We roll around, we play, we're Vegan. We clear the underbrush of excess foliage, we serve our purpose in the chain.

CHUCKY: And what purpose do they serve? Everyone else does something. My kind? "Pest management," you're welcome very much. You clear the canopy then offer yourself up to a higher predator - as you should. Not them. They won't even decompose properly. They torch themselves, freeze dry each other, build cement walled mausoleums so the worms can't even get a crack at 'em. Oh, and their contribution? Let's see; pollution, over-population, global warming, deforestation, eradication of entire species - the kidnapping and unlawful imprisonment of you and me! Their only positive contribution is that they will probably eradicate themselves someday, which I think would be great, because then the cockroaches - whom I happen to really like as a species as well as a snack - can finally have their day. They are a worthless species, Paulie, worthless!

PAULIE: Still, Chucky, kill? Geez, I dunno, I dunno.

CHUCKY: Here, you wanna' know? Here. *(hands Paulie the iPhone but Paulie won't take it)* Read it. Read the chain. *(Paulie won't read it)* From Owen to his buddy, Sal: *(reading text)* "Finally dumping that fat, pain-in-the-ass, banana-crapping Panda." Sal: "How much?" Owen: "Two G's." Sal: "Banana-crapping, pain-in-the-ass." Owen: "Hooters after?" "Double thumb-up Emoji." There you go. That's you, Paulie. The "banana-crapping, pain-in-the-ass" that scores a lousy two G's so Owen and Sal can eat wings at the "Hooters."

OWEN: *(off)* Phone, phone, where's my phone? *(They look to the doorway, know he's coming.)*

CHUCKY: Gimme one shot. Do your cuddle-bear routine, roll him over and give me one shot at that jugular. I've got the teeth. They're strong enough, I can pierce his jugular. If I get a clean shot, I can do it. *(PAULIE doesn't answer right away, confused, overwhelmed as OWEN returns.)*

OWEN: Hey guys, either of you see my phone? I'm sure I had it … *(He searches as CHUCKY looks to PAULIE.)*

PAULIE: *(playful growl)* Ahh-oow. *(PAULIE gestures for more hugs. OWEN notices.)*

OWEN: Oh, you want to cuddle some more? More cuddles for my cuddle-bear? Let's see, did it fall out when we were wrestling? Here, we were like this, like this - *(He and PAULIE wrestle and cuddle while OWEN searches. PAULIE turns OWEN away from CHUCKY. CHUCKY sneaks up behind OWEN, pounces and bites OWEN in the neck. Blood spews from his jugular.)*

OWEN: Jesus Christ, what the - ?!!! Get off! *(he squirms and tries to escape)* Help - !

CHUCKY: Hold him down! *(Paulie obeys as Owen weakens.)* There you go. Yeah. We got him! *(to Owen)* Who's extinct now, huh? Who's extinct now?!

(OWEN goes limp.)

PAULIE: *(numb)* We did it.

CHUCKY: We're free Paulie, free. Come on, let's go!

PAULIE: We did it.

CHUCKY: Paulie, let's go! *(CHUCKY slithers out the door. PAULIE doesn't move, alone, horrified, covered in blood, staring at the lifeless OWEN.)*

PAULIE: Just like them.-

> *The End -*

JUST SAY IT THREE TIMES

Erin Moughon

Originally Produced by Riant Theatre's Strawberry One-Act Festival in the Summer of 2016

July 15, 18, and 21, 2016 at Theatre at St. Clement's

Directed by Erin Moughon
Festival Produced by Van Fisher

CAST:
EMILIA: Bess Miller
JOANNA: Emily Long
APHRA BEHN: Kendra Augustin

CHARACTERS:

EMILIA: F, late 20s-early 30s, unhappy with her life, but unwilling to change her life

JOANNA: F, late 20s-early 30s, a little more freewheeling than Emilia, also unhappy with her life

APHRA BEHN: F, 17th century playwright, poet, and spy

SETTING: Emilia and Joanna's apartment

TIME: Now

Joanna and Emilia are drunk. Like super drunk. Like I didn't know you could get that drunk after college without passing out and/or vomiting drunk. They are also at home. And in their mid-late 20's. Maybe early 30s.

JOANNA: You know what? You. You're the best.

EMILIA: No, you're the best.

JOANNA: No, you…what were we talking about?

EMILIA: I don't know. Hey. The movie's over. When did that happen?

JOANNA: *(turning over an empty vodka bottle)* I think when we ran out of vodka.

EMILIA: That. That is the saddest thing I've ever heard.

JOANNA: I know right?

EMILIA: What can we do with an empty bottle?

JOANNA: Spin the bottle?

EMILIA: With just two people? If we had some more booze, we could play this new drinking game.

JOANNA: Hold on.

Joanna goes to the kitchen. There is a loud crash.

EMILIA: Is everything

    Joanna re-emerges with a bottle.

JOANNA: I'm good! I'm good!

EMILIA: I thought we drank everything.

JOANNA: Not this!

EMILIA: Is that peppermint schnapps?

JOANNA: Hehe.

EMILIA: Whaa-t?

JOANNA: You said schnapps. Hehe.

EMILIA: And now wha-t?

JOANNA: I said schnapps. Hehe. I said it again!

EMILIA: *(grabbing the bottle)* Give me that.

JOANNA: Okay. Okay. What was I doing?

EMILIA: Drinking game!

JOANNA: Woohoo!

EMILIA: You did not just woohoo.

JOANNA: Woohoo!

EMILIA: Oh lord.

JOANNA: What? Drinking games deserve woohoos. It's a rule. Or something.

EMILIA: I'm so glad I'm the only person here for that.

JOANNA: Shut up and explain the game.

EMILIA: It's called Ten.

JOANNA: Ten! Do I win?

EMILIA: I didn't…didn't…explain. Let me explain!

JOANNA: I didn't win?

EMILIA: We didn't start!

JOANNA: Really?

EMILIA: Look. It's called "Ten" and

JOANNA: Ten! I win again!

EMILIA: That's just the name!

JOANNA: You win by saying the name?

EMILIA: No, you win by naming ten things in…a time period. I don't know. Ten things until you get one wrong.

JOANNA: What ten things?

EMILIA: You pick a category. Something that has at least ten answers, but obscure.

JOANNA: So like ten colors?

EMILIA: Yeah, but obscure. Like ten non-natur…non-natur…man-made colors. Or something.

JOANNA: Okay. So you name a thing and I name ten things?

EMILIA: Yeah.

JOANNA: And what happens if I get it wrong?

EMILIA: You drink.

JOANNA: And if I get it right?

EMILIA: I drink.

JOANNA: Aw man.

EMILIA: What?

JOANNA: I was hoping to drink.

EMILIA: We can both drink.

JOANNA: Hurray! Who goes first?

EMILIA: Spin the bottle.

JOANNA: Sweet.

Joanna spins. It lands on Emilia.

EMILIA: Okay. Okay. *(pause)* Umm…

JOANNA: Come on! Come on! I want to drink!

EMILIA: Okay! I've got it.

JOANNA: Hurray!

EMILIA: Name ten

JOANNA: Yeah. Yeah.

EMILIA: Let me finish!

JOANNA: Sorry.

EMILIA: Okay. Where was I?

JOANNA: Name ten…

EMILIA: Oh yeah! Name ten female playwrights.

JOANNA: What?

EMILIA: Ten playwrights who identify as women.

JOANNA: Those exist?

EMILIA: Yes, they exist.

OANNA: Are you sure?

EMILIA: Just go.

JOANNA: I…um…well…there's the weird British one. And the other weird British one that's super violent. And the American one who…writes herself. I think? And…

EMILIA: Names.

JOANNA: What?

EMILIA: Name the women. Don't just vaguely describe them.

JOANNA: But I don't know names! I couldn't even name male playwrights! Except that English one who writes in that weird version of English with all the rhymes.

EMILIA: Oh my god.

JOANNA: What?

EMILIA: Did you pay attention at all in school?

JOANNA: Not to that. Give me some non-linear algebra, and I'm good.

EMILIA: You're so weird.

JOANNA: Oh yeah? You name ten female playwrights.

EMILIA: Okay. Caryl Churchill. Sarah Kane. Wendy Wasserstein. Danai Gurira. Aphra Behn.

JOANNA: Waitwaitwait. What was that last one?

EMILIA: Aphra Behn.

JOANNA: You just made that up.

EMILIA: She was the first female playwright. Well, English female playwright. First playwright to write in English who was a woman? First something something playwright.

JOANNA: Aphra?

EMILIA: Yeah.

JOANNA: That's a name?

EMILIA: Yes.

JOANNA: It sounds like the name you turn all the lights off and call out to get her to appear.

EMILIA: No. You're thinking of

Joanna has jumped up and turned off the lights.

JOANNA: We should do that! Whoa! Ow!

Emilia turns the flashlight feature of her phone on. Joanna has fallen.

EMILIA: You're going to kill yourself. Turn the light back on.

JOANNA: No! I've always wanted to try this!

EMILIA: It's not Aphra Behn.

JOANNA: Okay. What do I? Stand in the middle of the room? Spin around?

Joanna spins around slowly.

EMILIA: No. No spinning! It's not…

Joanna takes Emilia's phone and turns it off.

JOANNA: Aphra Behn.

EMILIA: Joanna. Stop. Give me back my phone. This is

JOANNA: Aphra Behn!

EMILIA: Where's the light switch?

JOANNA: APHRA BEHN!

Both pause for a moment.

EMILIA: See? I told you it wasn't the right person.

She turns on the light. Aphra Behn is standing in the middle of the room next to Joanna.

APHRA: Hello.

JOANNA: Holy shit!

EMILIA: Oh my god! What happened! What happened!

JOANNA: Holy shit!

Emilia grabs an umbrella and wields it like a weapon.

EMILIA: Who are you? How'd you get in here? Answer me!

APHRA: I'm Aphra Behn. You called me. Where am I?

JOANNA: Holy shit! I did it!

APHRA: Quite.

EMILIA: This is insane.

JOANNA: I am the best! Does this mean I win?

EMILIA: You're dead. Like dead dead. Like a couple of hundred years dead.

APHRA: Yes.

JOANNA: I think this means I win.

EMILIA: How are you here?

APHRA: You tell me. You summoned me.

EMILIA: This isn't happening. Did I die? Is this what alcohol poisoning feels like?

JOANNA: So your name is really Aphra?

APHRA: Yes.

JOANNA: What the hell kind of a name is that?

EMILIA: Joanna! We don't want to piss…it…her…off.

APHRA: It's the name my parents gave me.

JOANNA: And Behn?

APHRA: Husband's last name. He was German.

JOANNA: Cool.

EMILIA: Jo, this is not cool. You've somehow managed to conjure up an ancient playwright…

APHRA: Ancient? It's been less than 400 years.

EMILIA: Sorry. *(pulling Joanna to the side)* Now I'm pissing her off and she's still here and how did you do that anyway? What was in our drinks?

APHRA: *(picking up a bottle and smelling it)* Something foul, I can assure you.

JOANNA: Why are you here anyway?

APHRA: You summoned me. It doesn't happen often.

EMILIA: But you're a playwright. Not a mystic or witch or…Wait. Are you a witch?

APHRA: Spy. Novelist. Prisoner. Playwright. I don't think witch is usually listed in my accomplishments.

JOANNA: See? She's fine. *(picks up bottle and tries to drink from it)* We're out. Aphra, can I call you Aphra? Aphra, did you happen to bring anything with you? Anything to…anything alcoholic?

APHRA: I travel light.

Aphra begins to explore.

JOANNA: Yeah. That makes sense.

EMILIA: What are you saying? None of this makes sense! We are talking to a playwright from the mid-1600's, and you think that her not having any booze is making sense?

JOANNA: Well, if you travelled all that way and all of those years, would you bring a heavy bottle with you?

EMILIA: None of this makes any sense!

JOANNA: What do you mean?

EMILIA: That time travel would work because you said someone's name three times.

JOANNA: In the dark. Don't forget in the dark.

EMILIA: How could I? You're nuts. Maybe I'm crazy too.

APHRA: I would say that explains things.

EMILIA: What?

APHRA: Well, your domicile is filthy.

EMILIA: So?

APHRA: And you are both intoxicated.

EMILIA: It's been a hard week.

APHRA: And what exactly makes it so "hard"?

EMILIA: Excuse me?

APHRA: You were in the dark, drunk when I arrived.

EMILIA: Your point?

APHRA: You are unhappy. And this doesn't seem like the first time.

EMILIA: And you were happy all of the time?

APHRA: Hardly. But I did something about it. I turned my prison into my own world. Full of characters and laughter and wit.

EMILIA: So I'm supposed to become delusional?

JOANNA: Be nice!

APHRA: No. I expect you to do something. Make something of yourself. You sit and complain about your situation. Change it.

JOANNA: I wish I had your moxy.

EMILIA: Moxy? Since when do you say moxy?

JOANNA: Since an awesome lady from the past came to give me advice.

APHRA: Moxy?

JOANNA: Gumption. Uppity-ness. A real backbone. Um…um…

APHRA: I think I understand. Thank you.

EMILIA: And what has all of the moxy gotten you?

APHRA: It got me to travel here.

EMILIA: And for us?

APHRA: What do you want to do?

EMILIA: What?

APHRA: With your life? What do you want beyond this?

EMILIA: I…

JOANNA: Come on.

EMILIA: What?

JOANNA: Every other day. All you can talk about is

EMILIA: To you. That's different. Or to myself.

APHRA: There's your problem. You can't admit it to other people.

JOANNA: Why are you embarrassed all of a sudden?

EMILIA: I'm not embarrassed. I don't want to tell the crazy lady from the past or the ghost or the witch or whatever she is. The more she knows about me, the more she can do to me.

JOANNA: You're ridiculous.

APHRA: And why would I want to waste my time on you? You don't even think you are worth your own time.

EMILIA: And that's just about enough from you.

APHRA: Excuse me?

EMILIA: Where do you get off coming here and telling me how to live? Of course you could go and be a playwright and a poet and novelist? What else did you have to do? Your biggest concern was probably how to deal with your lice. What distractions did you have? No T.V., no internet, no real viable ways of employ.

APHRA: No encouragement. No one sticking up for me. No reassurances from my comfortable apartment living my comfortable life. Maybe having nothing to lose was a good thing. Maybe it is the best thing. Maybe you should try it. What are you so afraid of? Failing? Everyone fails. What of the people who never try? Are you content to waste away here with the might have been?

EMILIA: Why did you come here at all?

APHRA: You summoned me.

EMILIA: She summoned you.

JOANNA: Well, you're clearly the one who needs her.

EMILIA: And what about you?

JOANNA: Why are you turning on me? It's not my fault you're unfulfilled and sad and a drunk.

EMILIA: And what have you done with your life that is so amazing?

JOANNA: Nothing. And that's my fault. I don't blame you for my choices.

APHRA: And why do you make those choices?

JOANNA: I'm unhappy and scared, and I don't like being here. I don't know how I got here, but I don't like it.

APHRA: And where would you like to be?

JOANNA: Where you were.

EMILIA: What?

JOANNA: I think it would be amazing.

APHRA: You know it's not the fairy tale. Dirty jails. Lack of baths. Lice. Disease. Oppression.

JOANNA: I'm aware, but it's more than that. Look at all that you accomplished in spite of the circumstances. Maybe because of them! It seems like that's what I want.

EMILIA: How could you want that?

JOANNA: How could I not? You've never asked me what I wanted before. Maybe this is all for me.

EMILIA: What?

JOANNA: I'm not happy here. I think I could be happy there. Where she's...*(to Aphra)* you're from.

EMILIA: And what happens to Aphra? When you go back?

APHRA: I stay here.

EMILIA: Lovely.

JOANNA: So it all works out! We should change clothes!

EMILIA: Excuse me?

JOANNA: Not you and me. Me and Aphra. If she is staying here…

EMILIA: This is not happening.

APHRA: Is there a changing?

JOANNA: Back this way.

They exit.

EMILIA: *(to Joanna)* And what exactly are you planning on doing in the 1600s? You can't write! You're really terrible at it. Like scarily bad.

JOANNA: *(from offstage)* Maybe I'll invent Calculus!

EMILIA: Do you prefer to be burned at the stake, drowned, or stone, you evil witch?

JOANNA: Haha. Very funny.

EMILIA: I wasn't joking. Do you have any idea of what you're getting into?

JOANNA: Yes! *(re-emerging in Aphra's clothes)* How do I look?

EMILIA: Like you escaped from a Renaissance Faire.

JOANNA: Cool.

APHRA: Your garments feel strange.

JOANNA: You'll get used to them.

APHRA: Perhaps. I wore worse in service of the King.

JOANNA: Now I get to go back and try this new life. And you have someone to give you the kick in the pants you need.

EMILIA: Just a minute.

JOANNA: You know I'm an enabler. We've just been in this rut.

APHRA: Now carefully consider what you are about to do.

EMILIA: You're still drunk.

JOANNA: So? Why does that mean I don't know what I want?

EMILIA: I…it's…it's the kind of decision you need to make sober.

JOANNA: And why is that? I want to go back. I want to be Aphra Behn. I want to be Aprha Behn. I want to be

APHRA: Careful.

JOANNA: Aphra Behn.

The lights go out. There is a crash. The lights come back on.

EMILIA: What? Where's…?

APHRA: Who?

EMILIA: She was just here.

APHRA: Emilia. You're being silly.// Now come on. You need to clean this up.

At //, Emilia starts talking at the same time as Aphra.

EMILIA: //Being silly? Where's um…what's her name? And why do I have to clean it up?

APHRA: Because you made the mess. And you told me not to let you get away with stuff like this anymore.

EMILIA: And when did I say that?

APHRA: When I moved in.

EMILIA: Stop being ridiculous. You didn't move in. Someone else. Did you guys plan this?

APHRA: Plan what?

EMILIA: You and…and… I can't remember her…his? Her? Name.

APHRA: Here's a trash bag. Get going.

EMILIA: There was something on the tip of my tongue.

APHRA: Now there's something in your hand. Hop to it.

EMILIA: Hop to it? Since when do you say that?

APHRA: Since you started staring off into space like a crazy person. Now clean. You asked me to

EMILIA: What?

APHRA: What is it that you are always complaining about?

EMILIA: How I want to quit my job and get my life started. I feel like I should be in such a different place right now. Running the world.

APHRA: And running the world starts by cleaning your own stuff. And then working up from there. For a long, long time.

EMILIA: And where are you going?

APHRA: Dropping off a manuscript. New book of poems.

EMILIA: How many is that now?

APHRA: Lost count. Now clean.

Aphra exits. Emilia starts to clean. She picks up a book.

EMILIA: Aphra Behn. Huh. Weird name.

She goes back to cleaning. Something strikes her. She looks up.

EMILIA: Wait.

Black out. End of play.

LAMENT

Begonya Plaza

Premiered at Midtown Short Play Festival in New York City
October 29 & 30, 2016

Directed by Jonathan Libman

LENNY TAURO was played by Rolando Chusan.
KAREN BLIXEN was played by Solonje Burns
VINCE GIL was played by Cooper Lawrence.

CHARACTERS:

Lenny Tauro: 25, Paulo Cotillion's lover. Sensitive, flamboyant and sings. Wears a silk shirt, and neck scarf, and tight pants.

Karen Blixen: 27, the wife, an ex-ballerina. Still a diva.

Vince Gil: 28, newspaper reporter. Clean-cut, whip smart, and fast.

SETTING: New York City's recent past. A park bench across the street from a hospital. The beginning of fall.

DESCRIPTION: Paulo is dying of AIDS. His life partner, Lenny, is forced to stand idly by when Paulo's family handles everything. After all, only "family" is authorized. This is the New York of not long ago, when same-sex marriage was still illegal and progressive journalists are reviled for bringing such injustice to light. This is still a reality in many countries today. We must never forget.

SCENE 1

"Dido's Lament" by Henry Purcell, plays, while LENNY sits on a park bench across from a hospital in New York City, looking up at a window with cell phone in ear hanging up and putting it away.

(KAREN enters.)

KAREN: Lenny!

(LENNY stands. KAREN gives LENNY a forced embrace.)

LENNY: How is Paulo?

KAREN: Not good.

(LENNY starts to exit in the direction KAREN entered.)

Where are you going?

LENNY: To be with him.

KAREN: But you're not allowed.

LENNY: So you didn't talk to them?

KAREN: I tried. Really, but they can't change policy rules.

LENNY: Bull-shit!

KAREN: Only family is allowed. I'm sorry.

LENNY: I'm more family to him than any single one of you.

KAREN: Legally, I'm Paulo's wife.

LENNY: So demand that I be allowed by his side!

KAREN: Anyway, Paulo is under heavy anesthesia. He won't recognize you. It won't make a difference if you're there or not. The family wouldn't feel very comfortable anyway.

LENNY: You've always been a cold selfish bitch.

KAREN: Excuse me?

LENNY: The fuck'n pageantry of misfit wannabes circling around him, like vultures. Family! Yeah, right. Never did one of you ever call or visit Paulo, except to see what you could get from him. Always available for a "free" ticket to the ballet, and of course, the party afterwards. But invisible when it came to lending him a helping hand.

KAREN: I was hardly ever around.

LENNY: What are you doing here then?

KAREN: What's right.

LENNY: Too late for that.

KAREN: I didn't think he wanted to talk to me.

LENNY: But you still called to make a stink whenever his money hadn't reached you quick enough.

(KAREN pulls out her I-phone.)

KAREN: I took a photo of him for you, if you want I can forward it...

(LENNY looks up the window across the street.)

LENNY: You take pleasure don't you? You want to punish him for all your inabilities as a dancer.

KAREN: They're not inabilities, they're injuries, you fool.

(LENNY points up at window.)

LENNY: You're the fool who can't see that he needs me right now.

KAREN: I remember it like it was yesterday, your filthy smirk while he kicked me out leaving me to pick up the pieces on my own.

LENNY: You knew all along who he was.

KAREN: He promised me that we'd never divorce.

LENNY: You got everything you wanted.

KAREN: Not everything.

LENNY: For the past year every day and night I nursed him, cleaned him, fed him, massaged him, slept by his side, attentive to my Paulo's every need.

KAREN: I have nothing to do with hospital rules.

LENNY: But if you explain to them...

KAREN: I wish I had that kind of power!

LENNY: Melba, our house sitter just called me. Paulo's bitch of a sister had the audacity to go to our home and take Melba's keys, and kick her out. She has no right!

(LENNY breaks down.)

KAREN: Marcia is devastated, the poor thing! And she's just trying to do the best she can for her brother.

LENNY: That's my home too.

KAREN: I don't know about that...

(A FIGURE appears hiding from behind a tree, taking pictures, and eavesdropping.)

LENNY: Don't hate me because I was the one by his side, empowering Paulo to become the ballet icon of our time.

KAREN: By your side Paulo also became the victim of that, decease...
—I'm just saying.

LENNY: Is this how you justify keeping me away from his deathbed?

KAREN: Paulo, like you just said, is an iconic public figure, a celebrity, and doesn't need "certain" kind of publicity if you know what I mean. You're better off staying away, and whatever belongs to you, legally, will go to you, in due time.

LENNY: I never wanted anything but to be by his side. You can't understand that kind of love.

KAREN: Oh I understand. It's the law that doesn't understand. Now I need to get back inside.

(KAREN relishing in her power, exits.)

(VINCE appears and sits at other end of bench.)

VINCE: Fancy meeting you here.

LENNY: Vince, what are you doing here?

VINCE: My job.

(Stares across the street toward KAREN.)

And you? What are you doing here?

LENNY: Sitting on a park bench.

VINCE: In front of a hospital.

LENNY: Didn't even notice.

VINCE: It's not right, Lenny.

LENNY: What?

VINCE: That you're out here and Paulo's inside.

LENNY: No, it's not right.

VINCE: They can't hide you, no matter how hard they try.

LENNY: Paulo knows.

VINCE: The world knows.

LENNY: Just because you know?

VINCE: Gay people know, and we're pretty dispersed throughout the world.

(VINCE offers LENNY a cigarette.)

How is he?

LENNY: Dying.

(LENNY breaks down.)

VINCE: Aids?

LENNY: Plus other dreadful symptoms.

VINCE: Such beautiful talented soul.

LENNY: Please Vince, don't write hurtful shit, I beg you.

(VINCE pulls out from his pocket a recorder, turns it on, begins to improvise a dictation.)

VINCE: Like, uhh for instance... While the renown ballerino, Paulo Cotillion, agonizes his final moments of life in a hospital, his life partner, Lenny Tauro, is banned from sitting by the dancer's death-bed and holding his lover's hand. ...Mr. Cotillion's family have chosen to exploit the tragic circumstances and anti-gay policies to serve their purpose as a pretext to ostracize in order to take all that they can for themselves and preserve their pathetic position of privilege. Are you fucking kidding me? This is what I live for. To accurately cover LGBT issues. Otherwise how is the root of this homophobic bias unearthed? (beat) This is not just about you, Lenny. This sexist prejudice has implications which I'm going to happily uncover.... Otherwise how will opposition to this civil right once and for all be rectified? ...Love is a human right.

LENNY: Okay, enough already.

(VINCE shuts off the recorder.)

VINCE: The article will be ready for tonight's publication.

LENNY: I don't want to be a part of this. Can't you pretend you didn't see me?

VINCE: I know it's hard, embarrassing, and even damaging. But, it's the truth, and change only happens with the truth.

LENNY: How did you know?

VINCE: Your house sitter. Melba? She called me. Said she remembered me from that house party a few years back. Said, Mr. Cotillion had my little blurb of that celebration framed on his kitchen wall. Said she was scrubbing a pot when Paulo's sister arrived, and barely had time to take her cleaning gloves off while Ms. Marcia kept yelling: "vayase, vayase". I offered her money but she didn't accept. Also said,"They really, really love each other."

LENNY: What do I do?

VINCE: You go in that hospital and demand to see your partner, and husband if the legal system had granted you that civil right.

(LENNY sees a BUTTERFLY fluttering toward him.)

I'll follow right behind.

(LENNY doesn't take his eyes off the BUTTERFLY as it lands on his hand and after a moment flies off again.)

(VINCE watches mesmerized)

LENNY: Paulo has left us.

(LENNY lets out a cry looking up at window, and back at nearby BUTTERFLY.)

Rest, my sweetheart, till we're together again. - He's gone.

(VINCE looks out in front across the street.)

VINCE: ...Look at that. The cameras have arrived while the corpse is still warm.

(LENNY stares up at the window, peaceful.)

LENNY: Paulo knew I was here and he came to me to say goodbye. No more pain my love.

VINCE: Look at her, ha! Just look at that. She floats out with such drama! I might as well see what she has to say.

(LENNY starts towards KAREN.)

VINCE: Watch this.

(VINCE turns his recorder on.)

(KAREN enters stage, ready for cameras with red lipstick, jeweled hands on stomach, and chest.)

VINCE: Are you Mr. Cotillion's ex-wife?

KAREN: I am now the widow of Mr. Cotillion. Paulo passed a few minutes ago.

VINCE: My condolences.

KAREN: My precious husband. The two of us had such a busy schedule that we didn't get to spend as much time together as we would have liked, and for which I am deeply regretful. I was always away, and he was always dancing. After my injury I began to pursue another art, the art of painting. You see, I'm now a painter.

VINCE: What was the cause of Mr. Cotillion's death?

KAREN: My first collection will be on exhibit very soon, at the Gore Gallery.

VINCE: Was his death...

KAREN: I've decided I'm going to title it, Creative Consolation," in honor of my Paulo. Through art...

VINCE: What was the cause?

KAREN: To channel my profound pain. It will be a fascinating exhibit, I promise you that.

VINCE: Was it aids?

KAREN: Excuse me!

VINCE: Where is his lover? Paulo was gay?

KAREN: ...What you're talking about?

(KAREN laughs as she scampers away.)

VINCE: Everybody knows, Ms. Blixen! Will you and his lover share the Estate?

(VINCE turns off recorder.)

(LENNY, almost to himself, looking up at the sky softly sings, Dido's Lament.)

(KAREN returns and with VINCE listen to LENNY sing.)

LENNY: When I am laid, am laid in earth, May my wrongs create
No trouble, no trouble in thy breast.
Remember me, remember me, but ah, ah, ahhhhh! Forget my fate.
Remember me, but ahahahahaha forget my fate.

(LENNY bows his head. KAREN and VINCE follow.)

THE END

THE MIME CRIME
Jonathan Yukich

"The Mime Crime" premiered at Times Square's Manhattan Repertory Theatre in July 2016. The production was directed by the author. The cast was as follows:

THE MIME: Zach Fontanez
MARY, ETHEL, SWAYZE: Kiera Terrell
BOBBY, CAPOTE, FLARB: Josh Dill

CHARACTERS

THE MIME: ageless
BOBBY: early twenties
MARY: early twenties
ETHEL: late fifties, very loud
CAPOTE: an irascible poodle
DETECTIVE FLARB: middle-aged cop
DETECTIVE SWAYZE: middle-aged cop

CASTING NOTE: The play is written to be performed with only three actors. It is suggested that MARY, ETHEL and DETECTIVE SWAYZE be played by the same actor; BOBBY, CAPOTE and DETECTIVE FLARB can also be played by the same actor. The MIME is not to be doubled. Costume changes between scenes should be simple and expedient.

SETTING: A simple park bench on a bare stage.

SCENE

AT RISE: (A MIME. Blank expression – empty, inscrutable. Hold. A smile comes over him. He acknowledges the audience with a graceful wave. Flashes the "okay" hand sign. He moves a finger before his lips –shhh! – but soundless. Strikes a pose. Hold.)

(A young couple enters, BOBBY and MARY. They see the MIME.)

BOBBY: Hey, look – a mime.

MARY: What a dipshit.

BOBBY: Whoa.

MARY: Is he not?

BOBBY: He can hear you.

MARY: Good. He's lame.

BOBBY: I've never seen one up close like this.

MARY: Yeah? When I was little, they were all over this park.

BOBBY: What happened?

MARY: I think they were all shot.

BOBBY: Seriously.

MARY: Seriously, no one cares anymore. We have iPhones now.

BOBBY: I wish it would do something.

MARY: Come on. Let's go make out by the fountain.

BOBBY: Maybe if we gave it a quarter.

MARY: We shouldn't encourage him.

> *(The MIME comes unfrozen.)*

BOBBY: Look, he's waking up.

MARY: I should punch him in the nuts.

BOBBY: I think he's kind of cool.

MARY: How am I attracted to you?

> *(The MIME, carefree, merrily acknowledges BOBBY and MARY.)*

BOBBY: He's so excited to see us.

MARY: We're probably the first people to notice him in weeks.

> *(The MIME begins to walk in place.)*

BOBBY: Oh wow – how great is that!

(MARY scoffs. After a moment, the MIME performs the trapped in a box routine.)

BOBBY: *(CONT'D)*

>   *(Almost giddy.)*

Now he's trapped . . . like in a box or something. Oh brother! He's trapped in a box!

MARY: He's an asshat.

(The MIME begins to sew with needle and thread.)

BOBBY: What's he doing now? Oh, he's sewing! It's like he lives in his own world. Gee willikers, what I'd give to see what he sees!

MARY: *(Shouting at the MIME, viciously.)* Hey! You should jam that sewing needle in your eye!

BOBBY: Jesus, Mary. Behind the face, there's a human being.

MARY: He needs to hear this. Your art form, it's worn-out! You don't belong in this century! Do you hear me?

(The MIME motions for BOBBY to come closer. The MIME wants to give him a closer look at what he's sewing.)

BOBBY: He's signaling to me. He wants me to come closer.

MARY: He's ruining our date.

BOBBY: I can't walk away – it'd be rude.

(MARY sighs, totally put out. BOBBY moves closer to the sewing MIME.

The MIME calls him even closer. Closer still. BOBBY is just next to the

MIME, playing along, acting as though he is seeing what is being sewn.)

BOBBY: Wow. What is that you're sewing there? Mittens maybe?

>   *(MIME, always with a big smile, shakes his head no.)*

A blanket?

>   *(MIME shakes his head no.)*

A sweater?

>   *(MIME nods excitedly, pointing at MARY.)*

For Mary! A sweater for Mary. Aw Mary, he's sewing you a

sweater.

(The MIME stabs BOBBY in the chest with a needle. BOBBY reacts as if he's actually been stabbed and is bleeding out.)

BOBBY: *(CONT'D)* Oh god . . . god . . . Mary . . . !

MARY: Shut up, Bobby. It's not funny.

BOBBY: Mary . . . I can't . . . !

(BOBBY goes to the ground, shakes, twitches, dies. MIME continues to sew, contentedly.)

MARY: Are you happy now? Goddamn it! Bobby! Get up!

(BOBBY doesn't move. Turns to the MIME.)

Wipe that goofy grin off your face, you degenerate!

(The MIME stabs her in the right eye.)

Ahhh! What have you done!

(The MIME stabs her in the left eye.)

Ahhh! Oww! My eyes! You've blinded me! You crazy fucking mime!

(The MIME lifts needle to stab her again.)

AHHHHHHHHH!!!

(Blackout.)

2.

(As before, a MIME. Alone. Blank expression – empty, inscrutable. Hold. A smile comes over him. He begins to moonwalk, playing to the audience. Stops. He moves a finger before his lips –shhh! – but soundless. Strikes a pose. Hold.)

(A woman, ETHEL, enters on her phone, walking her dog CAPOTE on a leash.)

ETHEL: So Arthur goes in for another colonoscopy next week. I think he kind of likes getting them. I don't ask why. After forty years of marriage, you stop asking why.

(CAPOTE is smelling the MIME. Jerking the leash.)

Capote, get away from there. Capote!

(Back to phone.)

My dog, sorry. He's a poodle. Yeah, stupid, but sweet. We're in the park. Yes, the one where all those people have been murdered. How many now? Fourteen – really? I know it's been on the news.

ETHEL: *(CONT'D)*

(CAPOTE begins to hump the MIME'S leg. The MIME is unfazed.)

I'm not worried. It's broad daylight. I'm sure the killer's a long way from here.

Besides, I mind my business. Steer clear of psychos.

(Jerking the leash.)

Capote! Quit schtooping that statue!

(Back to phone.)

I'll tell you the problem, everyone's out of touch. People have stopped paying attention. It's sad, it really is. But what can one person do?

(CAPOTE begins to smell the MIME'S crotch.)

And I'll tell you something else, it's rude too. This brazen apathy. Makes you wonder, it does, what will it take for us to snap out of it?

(To CAPOTE.)

Have you gone poo? I don't have all day. Go poo.

(To phone.)

No, Claire, I was talking to the dog.

(CAPOTE begins to sniff around the MIME again.)

Yes, I should go too. We'll talk next week. My best to Herb.

(The MIME comes unfrozen. CAPOTE reacts, alarmed, barking.)

Where did he come from? It's a mime, Claire. Here in the park. Yes, the old-timey kind, the ones with the fruity berets.

(MIME begins to mime a series of lasso/rope tricks.)

They give me the willies. I've got to go. Capote's in a tizzy. Call you soon.

(Puts phone away. Tries to calm down the dog, who is disturbed by the MIME and is making it known with its yapping. The MIME begins to mime a lasso in the air, like a cowboy.)

ETHEL: *(CONT'D)* Capote! What's gotten into you! Sit! Capote!

(To the MIME.)

I hope you're pleased! Capote never acts like this. Do you have a license to perform here? Do you!

(The MIME hurls the mimed rope/lasso around CAPOTE'S neck. CAPOTE reacts as if he's actually been lassoed. A tug of war ensues between ETHEL with the real leash and the MIME with his fake lasso. In the back and forth, CAPOTE begins to strangle.)

ETHEL: *(CONT'D)* How're you doing that? Let go. You're hurting my dog. Stop! Let go of my dog!

(CAPOTE yelps, twitches, dies.)

YOU! You barbarian! You murdered Capote! You little creep! You'll pay for this! You'll . . . oh god, no . . .

(The MIME has another lasso; winds it up to snare ETHEL.)

What're you doing? Help! No . . . no . . .

(The MIME hurls the lasso at her.)

NOOOOOOO!!!

(Blackout.)

3.

(As before, a MIME. Alone. Blank expression – empty, inscrutable. Hold. A smile comes over him. He begins to mime lifting weights, at first very heavy, then very light. Stops bit. He moves a finger before his lips –shhh! – but soundless. Strikes a pose. Hold.)

(DETECTIVE FLARB enters, sits on bench, lost in thought. His partner, DETECTIVE SWAYZE, enters behind him.)

SWAYZE: How about a coffee?
FLARB: I'm good, thanks.
SWAYZE: What's on your mind?

FLARB: I can't figure this case. There's a maniac loose in this park and we got no leads. Not one. It's been weeks now.

SWAYZE: Maybe he knows something.

FLARB: Who?

SWAYZE: That mime.

FLARB: What mime?

SWAYZE: Right there.

FLARB: Oh, hell – I thought it was a birdbath. Look at him, the schmuck bastard.

SWAYZE: I bet he sees a lot.

FLARB: Maybe we should talk to him. Ask him some questions.

SWAYZE: Mimes don't talk. It's kind of their thing.

FLARB: We'll show our badges.

SWAYZE: It won't matter.

FLARB: Come on, it's just some gag he's doing.

SWAYZE: It's not a gag to mimes. They're very prideful.

FLARB: *(Derisive.)* About what?

SWAYZE: About what they do. Pantomime is the oldest form of communication. Before there was language, before there was writing, there was mime – the highest art form. It's how we told our stories, praised our gods.

FLARB: How do you know some much about this?

SWAYZE: My father was mime.

FLARB: Get out. And you never told me?

SWAYZE: It's not something you tell people. He used to perform in this very park. At that very spot. As a little girl, I'd come with him. Once we entered the park, he'd transform into this other thing, this mime. It was kind of a ritual. He was no longer recognizable as my dad. Crowds would gather – oh, how they loved him. He did all the classic bits, and even some of his own. People had such fun, and I was so proud. Then, I started noticing that, when we'd leave the park, it'd take him longer to change back to a real person. Until, finally, one day, he just didn't. He stayed a mime.

FLARB: No way.

SWAYZE: He never changed back. He'd go to work, mow the grass, even go to bed as a mime.

FLARB: That's commitment.

SWAYZE: It was more than that. It was like this other dimension had been opened to him. As if he was so focused on seeing the unseeable that it actually started to appear. His mind made something out of nothing. I think, in a way, we're all capable of that.

FLARB: Are you high?

SWAYZE: If only.

FLARB: Is your dad still alive?

SWAYZE: No. He died – right here, as a matter of fact.

FLARB: Christ.

SWAYZE: He was performing. Went into cardiac arrest, started to hemorrhage.

FLARB: Why didn't someone help him?

SWAYZE: They thought it was part of the act. He made a fortune in tips that day.

FLARB: Did he have any last words?

SWAYZE: He was a mime.

FLARB: I thought maybe –

SWAYZE: Nope. He did one peculiar thing, though. Just before his last breath he swiped some paint off his face with a finger, then smeared it on my face. As if to say –

FLARB: It's your destiny to become a mime.

SWAYZE: Yeah, right, something like that.

(Struck by the idea, but manages to let it go.)

Well, it wasn't for me.

FLARB: There was that woman, what was her name? Ethel –

SWAYZE: Rosenstein.

FLARB: Yeah, she was on the phone with her friend, remember?

SWAYZE: Yeah? So?

FLARB: Her friend said the last thing she mentioned was seeing a mime. Maybe it was him.

SWAYZE: Could be, I guess.

FLARB: Let's see what this guy knows.

SWAYZE: *(Dubious.)* Good luck.

FLARB: *(Approaching the frozen MIME.)* Hey buddy. This is Detective Swayze, I'm Detective Flarb. Can we have a few words? There have been some homicides here in the park. I was wondering if you might know anything about that.

(MIME doesn't budge.)

We'd appreciate your cooperation.

(MIME doesn't budge.)

Okay, pal, let's cut the crap. You either talk or I'm taking you in? Understood?

(FLARB moves toward the MIME, threateningly.)

SWAYZE: You shouldn't touch him. They really don't like that.

FLARB: Look at this guy. He's ignoring me. This is patent disregard for the law.

SWAYZE: You have to respect his ways.

FLARB: Oh, fuck that. Hey buddy. Hey! I'm talking to you! I said I'm talking to – you!

(FLARB pokes him, tauntingly, with his finger. On being touched, the MIME'S smile fades. His face becomes contorted, and he begins to make dull rumbling sounds, as if malfunctioning.)

SWAYZE: Now you've done it.

FLARB: Done what exactly?

SWAYZE: I have no idea.

(The MIME lets out a primal scream. It should be long and loud and unsettling.)

FLARB: That's it. I'm arresting him.

SWAYZE: For what?

FLARB: For freaking me out.

(The MIME mimes a gun. Points it at FLARB.)

Oh shit, he has a gun.

SWAYZE: It's not real.

FLARB: Call for back up.

SWAYZE: The gun's not real.

(The MIME is advancing on FLARB, who backs away.)

FLARB: Easy now. Let's not do anything rash.

SWAYZE: Flarb, listen to me – it's all fake. He's a mime.

FLARB: Right.

(Laughing it off.)

I got confused for a second. I thought, for a minute – sheesh, this is embarrassing! He's just a mime!

(The MIME fires the fake gun. We hear the gunshot. FLARB has been shot.)

Lawrence Harbison

FLARB: Is that fake too? 'Cause it really feels like I've been shot.

(The MIME shoots FLARB again.)

This joker's got talent.

(FLARB goes down. MIME stands over him. Fires once more. We hear the gunshot. FLARB is dead. Pause. The MIME looks at SWAYZE, who stands in disbelief. The MIME, still miming the gun, slowly walks to SWAYZE. The MIME hands her the gun. SWAYZE is now miming the gun, frightened. The MIME swipes paint off his face with a finger, smears it on SWAYZE'S face. Pause. The MIME'S sunny grin returns. He scampers off quickly. SWAYZE looks at the gun in her hand, then out at us, empty, inscrutable. She moves a finger before her lips – shhh! – but soundless. A smile comes over her. Hold. Fade.)

END OF PLAY

NON-REFUNDABLE

C.J. EHRLICH

NON-REFUNDABLE had its inaugural production in "Dewey 2016: Election Edition, an Evening of Comedies about Politics" in October 2016, at the Chappaqua Library Theatre, Chappaqua, NY.

Produced by The Friends of the Chappaqua Library
Contact: Katherine Whymark, chafriends@wlsmail.org
Directed by C.J. Ehrlich

CAST:
CASSIE: Katherine Whymark
WINONA: Dianne Roxy Pennington
HELGA: Julie Majchrzyk

SETTING: A shabby hotel room, somewhere in Eastern Europe.
TIME: Valentine's Day, contemporary.

CHARACTERS:

> WINONA (F, age flexible, any ethnicity), a social studies
> teacher at a middle school in Kentucky
> CASSIE (F, age flexible, any ethnicity), math teacher at the
> same school. Wears a very wrinkled dress
> HELGA (F, age flexible), burly, authoritarian Eastern
> European in a drab uniform
> Winona: pronounced as in "Winnie", not "Why-nona."
> "Moonch" is Winona's term of endearment for Cassie.

AT RISE:

Night. A spartan room in a former workers' holiday camp in Eastern Europe. A single bed, a window. A bathroom, off.

WINONA and CASSIE enter, looking like they slept in their clothes, if at all. They take in the room.

WINONA: There, Cass... What'd I tell ya. A bed. And look! A blanket. And a pillow! Mmm... Smell that fresh burlap.

Cassie screams.

CASSIE: Something ran across— Get it, get it, Winn—!

Winona checks under the bed, in the bed.

WINONA: Nothing. Clean as your reputation.

CASSIE: Oh god. I'm seeing things. So tired. So hungry. So tired—

WINONA: *(proud)* When Giggy and I stayed in Machu Picchu, the rooms were dug right into the earth. It was like being buried alive.

Cassie collapses onto the bed.

CASSIE: Wake me when the bags come.

WINONA: Up, up. It's a long march back to the dining hall. Ivan says at eight sharp they lock up the food tighter than Bibles under Stalin. Let's go get us some goulash!

Cassie groans. Winona tries to pull her up.

WINONA: *(cont'd)* OK, OK. You need fuel. Any granola bars left? Granola crumbs?

CASSIE: There's a jar of peanut butter, in my suitcase.

WINONA: It'll get here. Soon as they load up the wheelbarrows—

CASSIE: And push 'em up Mount Heart Attack.

WINONA: Hey. What's that smell? Kind of like... pork rinds?

CASSIE: *(laughing nervously)* Pork rinds! Who's hallucinating now?

(smelling her clothes)

Song-of-a-biscuit, it's old-people smell! Mothballs, gardenia tobacco, and that disgusting Nordic cough mixture.

WINONA: Cassie—"Moonch"... Be nice.

CASSIE: Our first vacation together. Why are we touring a bunch of other people's old countries with a bunch of other people's grannies? And a tour guide who hates Americans!

WINONA: We're with 'em 24-7. Might as well make friends.

CASSIE: How? The ones who hear, don't speak English. And I've had it with their Viking sing-alongs. Four hours on that median strip, wailing like it was Thor's sendoff!

WINONA: It stirred ancient race memories, when the bus caught fire.

CASSIE: And if we so much as hold hands, they're gonna chase us out of town with tar and pitchforks.

Cassie removes her dress, fans it in the air, keeps her slip on.

WINONA: There's the best scenery yet.

She starts massaging Cassie's shoulders. Cassie whimpers.

WINONA: *(cont'd)* Hey. What's this, bruise?

CASSIE: One of those grannies caned me. So she could steal our seats! Then faked she was asleep. The faking faker--

WINONA: You liked Herr and Frau Schmendermann.

CASSIE: Because you got her seat, when they dragged him off the bus.

WINONA: Boy, he went down like a house of cards, huh? This tour is not for the weak of heart.

CASSIE: You know what kept me going, grading midterms? One C after another— Jiminy Crickets, could they stop texting for five minutes, and learn similar triangles?

WINONA: What kept you going, moonch?

CASSIE: Imagining you and me, in this romantic hide-away where we can stop hiding away.

WINONA: Feel the romance. The Stasi could be spying on us right now!

CASSIE: If you wanted to be watched, we could've stayed home in Bulletsville.

WINONA: This camp was the height of luxury under Kublachev. All the trendy activities—shotput, hammer toss, artillery range—

CASSIE: See, when you say luxury, I think "spa," not "steroids."

WINONA: ...I'll call about the bags.

CASSIE: *(with knowing superiority)* Sure. And while you're at it, order a dozen roses and a big box of chocolates. On the "invisiphone."

Winona looks around. No phone.

WINONA: Ah. I'll yell out the window for the bags.

(peering out the window)

Oh... Aha. So that's it.

(turning back, mystery solved)

We overlook the dumpsters!

CASSIE: Brochure said "3-star or better." Are there negative stars?

WINONA: OK, it's a bit Spartan, but—

CASSIE: When you signed in, the desk clerk tried to mug you.

WINONA: He gave me back the watch. (beat) Imagine, Cass. Somewhere, out in that dark Bavarian forest... werewolves.

CASSIE: I'm going to splash some rusty water on my face.

Cassie exits. Winona reads loudly from a battered brochure.

WINONA: You know we're less than an hour from Bratislava's biggest gravel pit? Tomorrow, we tour the radium factory!

CASSIE: *(OFF)* My ovaries can't wait!

WINONA: And Spilberk Castle. Rated seven out of ten in Zagat's "Torture Chambers of Europe."

CASSIE: *(OFF)* Oh! You have got to be kidding. You have GOT to be—

(she re-enters)

You said "ho-tel." Not "hole toilet."

WINONA: Viva la difference! Oh no, sweetie—no—

Cassie starts to cry.

CASSIE: I'm sorry. I'm exhausted, I'm starving, my feet are on fire, I've been caned. It's, it's just so-- unfair.

WINONA: What is, moonch?

CASSIE: I am so, so tired of pretending we're just friends who teach at the same school. We finally get a chance to get out and it's a little taste of Hell.

WINONA: You know, Cass. If we worked in a rivet factory, this would be a slice of paradise.

CASSIE: And how the bejeepers could I think $399 all-inclusive made sense? For gosh-sakes, I'm a math teacher.

WINONA: When Giggy and I were in Nepal, we ate day-old momo—

CASSIE: I'M NOT GIGGY! Dysentery is not on my bucket list! We should be in Paris, ordering snails in bad French! Or in Rome, watching the gladiators. Or any big city with street lighting, a ladies' bar, and least one shop that sells pot pourri.

WINONA: Cass. Life is non-refundable. If you choose to be miser-
able—

CASSIE: Right! I sneak out with you for February break, instead of
visiting my nieces in Iowa, because I crave misery.

WINONA: So you can tell the Math department how I made you suffer?

CASSIE: The Math—what! Did you— tell Social Studies about me?

WINONA: Well I want to. Don't you want to?

CASSIE: No! Yes! I don't know, I didn't write the damn policy!

WINONA: We should sue! The union will back us. Right?

CASSIE: Sure. From the people who brought you the Six Days of
Creation, Adam and Eve wedding cakes, and the Second Coming
of Noah's Ark. Bulletsville Kentucky's first Save the Dykes rally!

*Cassie covers her mouth, shocked by her own words. Winona
shakes out Cassie's dress. An empty wrapper tumbles out.
Winona grabs it before Cassie can.*

WINONA: Pork rinds. The rest stop! You didn't save me a single rind.

CASSIE: You were off practicing your German on a border guard. The
geezers were stripping the shelves, like locusts. Oh! This whole
thing is wrong, wrong.

POUNDING on the door.

WINONA: Thank the goddess. The bags.

*Winona opens the door to HELGA, a large, humorless woman
in a drab uniform. Helga snaps to attention, salutes.*

HELGA: Welcome to Garni Vinarski Deluxe Holiday camp of many
star ratings in very democratic Slovakia.

CASSIE: It's great to be here.

HELGA: Hotel services. Room service, is no room service. Being
eating in room is to entice rodents. Meals hours, no exceptions!
Do not being early. Do not being late. You will be punished. Rec-
reation! Lake this week is 80% algae-free.

(slightly less militaristic:)

I ham providing Latvian couples massage, Moldovan eyebrow
massage. Also I ham to cleaning your room. If bribes permit.

WINONA: Uh uh. No bribes. This tour is All Inclusive.

HELGA: For extra American dollars, can be had tour of Brno post
office, casino, and historic houses of prostitutions. Ladies will be

diverted to vodka tearoom in Martyrs Square.

CASSIE: Where - is - our - LUGGAGE?

HELGA: Luggage truck is with flat tire. Repair truck, is with out-of gas.

WINONA: We'll get our own bags!

CASSIE: And carry them half a mile, up the mountain, in the dark?

HELGA: No.

CASSIE: No what?

HELGA: You cannot be leaving room. Visas please.

WINONA: The tour director has our paperwork. Ivan. We "ham to meeting him" in dining hall. You know, Ivan?

HELGA: These rooms, by lake, are residing in newly independent state of Mustovia. Long live Mustovia!

CASSIE: Long live Mustovia?

HELGA: Visa is required to pass between Slovakia and Mustovia. Is to say, to walk to dining hall.

WINONA: No, no. This is a package tour. Talk to Ivan.

HELGA: Ivan, in Slovakia. Dining hall, Slovakia. You, Mustovia.

CASSIE: We didn't see any signs of a border--

HELGA: Is dark. You make illegal crossing. One free! Now, illegal aliens, I vend you visa.

WINONA: You—Aha. I see, I see.

HELGA: Visa is include views of lake. No more sanitation pits.

CASSIE: And the right to leave our room? It's a bargain.

WINONA: No! We're paid in full. Guides, transfers. Hotels 3-star or better! No buying visas to go to dinner!

HELGA: If you are not to purchase visa, I must to make you with house arrest. Welcome, Mustovian criminals!

WINONA: This is outrageous! By what authority--

Helga puts on an official badge, takes out a set of handcuffs, and a taser.

CASSIE: Looks like authority to me, Winn!

WINONA: How much are the visas?

HELGA: How much you got?

CASSIE: Aha.

HELGA: Twenty... five. Dollars. Each... Also. Today only is include two bags pork rinds. One hundred percent Mustovian pigs.

Beat. They reach into their bras. Cassie counts the money, gives it to Helga. Helga stamps and hands over two handmade visas, and the pork rinds.

HELGA: *(cont'd)* Happy capitalist holiday proclaiming love. "Love."

Helga salutes, starts to exit. Then turns, to blow them a kiss with the hand holding the money. She laughs maniacally. Exits, Winona starts to laugh, then cry.

CASSIE: Oh. Oh! Don't cry, Winn. We have visas!

WINONA: Look at me. Can't even stand up to the Mustovian army.

CASSIE: But, they had tasers.

Winona nods tearily. Now Cassie cries.

WINONA: What, moonch, what?

CASSIE: Don't you get it, Winn? We're not compatible.

WINONA: We are very—

CASSIE: We're not vacationally compatible! You're Amelia Earhart and Annie Oakley, and, and Crocodile Dundee, and I'm-- a wimp. I can't even think of a famous wimp.

WINONA: Kim Kardashian?

CASSIE: *(crying harder)* I want a hotel with a mini-bar, and a huge bed, and a hot bath, and, and a phone to call for help when the Mustovian army invades your room. Which, admit it, you think is fun!

WINONA: So we're in the Tijuana of Eastern Europe. You gotta admit, the women are empowered.

CASSIE: Our ancestors lived like this before they came to the Land of the Free. Cripes on a cracker, why are we doing it on purpose?

WINONA: Sweetie... Moonch. We can be out of here in five minutes.

CASSIE: You mean, defect?

WINONA: We hike to the check-in. Pay the bribes. Get a haycart to town. Pull out the plastic. Zoom—Paris. Vienna. Or any of those other expensive cities everyone's been to.

CASSIE: You would ditch this 100% prepaid tour? For me?

WINONA: For you. In a second. For us!... What now?

CASSIE: I'm so selfish! You stand all night through three countries, and I eat all the pork rinds!

WINONA: Awww—

CASSIE: And three granola bars when you weren't looking. I'm an awful, terrible person.

WINONA: You're wonderful. Darn it! I'm sick of being bullied.

Everybody knows about Mrs. Marinakis and the new janitor. It's time to take a stand.

CASSIE: I'm a math teacher, not a community organizer!

WINONA: We're done tiptoeing. Everyone's gonna know.

CASSIE: We'll sit together in the faculty lounge?

WINONA: Let's not go nuts.

Cassie pulls Winona onto the bed.

CASSIE: Oh Winn. Let's do it. Occupy Principal Gunderson! But first. Let's limp to dinner and get drunk on local hooch. Listen to old-people stories. You gotta love old people. They've lived.

WINONA: Yes! Then stumble back to our upgraded room and explore.

They embrace.

CASSIE: I want to drink vodka in Martyrs Square, and see the gravel pits. With you! You know. Years from now, we'll be the only couple we know who took a romantic vacation in a country that doesn't exist, with no visas.

They kiss.

WINONA: Wash your face, my illegal alien, and let's grab that goulash. We can sit with those sisters from the back of the bus.

Cassie exits. Winona lies back.

CASSIE: *(OFF)* Honey! You bring any... toilet paper?

Winona's only answer is a slow snore.

END OF PLAY.

OUR TEN

Mark Harvey Levine

Our Ten was first produced in August 2016 by Changing Scene Theatre Northwest in Tacoma, WA. It was co-directed by Karen Hauser and Pavlina Morris.

CAST:
LAUREN - Shawna Fancher
HAILEY - Chelsea Pedro
MADISON - Lauren Gallup
GUS - Mark Peters
CLAY - Tom West
JASON - Sean Kilen
RADIO VOICES - Skye Gibbs, Jenny Kindschy, Dan Lysne, Susan
    Moblo, Tamara Nelson

CHARACTERS:

OUR TEN can be performed with as few as six actors. The parts can be divided this way:

Actor 1(F) 20's-40's: Lauren - thoughtful, kind

Actor 2(F) 20's: Talk Radio Caller - troubled / Hailey - immature

Actor 3(F) 20's-50's: Talk Radio DJ - cynical / Commercial - manic / Madison - shallow

Actor 4(M) 30's-50's: REGGAE Station DJ - calm / Commercial Disclaimer - rapid / Gus - stodgy

Actor 5(M) 20's-40's: Top 40 Morning DJ Gregg - vapid / Clay - naive

Actor 6(M) 20's-30's: Top 40 Morning DJ Steve - fake / Jason - vacuous

TIME: The present.
SETTING: The 10 freeway in Los Angeles.

The 10 freeway in Los Angeles, morning rush hour. Lauren sits in her car (represented simply by a chair), not moving. She frustratedly listens to the radio.

REGGAE station DJ: It's 8:15 in Los Angeles, and it's going to be another beautiful day. The marine layer is expected to burn off pretty early, leading to highs in the low eighties by the beaches, reaching up to nearly a hundred in the valleys, with—

She hits a preset button changing the station to—

TALK RADIO CALLER: And I'm worried, y'know?

TALK RADIO DJ: Uh huh.

TALK RADIO CALLER: Cause the economy, you know, it's affecting people in weird ways.

TALK RADIO DJ: Uh huh.

She hits another button—

TOP 40 MORNING DJ GREG: — 10 freeway is backed up from the Crenshaw exit all the way to downtown, and the 605 has two lanes closed down due to a lady giving birth to twins!

TOP 40 MORNING DJ STEVE: Twins?

TOP 40 MORNING DJ GREG: Yep twins. Right in the #3 lane.

TOP 40 MORNING DJ STEVE: Shouldn't that be the #2 lane?

They both laugh too hard at their own joke.

LAUREN: *(looking out at the traffic, banging on her steering wheel)* Come on! Let's go!

She hits the radio again—

COMMERCIAL: — hurry in now and start saving! Sale ends September 18th. Or visit us at www.-

She hits the radio again, back to the—

REGGAE DJ: — listening to KSMG, my children, broadcasting from the top of Mt. Wilson, in the city of Los Angeles, Los Angeles County, California, United States of America, Continent of North America, Western Hemisphere, the Earth, the Solar System, the Universe, the Mind of God... A ClearStar Station.

She hits the radio again, back to the—

TALK RADIO CALLER: — I mean I was crying during the last election.

TALK RADIO DJ: Oh I know.

TALK RADIO CALLER: I'm just...really worried about things...the direction this country is taking...

LAUREN: God!

She hits the radio again, back to the—

TOP 40 MORNING DJ GREG: — that even legal?

TOP 40 MORNING DJ STEVE: Having a baby?

TOP 40 MORNING DJ GREG: On the 605!

TOP 40 MORNING DJ STEVE: I think as long as she did it hands-free...

They both laugh too hard again. Lauren hits the radio again, switching to —

COMMERCIAL DISCLAIMER: *(said very fast)* limitedtimeoffernotavailableinstoresoffernotvalidinVirginiamaycausehighbloodpressuredizzinessheartattackstrokeblindnessthoughtsofsuicideordeathusewithcautionresultsmayvarybatteriesnotincludedMSRP—

Lauren punches the button again.

TALK RADIO CALLER: Nobody knows where to turn.

TALK RADIO DJ: There is nowhere.

TALK RADIO CALLER: No, there really isn't.

Lauren punches the button again.

LAUREN: *(sighing)* I'm going to be late.

TOP 40 MORNING DJ GREG: Uh oh. Now we've got word that a guy is standing on an overpass of the 10 freeway, threatening to jump.

TOP 40 MORNING DJ STEVE: It's probably the father.

TOP 40 MORNING DJ GREG: The father of the twins!

They laugh.

TOP 40 MORNING DJ STEVE: Hey you're killing yourself on the wrong freeway!

They laugh.

TOP 40 MORNING DJ GREG: Well, that's probably what's backing up the 10.

They laugh.

TOP 40 MORNING DJ STEVE: Yeah, that'll do it.

They laugh. She punches a button.

REGGAE DJ: — word from the 10 freeway, my children. There's someone on the Crenshaw overpass... threatening to jump. Police are on the scene, trying to coax him back onto the bridge.

LAUREN: Oh great...

REGGAE DJ: So, stay away from the 10 freeway if you can, and say a little prayer for that man, my children. It's a rough world out th— .

She turns off the radio. Lights change. Other people in cars (chairs) join her. They all crane their necks to see something off in the distance. Then they get out of their cars. The following dialogue should be very overlapped.

CLAY: What's going on?

JASON: — There's a guy trying to kill himself—

LAUREN: — Some guy trying to commit suicide—

CLAY: — What? —

HAILEY: — There's a guy on the bridge—

MADISON: — I heard it on the radio—

GUS: — What's the problem now?—

HAILEY: — He's threatening to jump—

LAUREN: — See him, way up there?—

CLAY: — Oh man—

HAILEY: — On the overpass—

MADISON: — Oh there he is!—

GUS: — I don't need this—

JASON: — Look at all the cops—

MADISON: — I can totally see him now— *(she takes a picture with her phone)*

GUS: — I have to get to work—

CLAY: *(to Lauren)* Hey.

LAUREN: Hi.

HAILEY: — How long has he been up there?—

GUS: — I don't know. But I have to get to work—

MADISON: — He's on the outside of the fence, standing on a little ledge—

JASON: — It's weird to be standing out here—

CLAY: — I know!—

LAUREN: — I don't think I've ever stood on the freeway before—

HAILEY: — You think he's going to jump?—

CLAY: — I hope not—

LAUREN: — It feels like breaking the rules—

MADISON: — How did he even get out there?—

JASON: — Where do you work?—

LAUREN: — Santa Monica—

CLAY: — I work in Culver City. I'm going to be late—

HAILEY: — I hope they get him down—

GUS: — We're all going to be late because of this guy—

LAUREN: — How about you?—

JASON: — I'm in Market Research. In Westwood, near UCL—

They all react — the man has jumped.

CLAY: Woah!

LAUREN: Oh God.

HAILEY: He jumped.

MADISON: Oh my God.

JASON: Okay. Scrape him up so we can go.

Lauren looks at Jason in disbelief. They all overlap each other as before.

GUS: — This town eats people up—

LAUREN: — They're getting him—

HAILEY: — Wow, that was fast—

Madison takes another picture with her phone.

MADISON: — I'm totally posting that—

CLAY: — They had an ambulance waiting—

GUS: — But that's life, y'know?—

JASON: — Alright. Back in our cars—

MADISON: — Have a good day!—

CLAY: — Nice... meeting you. I guess—

LAUREN: — Yeah... um... bye—

JASON: — Laters!—

GUS: — You just gotta keep moving...

They all get back in their chairs. Lights change to denote passage of time.

LAUREN: *(writing on her blog)* I can't believe I saw that. I can't believe that just happened. And we'll never find out about that poor man. Who he was, or why he did it. It's not... remarkable enough to be on the news... or even in a newspaper. I wonder if it would be in the paper. Does anybody still get the paper? Comment below if you do.

JASON: *(on Twitter)* Saw a guy try to snuff it on the 10 today.

MADISON: *(on Instagram)* This is a picture of a man who tried to kill himself on a freeway overpass here in LA.

LAUREN: I Googled to see if I could find out anything about him. I found a small item on a local news site. It was just two lines of text. The first line talked about how a young man had jumped off the Crenshaw overpass in an attempt to end his life.

JASON: Hashtag Suicideispainless.

CLAY: *(on Facebook)* Clay is feeling sad. No.

HAILEY: *(texting)* You guys! I totally saw someone jump onto the freeway today.

LAUREN: The second line simply read "He survived, with moderate injuries." That's it. "He survived, with moderate injuries."

MADISON: It's a little blurry, but if you look close you can see him.

JASON: Hashtag Unlessyouhitthepavement.

GUS: *(talking to friends, drinking a beer)* No, I don't post things on Facebook or the Twitter or anything.

LAUREN: It made me think about death, and our lives. And what we leave behind. I leave behind this blog, I guess. I might even be dead by the time you read this. Crazy, huh? The dead speak!

CLAY: Clay is feeling upset. Clay is horrified? No.

JASON: Hashtag Faceplant.

HAILEY: It was super weird.

LAUREN: But I never did find out why that guy wanted to kill himself. All I ever got were those two lines of text. I guess he lost hope. Or lost his connection to other people. I'm sure he felt alone.

MADISON: And this is after he jumped.

CLAY: What's a good emoticon for seeing a suicide?

HAILEY: I mean, like... really, really weird.

GUS: I just tell my wife, and then she tells the other wives, and they tell their husbands. That's my social media.

JASON: Hashtag GoAheadAndJump.

LAUREN: I think we need to just stop and wave to other folks more. I mean metaphorically. Don't do this on an actual freeway in Los Angeles, you might get shot. Just... metaphorically. Step out of the car. Stand on the pavement. And say hi.

MADISON: No filter!

HAILEY: You guys, I'm weirded out. Take me to a movie or something.

LAUREN: We're all so connected. And so not. We're all just zooming past each other, trying to get somewhere. Alone in our little chairs.

CLAY: I guess the shocked emoticon. Yeah.

GUS: I feel for the guy, y'know? Because life is hard. They don't tell you how much hard work it is. It tears at you bit by bit.

LAUREN: And we survive, with moderate injuries.

END OF PLAY

POP STAR

David MacGregor

Ohlone College Playwrights Festival, Nummi Theatre
(Fremont, CA), May 5-6, 2016

Producing Director – Michael Navarra
Director – John Vargas

SUZIE – Bre Vallado
BEN – Greg "Juice" Burhyte
TORIN – Brandon Kibbee

Stage Manager – Bobby Rodriguez
Lighting Designer – Amy Broussard

SETTING: An office.
TIME: Now and then.

CAST
SUZIE: A talent agent in her 20s-50s
BEN: A talent manager in his 20s-50s.
TORIN: A pop star in his late teens-early 20s.

NOTE: Specific cultural references can be updated if so desired.

In a typical office, SUZIE sits behind a desk while BEN paces. It's very tense as they each compulsively check their phones every five seconds.

BEN: He's coming, right? You talked to him?

SUZIE: Yes, I talked to him! He'll be here! He's very punctual.

Phones are checked again, until there is a noise offstage.

BEN: That's him!

BEN and SUZIE begin jabbering business-speak into their phones as TORIN enters. He's a good-looking young man with an easy smile and demeanor. BEN and SUZIE hold up fingers indicating TORIN should wait. The phone calls end simultaneously.

SUZIE: There he is!

BEN: Torin, my main man!

SUZIE kisses TORIN multiple times on both cheeks as BEN tries to perform some kind of elaborate handshake, then settles for a simple, old-fashioned one.

BEN: God, you look great! Doesn't he look great, Suzie?

SUZIE: He always looks great! And you know why? Because he is great!

TORIN: Thanks, guys. So what's up?

BEN: WHAZZUP!!!???

SUZIE: Torin in da house!!!

BEN and SUZIE execute a disturbing little bump and grind routine as they sing.

BEN AND SUZIE: He's a rock star! He's got it! He's our rock star! We got it!

BEN and SUZIE end their routine by "raising the roof" with their hands, then salaaming to TORIN.

TORIN: You said you wanted to see me?

SUZIE: Yes, yes, we did. Have a seat, Torin.

BEN ushers TORIN to a chair, then stands behind him, sometimes pacing, sometimes giving TORIN a shoulder massage. SUZIE sits back down behind the desk.

SUZIE: So, how are things?

TORIN: Good! I finished the concert tour six weeks ago and the new album's on track to be released in three months.

SUZIE: That's great!

BEN: That's fucking outstanding!

SUZIE: But what I meant was, what are you up to now?

TORIN: Right now? Just relaxing playing some video games with friends...oh, and I've been visiting Civil War battlefields. They're amazing!

BEN: Well, sure! I feel you! Civil War battlefields...that's on my bucket list! Are you kidding me?

SUZIE: History is so great, isn't it?

TORIN: Yeah! In fact, I was just at Gettysburg last week at this place called Cemetery Ridge, which they left exactly the same as it was back in 1863, and I started thinking about what happened there, you know, Pickett's Charge, and all the men who died, and I just started crying. And I'm feeling a little embarrassed, but then, like twenty yards away, there's this huge guy, and he's just sobbing. And his wife is trying to console him and he says to her, "It hurts my heart, Mama." And it does. It really does. It's incredibly moving.

SUZIE: Right.

BEN: And don't you be ashamed of crying. I'm a huge fan of crying and you are a rock star!

SUZIE: Absolutely! But Torin, the thing is, and Ben and I were talking about this, we're concerned that you might be dropping off the public's radar a little bit.

TORIN: I was just on a seven-month international concert tour that made fifty million dollars.

SUZIE: Which ended six weeks ago.

BEN: And in entertainment terms, that's like when dinosaurs ruled the earth.

SUZIE: Bingo! And with the album not coming out for another three months, that's a concern. We need to keep your Q Score up to get the traction we're looking for on the album.

BEN: Exactly! So, as your agent and manager, it is our responsibility to keep your name out there, up there, and in there. Capisce?

TORIN: I think it's pretty out there. When I buy a gallon of milk at the drug store, half the magazines on the counter have my face on them.

BEN: Only half?

SUZIE: See, that's a problem. The public has the attention span of a brain-damaged mosquito and we cannot allow you to go four or five months off the grid. So, Ben and I have come up with a little publicity booster for you. Ben?

BEN: Okay, here's what we've set up. You're going to love this! First, you get legally drunk, which is going to be a blood alcohol level of at least zero point eight. Then, around midnight or so, you get in your Lamborghini, head out to Highway 42, and crank that baby up to 150, 160 miles an hour. We'll make a call to the state police saying there's some maniac on Highway 42, you'll get pulled over, and when you get out of the car, you say...

BEN holds out his hand and snaps his fingers. SUZIE gives him a sheet of paper, which he hands to TORIN, who reads it out loud.

TORIN: "What the fuck is this? This is bullshit. Who the fuck do you think you are? Do you know who I am?"

SUZIE: And that's the important line, "Do you know who I am?" Make sure the cop isn't in the way of his dashboard camera. We want that nice and clear for TV and the Internet.

TORIN looks from to SUZIE to BEN in disbelief.

TORIN: I don't talk like this.

BEN: Well, no, of course not! But you're drunk! You're out on a wild, midnight rampage! That's the way you roll! No laws, no limits, you're a rebel!

TORIN: And I don't own a Lamborghini.

BEN: You don't own a Lamborghini?

(to SUZIE)

Why doesn't he own a Lamborghini?

SUZIE scribbles down a note.

SUZIE: I'm on it, I'm on it!

BEN: I make another call to the paparazzi who will be at the police station by the time you arrive. You swear some more, try to cover your face, but not really, maybe throw a punch or two, and we're golden.

TORIN: You're saying you want me to become a criminal?

SUZIE: No, of course not! Not a real criminal!

BEN: Not a criminal criminal!

SUZIE: A celebrity criminal! There's a big difference.

BEN: Huge difference! And you've got to give your fans—

SUZIE: Your core fans—

BEN: —a little something extra once in a while to prove that you still have it. We're talking street cred, my man!

SUZIE: And I'm sorry, but with all due respect, having a bit of a cry at some cemetery isn't going to do that.

BEN: You will not be tamed! Yes, you sing catchy pop tunes, but you're tortured and sad and lonely.

SUZIE: Incredibly lonely, which is why you go out for drunken, late-night reckless drives by yourself. To kill the pain!

BEN: That's what your public wants, someone to worry about...

SUZIE: ...to care about...

BEN: ...someone they could love and save if they ever actually got the chance to meet you, which, don't worry, they won't.

SUZIE: And that's what we're selling here, Torin. We're selling hope. But you need to give your fans something to hope for—

BEN: —which you're not doing if you're happy and well-adjusted and taking tours of historical sites.

TORIN: I don't know. You're asking me to break the law.

BEN throws his hands up in exasperation.

BEN: You see? What did I tell you, Suzie? I give up. You can't help someone who doesn't want to be helped.

SUZIE: Ben, let me handle this.

(to TORIN)

Okay, we didn't want to bother you with the whole big-picture thing, because that's our job. But the big picture is this. You're a very attractive and bright young man—

BEN: He's a fucking genius! Everyone knows that! MENSA should be asking to join you!

SUZIE: —and you know this whole "pop star" thing is going to fade away. That's just how these things work. Now, we talked about getting you into movies and acting, remember that?

TORIN: Sure! I'd love to act.

SUZIE: Okay then! Look at this whole drunk driving arrest deal as research.

TORIN: How is it research?

SUZIE: This is what actors do! It's not enough to simply imagine a role! You can't just pretend! You need to know what it's like to be drunk and see those police lights in your rearview mirror! Know what it's like to be booked and photographed and thrown into a cell with convicted felons! You need to see it and taste it and smell it so you can draw upon those experiences when you're making a movie!

TORIN: So, Method Acting?

BEN: There you go! Brando, Pacino, Hoffman...all those nut jobs! When Jim Carrey made those Dumb and Dumber movies, he wasn't just playing dumb, he was really that dumb! He immersed himself in complete, moronic, idiotic, stupidity. And he did that for us!

SUZIE: For all of us!

TORIN: So this would be research?

SUZIE: The best kind of research! Not just reading about it, but living it.

BEN: And hello! Bonus! The Twitterverse would explode! Ooh, best idea yet! We'll get you a dash-cam for your drunken drive, then leak the footage to TMZ and Buzzfeed!

SUZIE: Oh my God, I just got moist.

BEN: Me too!

(to TORIN)

So, that's the plan! What do you say, big dog?

TORIN stands up to think.

TORIN: How fast did you want me to go again?

BEN: Minimum one-fifty. But hey, if you're feeling it, crank it up, bad boy! Let the Lambo unwind!

TORIN: But I don't think I've ever gone over eighty-five. How about this? I'll go...ninety, and I don't need to be drunk or have a Lamborghini, I'll just use my Jeep. How would that be?

SUZIE: What part of this are you not getting?

BEN: Aside from everything?

TORIN: I'm just not comfortable with getting drunk and driving a sports car a hundred and fifty miles an hour for publicity.

BEN: I don't know what to say. I thought you were serious about your career.

SUZIE: Ben! Stand down, okay? We'll...we'll just have to come up with someone else—something else!

TORIN: Okay, that would be great.

(an idea strikes him)

I like helping out at animal shelters and talking at teen centers!
SUZIE: We'll keep that in mind.
TORIN: Great. Well, thanks you guys. Thanks for understanding.
BEN: We'll call you.

There's an awkward moment as TORIN looks around, but BEN and SUZIE avoid eye contact. TORIN exits.

BEN: And you can stick a fork in his ass, because he is done.
SUZIE: It's so sad. I mean, we tried, didn't we?
BEN: Hey, there's some people you just can't help.
SUZIE: Well...onward and upward. What do you got for me?
BEN touches his phone and does a quick scroll.
BEN: Nebraska girl. Sixteen. Farm-raised and corn fed, blue eyes, size two, slightly pigeon-toed. You?

SUZIE scrolls on her phone.

SUZIE: Twin brothers from the Bronx. Eighteen. Bi-racial with green eyes, but complexion issues...
BEN: *(checking his phone)* Emo suburban kid, nicely tatted, good hair—
SUZIE: Can he actually sing?

BEN bursts into laughter and SUZIE joins him. BEN points at SUZIE.

BEN: You still got it!
SUZIE: *(pointing back)* You still got it! You know what? I'm saying farm girl. America's new Dairy Queen!
BEN: Sold! Let's ride that pony till she drops!

They touch their phones together, toasting their new plan, then start tapping maniacally at their phones as lights fade.

END OF PLAY.

SPEED MATING

David Guaspari

Produced by Playwrights Roundtable, Summer Shorts 2016
Orlando Shakespeare Center July 15-31, 2016

PATTI: Carmen Borja
CHICK: Thomas Rivera
SAM: Jake Teixeira
FRANCES: Vanessa Toro

Director: BeeJay Clinton

CHARACTERS:

Chick	male, about the same age as all the others
Sam	male
Patti	female
Frances	female

SETTING: The present. Summer. A field.

AT RISE: CHICK and SAM curled up on one side of the field, PATTI and FRANCES on the other. All seem to be asleep. An alarm clock beside CHICK rings. He bolts upright, silences the clock, and shakes SAM.

CHICK: Rise and shine! We're the men of the hour!

SAM: What year is it?

(CHICK checks the clock.)

CHICK: Eighteen.

SAM: I'm beat … I woke up at 12 and could not get back—

CHICK: Our one and only chance to *mate*. Here's the program.

(CHICK hands a piece of paper to SAM.)

SAM: *(Reading)* "Years 1 through 17: pupate. Year 18, minutes 1 to 60: Emerge … Mate …" Where's page two?

(CHICK has begun a sort of disco-inspired twitching.)

CHICK: Wherever.

SAM: Seventeen years of sucking sap from tree roots …

CHICK: And now it's time to *work* on those *moves*.

SAM: … an hour of meaningless sex …

CHICK: Yesssss!

SAM: … and then?

CHI

CK: Retirement … travel … whatever.

SAM: Look. There's no number. If there *is* a page two shouldn't this say "one"? And if there's not? If this is all there is? Sucking sap; a burst of whoopee, which I'm not even sure what that amounts to; then nothing? forever?

CHICK: Bummer. Call me if you find page two. I'll be emerging.

(SFX: Alarm clock. PATTI and FRANCES spring awake.)

PATTI: Party time!

FRANCES: *(Studying the clock.)* Behind schedule already. Two full minutes.

PATTI: Two minutes into party time!

FRANCES: In another 58 we'll be dead. How did you talk me into buying such a cheap biological clock?

(PATTI primps, sprays herself and FRANCES from an atomizer.)

PATTI: Don't forget your pheremones.

FRANCES: You're just going to rush out there? With no plan? Have you got the faintest idea how to … Do It?

PATTI: I think that part just happens.

FRANCES: Or what comes next?

(Showing PATTI a thick glossy bridal magazine.)

Be glad we're not fireflies. Afterward … we'd be supposed to bite their heads off and eat the rest.

PATTI: Eeeeuuuuggh.

(SAM and CHICK emerge, SAM still clutching the program.)

CHICK: Wow! Who knew it would be so big? Or so bright? It makes you feel … I don't know … feel so …

SAM: Pathetic? Worthless? Insignificant?

(PATTI and FRANCES emerge.)

CHICK: Girls!

SAM: What makes you think so?

FRANCES: *There's* two who'd look better without their heads.

CHICK: I know'em when I see'em—

PATTI: I think they're cute.

FRANCES: They can't be the only things under that rock.

CHICK: —and know how I feel, deep down. I feel the need … to fly!

SAM: "Emerge. Mate." Where does it say "fly"? Someone could get killed.

CHICK: A Mating Flight!

(CHICK takes off and frantically flits about, buzzing and showing off his moves. SFX: Ticking clock.)

PATTI: Wow! Will you get a load of *that*?

(FRANCES consults her magazine.)

FRANCES: Hymenoptera? … Nope … Lepidoptera? … Don't think so … Diptera? … I don't know *what* that is.

PATTI: I'd bite its head off any day.

(CHICK lands beside SAM. The ticking clock stops.)

CHICK: I'm a natural! Who needs a program?

SAM: Someone hoping for an encore?

FRANCES: *(Reading from her magazine)* "The male accompanies his acrobatic flight with a wide variety of sounds—buzzes, clicks, and ticks—all designed to attract and impress a mate."

PATTI: I'm impressed.

FRANCES: "But the female is fussy. This is the big decision of her life—and on it depends the fate of her species. She will reject many suitors and choose the fittest she can find."

PATTI: I'll take him.

(PATTI launches herself unsteadily.)

FRANCES: Fitness! Fitness! Decision-wise, this is major!

(PATTI wobbles away.)

Slut!

CHICK: Here comes one. Go for it.

SAM: You're the natural.

CHICK: Takin' a breather. Go ahead. There's more where that one came from.

SAM: You want me to skip right to the end of the page?

CHICK: Live a little.

SAM: I've seen the bottom line: "Mate." The End? No way I'm going there without knowing what's next.

(SAM, backing away from PATTI, bumps into FRANCES. Startled, she turns fiercely—as though as though she's going to bite his head off—then recovers her composure.)

FRANCES: What are you doing? Where are you going? What *are* you?

SAM: Is that a trick question?

(FRANCES makes a sound effect: the sound on a quiz show that means "wrong answer.")

FRANCES: Your job is to impress. You're supposed to be up there, buzzing, twitching, flitting …

SAM: Not till I've seen the rest of this.

(SAM shows FRANCES the program.)

FRANCES: Still using the cheat sheet? What have you been doing for the last 17 years? What a species! We might as well throw in the towel, just go extinct.

(SAM seizes FRANCES's bridal magazine and starts eagerly turning its pages.)

SAM: Is this the rest of the program? My god—whoever god is; my vocabulary's rudimentary—look at the size of the thing! I knew it! I knew we were creatures of destiny!

(SAM stops turning pages.)

Woah. Glad I'm not a firefly.

FRANCES: What should matter to you is whether *I'm* a firefly.

(PATTI lands beside FRANCES.)

PATTI: I'm in love. And it's forever.

FRANCES: *(Checking the clock)* Or 30 minutes, whichever comes first.

PATTI: Did you see where he went?

(Finally noticing SAM, but continuing to speak to FRANCES.)

Aren't you the sly one? Nag nag nag. Fitness. Selectivity. *After* you've already got yours. So … have you two … you know … already …? What was It like?

FRANCES: Be serious. You call that fit?

PATTI: It looks all there to me.

FRANCES: It hasn't got a clue. You know how it got here? On foot.

PATTI: But you found each other. That's love. Kismet. What else is life for?

FRANCES: Life is not for romance. It's for selection.

(SFX: Ticking clock. PATTI searches the sky.)

PATTI: It's him!

(CHICK lands behind PATTI. The ticking sound stops.)

CHICK: What's happ'nin'?

(PATTI turns fiercely, ready to bite his head off, then melts.)

PATTI: It's you!

(CHICK shows some moves.)

(To FRANCES) It's him. (To CHICK) I want to have thousands of your babies.

FRANCES: You intend to propagate with that?

PATTI: Mine didn't *walk* here.

FRANCES: And you think that one's mine?

CHICK: My man! Finally gettin' jiggy with the ladies!

PATTI: We'll fly away and live happily ever after.

SAM: *(To PATTI)* Dream on. You think your life could amount to more than one frantic hump?

CHICK: Absolutely. Come on out to the swamp, Tonto. It's bam, bam,

bam, non-stop. Unbelievable. Enough to kill a man.

PATTI: Life *has* a meaning: find true love and raise healthy babies I've already chosen names—Aaron, Abby, Abdullah, Abe, Abner, Adam, Adelle, Adolf, Adrian, Agamemnon—

FRANCES: It's about improving the species—by ruthlessly weeding out the unfit.

CHICK: Bummer. I say, Let's avoid extinction while the sun shines.

(SFX: Ticking clock. The sound grows slowly louder until the final blackout.)

Ladies? They're playing Our Song.

(CHICK launches another Mating Flight.)

PATTI: I'm so nervous. Will he respect me in the morning?

FRANCES: I wouldn't worry about that.

(PATTI launches herself.)

PATTI: Wish me luck!

(PATTI and CHICK exit, mating. SAM starts to walk away.)

FRANCES: Where do you think you're going? You're going to let their kind populate the next generation?

SAM: It's no skin off my—

(Pointing to his nose)

I don't even know what this is! I'm thirty minutes old! I need vocabulary! What words can I have for my situation?

FRANCES: Hexapods like us have obligations to the species. You and I are not prisoners of blind instinct. We're on the same page.

SAM: Page one?

FRANCES: That's the page we've got. Duty calls.

SAM: Give me one good reason.

(FRANCES makes a clumsy "mating flight" move.)

You call that a reason?

(SAM makes a clumsy, involuntary move in reply.)

FRANCES: This is it. The real thing: sexual selection.

SAM: You're trying to distract me.

(SAM makes another involuntary move. They both start to move.)

2017 The Best Ten-Minute Plays

Now what?

FRANCES: I think the rest just happens.

SAM: And after page one?

FRANCES: Whatever.

SAM: So ...?

FRANCES: So we fly. Ready?

SAM: We fly!

(As they launch themselves—

SFX: Alarm.

—SAM and FRANCES keel over slump, simultaneously. BLACKOUT.)

TIGHT CURLS TODAY

Jennifer Barclay

Originally produced at the Samuel French Off Off Broadway Short Play Festival, August 11, 2016 at Classic Stage Company in New York City. The cast was DEBS: Stephanie Weeks, RACHELLE: Allyson Morgan, HILDY: Pearl Rhein. Directed by Jessi D. Hill.

SETTING: A hair salon with three hair-dryer chairs (the kind that look like space-age helmet contraptions).

CHARACTERS (3F):
Hildy: the eldest
Debs: the middle
Rachelle: the youngest

NOTE: Time moves differently here.

It's hard to hear when your head is stuck in a hair-dryer chair.

HILDY: I use vegetable oil.

DEBS: *(hasn't heard)* What's that?

RACHELLE: *(hasn't heard)* What's that?

HILDY: Vegetable oil. That's what I use.

DEBS: Sure. Sure. Well, it's slick.

RACHELLE: What, peanut? Olive? Coconut?

DEBS: Coconut's not a vegetable, Rachelle.

HILDY: Can't use peanut. Roy's allergic.

RACHELLE: So that matters? Allergies? I mean

HILDY: Waddaya mean? Of course allergies matter.

RACHELLE: But I mean, even when you're talking about...

DEBS: Why wouldn't allergies matter?

RACHELLE: I mean, if you're putting it up his you-know-what?!

DEBS: SHHH!

The women look around, mortified. They stick their heads back under their respective dryer contraptions.

Time passes.

DEBS: I got tight curls today. For a change.

HILDY: You always get tight curls.

DEBS: *(hasn't heard)* What's that?

HILDY: I said what a nice change of pace.

DEBS: Yes, yes it is.

RACHELLE: Bobby must be, what? Five?

DEBS: He's four.

RACHELLE: But he's big.

DEBS: He's normal. Fiftieth percentile.

RACHELLE: Bet he keeps you running.

DEBS: He's pretty sedentary, actually.

RACHELLE: Growing up, all I did was watch cartoons. That hedge-hog. And the talking broom. Those were my favorites. If something came out of my vagina, something besides the normal fluids, I would be terrified.

HILDY: Not if it'd been baking inside of you for well over 9 months and you couldn't wait to giddyup.

DEBS: How's that handyman of yours?

HILDY: He fixed my toilet.

DEBS: And?

HILDY: And my sink.

DEBS: And?

HILDY: *(a naughty grin)* And my dry streak.

RACHELLE: It doesn't sound like a dry streak if you and Roy are playing with vegetable oil.

HILDY: That's only on Sundays. Married sex is only on Sundays.

DEBS: My knees crack. When I walk downstairs. It's very loud. It's kind of embarrassing. Does that happen to either of you?

HILDY: No.

RACHELLE: No, for me it's my ankles.

RACHELLE: That's not how it's going to be for me and Buddy. We're not gonna just have Sunday sex.

HILDY: Soon you'll be asking for my handy man's digits.

DEBS: And buying peanut oil.

RACHELLE: Buddy and me have selected only sunflowers for our wedding because we always want to be facing into the light. Into our future. And we're giving all our wedding money to charities. Ones that deal with deformed children. And instead of a honeymoon, we're going to build some houses in Botswana--

DEBS: Is this the impotent guy?

RACHELLE: Buddy. My fiancee.

HILDY: *(to Debs)* Yeah, he's the impotent guy.

Rachelle fumes and sticks her head back under the dryer. The other two follow suit.

Time passes.

HILDY: Bobby is what, 16?

DEBS: Bobby? 18, actually.

HILDY: He's graduating, then?

DEBS: No, he's killing himself.

HILDY: *(not hearing)* What's that?

DEBS: No, he's giving of himself.

HILDY: I didn't hear you.

DEBS: I said he's joining the army.

RACHELLE: I use a frozen banana. Peeled.

DEBS: *(admonishing)* Rachelle.

RACHELLE: I'm not ashamed of it. It's our thirteenth anniversary this week, and I prefer Chiquita Banana to Buddy's advances.

DEBS: I never thought of freezing it.

HILDY: B-12 is important.

DEBS: I have a B-12 deficiency.

RACHELLE: I have lupus. But it's not serious.

DEBS: I have slight anemia.

RACHELLE: And minor scoliosis.

DEBS: I've got a thing called vaso-vago-syncope. It sounds like a band.

HILDY: I have a lump in my breast.

RACHELLE: Good god.

HILDY: But I don't think it's the kind of lump you have to worry about. I think it's just a, what do they call it? Fleshy deposit.

RACHELLE: Still you should get it checked out.

HILDY: Of course I'll get it checked out.

(realizing, to Rachelle)

I've eaten bananas at your house. I've eaten banana splits.

RACHELLE: I'm not going to apologize. I'M DONE APOLOGIZING!

The three women put their heads back under their hair dryers.

Time passes.

DEBS: I'm getting tight curls today.

RACHELLE: Oh, that'll be nice for a change.

HILDY: How's your plumbing, Debs?

Beat: Debs ignores her.

HILDY: Debs? Just wondering how's your plumbing?

RACHELLE: Sometimes my toilet won't stop running. It runs and runs and runs and I know I should stick my hand in there and fix it because who else is going to do it? It's not like anybody is around to help, because evidently I talk to much. And too loud. And I snore when I'm awake. So I'm all alone. But the toilet doesn't bother me, I find, if I just close the door.

HILDY: Debs!

DEBS: YES YOUR HANDY MAN IS VERY HANDY, VERY HANDY INDEED, IS THAT WHAT YOU WANT ME TO SAY?!

HILDY: There's a blockage. In my sink. That's all.

RACHELLE: *(to Debs)* Isn't the handyman young enough to be your son?

HILDY: Rachelle!

RACHELLE: What?

HILDY: I told you!

RACHELLE: What, I'm not allowed to say "son"?

HILDY: Not to Debs. It's inconsiderate.

RACHELLE: I wasn't even referencing--

DEBS: I SAW BOBBY THE OTHER DAY.

Silence.

HILDY: Oh, Debs...

DEBS: He wasn't a ghost. He wasn't a saint. He was just wearing jeans and fruit-of-the-loom, he was just 25 like he was the last time I saw him. But he had this mole on his face. A very large mole. I thought it was chocolate and I tried to rub it off, but it stuck. It was permanent. And I'd never noticed it before. What kind of a mother never notices that her son has a mole on his face?

Beat.

HILDY: I have to pee. My bladder isn't what it used to be. Excuse me, I have to pee.

Hildy exits. Debs and Rachelle put their heads back under their dryers.

Pause: time passes.

DEBS: I'm getting tight curls today.

(beat)

I said—

RACHELLE: That's nice, Debs.

DEBS: How's the handyman?

RACHELLE: I'm alone, Debs. I'm all alone.

Beat.

DEBS: Bobby would have been 40. Today. Today would have been over the hill.

RACHELLE: That's very sad.

DEBS: Is it?

RACHELLE: I don't know what to say.

DEBS: I heard that Hildy left you her magazine collection.

RACHELLE: Yes, she did.

DEBS: She left me her kitchen. Bottles and bottles of peanut oil. She looked younger in the casket, wouldn't you say? I think she looked lovely. And her perm, it never looked better.

RACHELLE: I'm all alone.

DEBS: No, you're not.

RACHELLE: What happened? Debs? What's happening to us? We're all alone.

Debs reaches out her hand. Rachelle looks at it for a minute. Then she takes hold of it.

They hold hands. Their perms bake.

End of play.

TRUDY, CAROLYN, MARTHA, AND REGINA TRAVEL TO OUTER SPACE AND HAVE A PRETTY TERRIBLE TIME THERE

James Kennedy

"Trudy, Carolyn, Martha, and Regina Travel to Outer Space and Have a Pretty Terrible Time There" had its world premiere at the 2016 Humana Festival of New American Plays at Actors Theatre of Louisville on April 9th, 2016. The production was directed by Jessica Fisch, the set design was by Justin Hagovsky, the costume design was by Christopher Kastle, the lighting design was by Dani Clifford, the sound design was by Sam Kusnetz; the dramaturg was Jessica Reese and the stage manager was Paul Mills Holmes.

The cast was as follows:

MARTHA: Shirine Babb
CAROLYN: Renata Friedman
TRUDY: Rachel Leslie
REGINA: Brenda Withers

CHARACTERS: TRUDY
CAROLYN
MARTHA
REGINA
and
PATRICE (whom we never meet)

All five are young astronauts.

TIME: Now.
PLACE: The control room of a sleek American spacecraft traveling
through the outer reaches of the known galaxy.
Inside a spaceship in the most outer of all space.
The four astronauts sit in four chairs, strapped in.
There is a fifth chair that is empty.

It's incredibly boring in outer space. I mean so fucking boring.
Still, there is work to be done; buttons to be pushed, switches
to be flipped, knobs to be turned. Martha is asleep. Everyone
else is looking out into the abyss, occasionally busying them-
selves with astronaut tasks.

CAROLYN: What are your hobbies, Regina?

REGINA: I like to make soap. And candles.

CAROLYN: Really.

REGINA: My idea of a perfect day is staying inside, making soap, and watching documentaries about the KKK.

Trudy and Carolyn consider this.

CAROLYN: Wow. Huh. That's, uh…not something I think I would ever…ever do…to pass the time…or express myself creatively.

REGINA: Don't knock it til you try it.

CAROLYN: I guess.

REGINA: It's really powerful. And humanizing. I think it's important to remind ourselves of our capacity for evil. Those KKK members are so hateful…probably beyond repair. But they didn't come into the world that way, right? Something had to happen to make them that way, which I think is really a big metaphor for the demons inside all of us. And watching that footage while making soap… smelling lye, and vanilla extract…remembering how beautiful the planet earth is…giving myself a tool to cleanse away the grime of daily life…those days really do remind me of my place within it all. Ya know?

Trudy and Carolyn consider this. Simultaneously:

CAROLYN: That's deep.   TRUDY: What is wrong with you.

REGINA: Well, you think about this stuff too, right?

TRUDY: No.

CAROLYN: I think about…things…sure. But…the way you put that, was—

TRUDY: Really upsetting.

CAROLYN: Not that upsetting, but it was pretty—

TRUDY: I'm very upset right now.

REGINA: I thought we had reached a place where we could be really honest with each other and stuff.

TRUDY: No, Regina, we absolutely have not reached any sort of place where it would be appropriate to share that, in fact I cannot imagine any context at all any place ever where I would want to know any of that. Quite frankly I'm already very upset about the fact that I haven't sat on a real toilet in nineteen weeks nor have I worn a pair of sweatpants nor have I felt gravity nor have I eaten anything that wasn't freeze-dried nor have I punched a punching bag and also I have no idea how the Steelers are playing this season which is really difficult for me and now I have to picture you in your underwear and a pair of rubber gloves making bath salts and fetishizing the KKK. I am only a human woman, Regina, and I do not have the emotional capacity for all of this, nor does Carolyn.

REGINA: I appreciate your humanity, Trudy. Your emotional honesty is beautiful.

TRUDY: I would highly suggest that you stop speaking to me for an indefinite amount of time because, to let you in on a secret that actually isn't a secret except that you can't open your eyes to your reality: you, Regina, are right now in the lead to be the next one.

Regina processes this information.

REGINA: Is this true, Carolyn?

CAROLYN: ...I'm still on the fence about it...but you might want to give it a rest.

Martha makes a noise in her sleep.

CAROLYN: How is Martha still asleep.

REGINA: Some people can sleep anywhere.

CAROLYN: It's gotta be going on thirteen hours now.

REGINA: I think it's only been three or four.

TRUDY: No way.

REGINA: No, I'm sure of it, I keep checking my watch.

CAROLYN: I hate this.

TRUDY: We all hate this.

REGINA: I don't hate this.

TRUDY: Three out of four of us hate this.

REGINA: You can't speak for Martha.

TRUDY: Trust me, Martha hates this.

REGINA: Patrice didn't hate this. Patrice was having a great time.

TRUDY: Yeah, and look where she ended up. Not having such a great time anymore, which is her own fault, so if you do want to include Patrice in this, I would posit that in fact four out of five of us would do absolutely anything to be absolutely anywhere else right now.

Rest.

CAROLYN: I thought I would get used to the fact that time doesn't work up here, at least not in any real way...every hour looks exactly the same. I can't keep up, my body is so confused.

Martha makes another noise in her sleep.

REGINA: But still...yes, it's been somewhat of a...well, challenging adventure...I for one certainly thought there'd be more to...I don't know...do. But then all of those stars...it's been nineteen weeks and I'm still so overwhelmed...

TRUDY: So many freaking stars.

REGINA: They're so beautiful.

TRUDY: I hate myself.

REGINA: Think about it, though. We're the only four people in the entire universe with this view...the only four human beings who have ever seen this.

CAROLYN: Huh.

REGINA: That makes it worth it. Just, all of this beauty—

Martha makes a really ugly gross sleeping noise. Carolyn considers her.

CAROLYN: How far would you go with Martha?

TRUDY: How far?

CAROLYN: Yeah. You know, like first base, second base...

REGINA: Oooooooh!

TRUDY: Absolutely not.

CAROLYN: You don't think about these things?

TRUDY: I'm not about to discuss any of this with any of you.

REGINA: But we're you're friends.

TRUDY: Nuh-uh.

REGINA: Well, I'd certainly want to...snuggle...with her.

CAROLYN: Solid answer.

TRUDY: There's no snuggling in outer space.

CAROLYN: Not with that attitude.

TRUDY: If you want to unfasten your seatbelts and float away into the abyss, by all means, be my guest, I would finally get some peace and quiet.

CAROLYN: Just look at her little face though...perfect and yummy...

REGINA: It's true, she's so beautiful, I've been jealous since day one…

Martha chokes on her own phlegm and jolts awake.

MARTHA: Hey.

CAROLYN: Good morning, princess.

MARTHA: How's it going?

TRUDY: You know exactly how it's going. Nothing has changed in nineteen weeks, what a dumb question.

MARTHA: *(yawning)* Wow, ok, I'm just making polite conversation here…

CAROLYN: Trudy's in a bad mood today.

MARTHA: There must be something magical about a lack of gravity combined with filtered oxygen, because I just keep sleeping so well!

REGINA: It's true, you have.

MARTHA: I've been documenting my sleeping patterns since we blasted off, actually, and it's super fascinating. I'm a terrible sleeper back home, but up here, it's the exact opposite. I wonder why that is? *(She goes to get her sleep journal but notices the empty chair)* Where's Patrice?

An uncomfortable moment.

REGINA: There was a bit of…an incident.

MARTHA: An incident?

REGINA: Yes…and now Patrice isn't here anymore.

MARTHA: She's not here?

CAROLYN: No.

MARTHA: Well where is she?

Regina, Carolyn, and Trudy look out into the abyss. After a moment, Martha realizes.

MARTHA: No!

TRUDY: Oh yes, Martha.

REGINA: We can explain—

MARTHA: You ejected her?

CAROLYN: It's complicated…

TRUDY: It's really not. She was getting on our nerves. Wasn't she getting on your nerves?

MARTHA: Well—yes—she was—she is annoying—she was annoy-ing?—oh my god, but you ejected her.

TRUDY: We took a vote.

MARTHA: I didn't vote.

TRUDY: I voted for you.

REGINA: She does that sometimes.

TRUDY: You were asleep.

MARTHA: When did this happen?

CAROLYN: A while ago.

REGINA: *(checking her watch)* Two hours, give or take…

MARTHA: And now she's…

CAROLYN: Floating…forever…bouncing around between the stars and planets and meteors.

REGINA: Do you think she's already…you know…

CAROLYN: It's been over two hours, Regina. Of course she's already—

TRUDY: She deserved it.

MARTHA: Oh my god.

TRUDY: I hope she got sucked into a black hole.

MARTHA: I didn't know we could—

CAROLYN: They told us at training how to do it—

MARTHA: Right, fine, but I didn't think we actually would ever—

CAROLYN: The rules don't apply once you leave the Milky Way.

MARTHA: Wow.

> *Rest.*

MARTHA: Now what?

CAROLYN: We keep moving forward. Stay focused on the mission. Keep looking.

REGINA: Right.

TRUDY: It'll be much easier now.

MARTHA: What are we even looking for?

> *A moment of slow realization.*

TRUDY: What did you say?

MARTHA: I mean, we've been out here for nineteen weeks…plus the two months of training prior to the mission…and maybe it's because my brain is still waking up from that nap, but I can't remember anyone ever telling us what we're supposed to be looking for, or how long it's supposed to take.

CAROLYN: Wait, c'mon, they told us//

REGINA: Of course they told us…Carolyn, I thought I remember you saying—

CAROLYN: Lemme think for a sec. We're looking for…important…outer space…science…stuff.

MARTHA: But even if we find anything, who do we report to? How do we contact them?

TRUDY: Oh my god.

CAROLYN: I thought Regina was in charge of that.

REGINA: It's definitely not me. Trudy?

TRUDY: I'm only responsible for this lever.

REGINA: Well what does the lever do??

TRUDY: I don't know, I'm just supposed to keep pushing the lever!!

REGINA: Martha?!

MARTHA: I'm in charge of documenting our findings.

TRUDY: What findings?!

REGINA: You mean you're not in charge of navigation?

MARTHA: I thought you were in charge of navigation!

CAROLYN: Wait! Maybe Patrice was in contact with home base? She was always whispering things--

TRUDY: She was just talking to herself.

CAROLYN: No one was in contact with anyone this entire time???

TRUDY: This isn't happening.

MARTHA: So we were sent into space with no way of contacting home, with limited food and supplies…

CAROLYN: We don't even know how to turn this spaceship around—

REGINA: We don't know where we are in the entire galaxy—

CAROLYN: Martha what do we do??!?

MARTHA: Everybody stay cool. Let me be rational for a second.

Everyone tries to stay calm with varying degrees of success.

MARTHA: Taking ten steps back: why did we sign up for this?

TRUDY & CAROLYN: Money.   REGINA: It's always been my dream to be an astronaut.

MARTHA: Right. Okay. But now, I'm wondering…even if the money were to magically appear…if we can't turn this spaceship around, and we don't know how or if we're ever going to go home…what would the money be good for?

CAROLYN: You mean, we—

TRUDY: YES, Carolyn. That is what she means. This has all been a joke from the beginning—a joke we ALL fell for, which is what happens when you just trust everything people tell you. We trusted those friendly, polite NASA motherfuckers and look where we ended up.

MARTHA: I can't believe I didn't realize this earlier.

CAROLYN: It's not your fault, we were lied to. Somebody will fix this.

TRUDY: This is the worst day of my life.

CAROLYN: SOMEBODY WILL FIX THIS I JUST NEED TO BE-LIEVE THAT SOMEBODY WILL FIX THIS.

A big moment of wallowing.

REGINA: Well…if we're going to die…because everyone has to die at some point, right? At least we get to go surrounded by all of this beauty. And…and, we get to spend our final days together! Just the four of us! We're ultimately very lucky, when you think about it.

TRUDY, CAROLYN, and MARTHA look at each other.

TRUDY: All in favor?

CAROLYN: I.

MARTHA: I.

REGINA: What?

REGINA is ejected into space.

End of Play

YOUR LIFE CHOICES

Maya Macdonald

The Flea Theater #serials @theflea
Produced by Cleo Grey & Crystal Arnette 7/2015
Directed by Suzanne Karpinski
CHASE: Crystal Arnette
ALEX: Miles Butler
HARRIET FISHFLOW: Jordan Carey
FLAHIVE: John Paul Harkins
RINGO: Jeremy Rafal

CHARACTERS:

RINGO: 58 the manager. high strung, angry and clinical. wildly
    unhappy.
CHASE: 30 the top caller, the alpha. wins at everything work oriented.
ALEX: 27 the second to top caller.
FLAHIVE: 35 hates his job almost as much as he hates himself. Hasn't
    brought in a sale in months.
HARRIET FISHFLOW: 32 a mysterious woman

LOCATION: A telemarketing office during an enormous storm.

(A telemarking room with an apocalyptic feel, but mostly because outside of this room it is in fact the apocalypse. Outside are the sounds of the worst storm you've ever heard. CRASH! BANG! SCREAM! A BABY CRIES! A GIRAFFE SQUEALS! What.The.fucccck is going on out there? It's unrecognizably dangerous and scary. You shouldn't be at work, but here you are.

At the center of the room is an enormous pile of "leads." A lead is a piece of paper with the name, address and most importantly the phone number of someone it is your job to call. They are used, reused, stained, rotting, multi-colored, discolored, but most of all: there are A LOT of them. This bitch is everest and you could climb it, but you won't. You're not allowed.

The only thing pristine is a large dry erase board with names written in columns that then correspond with totals. This is what you're brought in and simultaneously what you are worth. And we can see that CHASE is worth the most. ALEX a close second. And FLAHIVE is a no good fucking nothing.

Three desks with three phones face forward

CHASE and ALEX enter talking. ALEX hangs on every word...)

CHASE: ...but like, then I was looking through his email while he was showering...

ALEX: Wait, you guys still get email? I thought you lived in zone 8Q??

CHASE: We do. But his parents are in Zone Q-12 and sometimes we go over there to check Facebook.

ALEX: whhhhhoa. They still have Facebook in Q-12??

CHASE: They have Facebook *and* running water.

(Whoa. This is seriously impressive)

ALEX: Damnnnnn. I thought no one had running water after ADRIA.

CHASE: If you have the money to live in Q-12 then apparently you still get to check Facebook. I haven't even had electric since Hurricane SANDRA.

(They continue to get ready, taking leads out of the huge pile,

turning on their headsets)

ALEX*:* What do you think though?

CHASE*:* He'll proposes by September. Latest.

ALEX: No, I mean. About the world ending tonight? It's (say the date of whatever day it is today). They say today is the day.

(A beat. The wind continues to howl and things keep breaking. Sounds pretty rough outside...)

CHASE: Whatever, they always say that.

FLAHIVE: hummhummhummhumm.

CHASE: Hey, Alex look who it is?

ALEX: You gonna sell anything this week, Flahive or are you gonna leave it to the professionals?

FLAHIVE: hummhummmmmhummmmmmmm

CHASE: What are you singing?

FLAHIVE: This song just popped into my head the other day. I can't remember the name of it...

CHASE: How can you afford to listen to music? You got a trust fund we don't know about?

FLAHIVE: No, it just sorta popped into my head the other day I realized I haven't had a song stuck in my head for like...a year at least

CHASE: *(To Alex)* I can't believe Ringo hasn't fired his ass yet.

ALEX: Me either.

FLAHIVE: Do you think the world is really gonna end tonight? They say this is the big one.

CHASE: They always say that.

ALEX: Yeah, but the East River is getting pretty bad. And the L Train? It wont be running all weekend.

FLAHIVE: I guess I'm just hoping that the world really does end, cause it would just save me the time of offing myself.

CHASE: Uhhhh. Another suicide threat from Manhattan's bottom caller.

ALEX: How you gonna do it this time?

FLAHIVE: I was thinking just a bunch of pills. A few fist full. I'm serious this time.

(A long beat)

CHASE: I was thinking of getting a new case for my phone.

ALEX: yeah?

CHASE: cause then like.it would feel like a whole new phone.

FLAHIVE: Your phone doesn't even *work* anymore. No one's does!
   Why do you even carry it around?

   *(They organize their leads. The chaos outside continues. After
   a beat, RINGO enters, they come to attention ready to work)*

RINGO: okkkkkay team!!
are we ready to do some Telemarketing?!?!

   (They cheer cult-ishly)

FLAHIVE: (*humming*)hummmhummmhummmhummumm

RINGO: Stop with the humming and get your leads!!!

   *(FLAHIVE stumbles to the huge pile and grabs some leads
   and sits down. They all get   ready for RINGO's big speech,
   some with more enthusiasm than others. A beat as he gears
   up into action. The storm becomes more and more scary
   outside)*

RINGO: Okkkkkay team.
   So I just got word that 23rd street is basically all gone
   blamo
   wiped away like shit
   so we're gonna remove all leads with the area code 37862
   and any leads that are the color purple
   and also 5th ave is missing
   I don't think it's gone yet
   all I know is that it's not where they left it, so lets just remove
   all leads from the room that are in Section H37 and….8Q4 just
   to be safe.

   (They obediently remove said leads)

   Alright team.
   Tonight might maybe be our last day on earth.
   so…
   it might be difficult
   to get people
   to pick up their phones
   So
   I'm gonna need you
   to dial
   faster

Is that right CHASE?

CHASE: That's right, Ringo!!

I'm gonna dial

till my fingers bleed!!!

RINGO: That sounds like a top caller!!

What about you, Alex??

You gonna let Chase take all your leads or are you gonna spend your last night on earth as a TOP CALLER??

ALEX: I'm gonna dial until my BONES CHIP!

(Lighting cracks)

RINGO: That's right!!!!

And what if they make excuses

like "it's the last Day on Earth and I want to spend it holding my loved-ones close" what're you gonna do?

CHASE: I'll HAUNT their last moments on EARTH until I CLOSE!!!

RINGO: That's what I like to hear!!!!

be a tiger

your inner tiger

or if your inner tiger is a kitten then be a kitten

but a kitten that gets what it wants

be the kitten

and get Ringo what he needs

(RINGO exits. The callers all start to dial. Since they are in headsets they can move freely around the room, sometimes being able to identify who they are talking to, sometimes not)

CHASE: hellohi, this is Chase! Hope you're having an eventful End of the World!

(She laughs exaggeratedly)

hahahah funny funny hilarity

we are laughing together

we are laughing together because I made a joke that we are at laughing at right now.

I'm calling real fast to invite you to participate in a limited time only completely tax deductible experience where I will permit you to purchase the thing I am selling right now…

(She listens to the person talking)

Right, so I understand that the world is probably ending right now, but like. If that's the case? Than why save your money?

ALEX: hithere hellohi!!

heyhi this is Alex and i'm calling to talk to you about a really totally special offer we're running

and it's a limited time only

because like

our time it really limited?

yeah yeah that's a joke about the world probablydefinitely dying right at this time

yeah, no, it's not something you *need* but like you want it, you want to have it and I am selling it to you…

FLAHIVE: hummmhummmhummmmhmmmmmmm

RINGO: Flahive! What're you singing?

FLAHIVE: I can't remember the name.

It just got stuck in my head.

(RINGO removes a huge sheet of paper from the board and hands it to FLAHIVE)

RINGO: Harriet Fishflow's Amex is still on digit off!

Stop humming and close the deal!

(He hands it to him and stomps off)

FLAHIVE: heyHihello, this is Flahive and I'm calling to speak to Harriet Fishflow…

HARRIET FISHFLOW: This is she.

FLAHIVE: This is uhhh FLAHIVE: Joe FLAHIVE: and I'm calling-from MidtownThingsYouWantButDon'tNeed

HARRIET FISHFLOW: Joe Flahive?

Do you still wear clip on bow-ties?

FLAHIVE: What?

(He touches his bow-tie. It unclips into his hand)

Yeah.

How did you know that…

HARRIET FISHFLOW: I went to PS9 with you. It's…Harriet. Fishflow…

You sat behind me in Biology.

And you used to call me-

FLAHIVE: Oh god.

Don't even say it.

I'm so sorry.

I was so mean to you.

HARRIET FISHFLOW: Yeah, you were pretty mean. But when you're cursed with the last name Fish-Flow.

FLAHIVE: Yeah, that must be rough.

HARRIET FISHFLOW: So, what were you calling about?

FLAHIVE: Oh, right. Everyone in the office has been trying to track you down.

We need the last digit on your Amex.

HARRIET FISHFLOW: It's 6.

FLAHIVE: You know…I do remember you.

HARRIET FISHFLOW: No you don't!

FLAHIVE: No, I do.

I remember you now. I.

I liked you.

A lot.

That's probably why I was such a dick to you.

HARRIET FISHFLOW: Great game.

FLAHIVE: I know, right?

(They laugh)

No, but. I liked how you sorta always seemed like quietly angry about everything.

HARRIET FISHFLOW: Yeah. That's aways been my thing.

FLAHIVE: Mine too.

(A large crash)

Shit, what was that?

HARRIET FISHFLOW: Oh. I think a lamp-post fell. Across the street.

FLAHIVE: What zone are you in?

HARRIET FISHFLOW: H37

FLAHIVE: Isn't that evacuated?

HARRIET FISHFLOW: Yeah. They all left.

FLAHIVE: Why are you still there?

HARRIET FISHFLOW: What difference does it make?

FLAHIVE: But

They say this is the big one, don't they? Shouldn't you find somewhere to go…

HARRIET FISHFLOW: I mean, this probably sounds really movie of the month, but I don't really have like…too much to live for?

I'm kinda ready to meet my maker.

(humming to herself the same tune as FLAHIVE was earlier)

So Give Me More More More Till I Can't Stand

FLAHIVE: Wait. What're you humming?

HARRIET FISHFLOW: This song. I haven't heard music in like over a year, but I can't get it out of my head. It's driving me crazy...

FLAHIVE: its the one with the...

there's a piano solo in the middle and...

its a fast song

HARRIET FISHFLOW: a fast song? No, it wasn't fast...

FLAHIVE: No, it was, but if you were to play it slow if you were to play it slow it would be sad.

(Suddenly, weirdly they begin singing a song together that they remember from long ago before all the power went out and all the things)

HARRIET & FLAHIVE: So give me more more
till I can't stand
Get on the floor, floor
Like it's your last chance
If you want more more
than here I am
And I ain't paying my rent this month
I owe that
But fuck who you want
and fuck who you like
Dance our life,
there's no end in sight
Twinkle, twinkle little star...

(The sound of a busy signal. And thunder! And lightning flashes! And water flooding!)

FLAHIVE: Hello?

Hello...

Harriet?

(And boom! The power shuts off)

CHASE: What the fuck was that!?

(The room shakes)

RINGO: It's the big one!!

ALEX: THIS IS IT!!

(ALEX is prepared and takes out a truck of things and begins to rally to the rescue)

CHASE: I've never in my whole life been happy
I've been chasing bullshit ideas that aren't real
I'm not ready I'm not ready!

(Something huge falls)

ALEX: Follow me everyone!!

(They do)

Everyone get behind the barricade.
I'll call for help!

(FLAHIVE gets up to leave)

CHASE: Flahive, where are you going??
FLAHIVE: I have to find her.
ALEX: You can't go out there! It's not safe!
CHASE: Everything out there could be gone!!
FLAHIVE: I don't care!

End of Play

10-MINUTE PLAY PRODUCERS

Actors Theatre of Louisville
www.actorstheatre.org
Amy Wegener
awegener@actorstheatre.org

Acts on the Edge, Santa Monica
mariannesawchuk@hotmail.com

American Globe Theatre Turnip Festival, Gloria Falzer
gfalzer@verizon.net

Appetite Theatre Company
Bruschetta: An Evening of Short
Plays
www.appetitetheatre.com

Artistic Home Theatre Co.
Cut to the Chase Festival
Kathy Scambiatterra, Artistic Director:
artistic.director@theartistichome.org

Artist's Exchange, Cranston RI
Rich Morra
rich.morra@artists-exchange.org

Artistic New Directions
Janice Goldberg - Co Artistic Director - ANDJanice@aol.com
Kristine Niven - Co Artistic Director
- KNiven@aol.com
www.ArtisticNewDirections.org

The Arts Center, Carrboro NC
10x10 in the Triangle
Jeri Lynn Schulke, director
theatre@artscenterlive.org
www.artscenterlive.org/performance/
opportunities

A-Squared Theatre Workshop
My Asian Mom Festival
Joe Yau (jyauza@hotmail.com)

Association for Theatre in Higher
Education New Play Development
Workshop
Contact Person: Charlene A. Donaghy
Email: charlene@charleneadonaghy.com

Auburn Players Community Theatre
Short Play Festival
Bourke Kennedy
email: bourkekennedy@gmail.com

The Barn Theatre
www.thebarnplayers.org/tenminute/

Barrington Stage Company
10X10 New Play Festival
Julianne Boyd is the Artistic Director
jboyd@barringtonstageco.org
www.barringtonstageco.org

Belhaven University, Jackson, Mississippi
One Act Festival
Joseph Frost, Department Chair
theatre@belhaven.edu

Black Box Theatre
FIVES New Play Festival
Producer: Nancy Holaday
(719) 330-1798
nancy@blackboxdrama.com

Blue Slipper Theatre, Livingston,
Montana
Marc Beaudin, Festival Director
blueslipper10fest@gmail.com
www.blueslipper.com

Boston Theatre Marathon
Boston Playwrights Theatre
www.bostonplaywrights.org
Kate Snodgrass (ksnodgra@bu.edu)
(Plays by New England playwrights
only)

Boulder Life Festival, Boulder, Colorado
Dawn Bower, Director of Theatrical Program
dawn@boulderlifefestival.com
www.boulderlifefestival.com

The Box Factory
Judith Sokolowski, President
boxfactory@sbcglobal.net
www.boxfactoryforthearts.org

The Brick Theater's "Tiny Theater Festival"
Michael Gardner, Artistic Director
mgardner@bricktheater.com
www.bricktheater.com

Broken Nose Theatre
Benjamin Brownson, Artistic Director
Bechdel Fest
www.brokennosetheatre.com/bechdel-fest-3
ben@brokennosetheatre.com

The Brooklyn Generator
Erin Mallon (contact)
brooklyngenerator@outlook.com
website: https://www.facebook.com/TheBrooklynGenerator/info

Camino Real Playhouse
www.caminorealplayhouse.org

Chalk Repertory Theatre Flash Festival produced by Chalk Repertory Theatre
Contact person: Ruth McKee
ruthamckee@aol.com
www.chalkrep.com

Chameleon Theater Circle, Burnsville, MN 55306
www.chameleontheatre.org
jim@chameleontheatre.org

Changing Scene Theatre Northwest
ATTN: Pavlina Morris
changingscenenorthwest@hotmail.com

Cherry Picking
cherrypickingnyc@gmail.com

Chicago Indie Boots Festival
www.indieboots.org

City Theatre
www.citytheatre.com
Susan Westfall
susan@citytheatre.com

City Theatre of Independence
Powerhouse Theatre
Annual Playwrights Festival
Powerhouse Theatre
www.citytheatreofindependence.org

The Collective New York
C10 Play Festival
www.thecollective-ny.org
thecollective9@gmail.com

Colonial Playhouse
Colonial Quickies
www.colonialplayhouse.net
colonialplayhousetheater@40yahoo.com

Company of Angels at the Alexandria
501 S. Spring Street, 3rd Floor
Los Angeles, CA 90013
(213) 489-3703 (main office)
armevan@sbcglobal.net

Core Arts Ensemble
coreartsensemble@gmail.com

Darkhorse Dramatists
www.darkhorsedramatists.com
darkhorsedramatists@gmail.com

Distilled Theatre Co.
submissions.dtc@gmail.com

Driftwood Players
www.driftwoodplayers.com
shortssubmissions@driftwoodplay-
ers.com
tipsproductions@driftwoodplayers.com

Drilling Company
Hamilton Clancy
drillingcompany@aol.com

Driftwood Players
www.driftwoodplayers.com

Durango Arts Center 10-Minute Play
Festival
www.durangoarts.org
Theresa Carson
TenMinutePlayDirector@gmail.com

Eden Prairie Players
www.edenprairieplayers.com

Eastbound Theatre 10 minute Festival
(in the summer: themed)
Contact Person: Tom Rushen
email: ZenRipple@yahoo.com

East Haddam Stage Company
Contact person: Kandie Carl
email: Kandie@ehsco.org

Eden Prairie Players
www.concordspace.com/2012/11/18/
submit-concords-1010-play-festival/
Reed Schulke (reedschulke@yahoo.com)

Edward Hopper House (Two on
the Aisle Playwriting Competition)
Nyack, NY
Rachael Solomon
edwardhopper.house@verizon.net
www.edwardhopperhouse.org

Emerging Artists Theatre
Fall EATFest
www.emergingartiststheatre.org

En Avant Playwrights
Ten Lucky Festival
www.enavantplaywrights.yuku.com/
topic/4212/Ten-Tucky-Festival-
KY-deadline-10-1-no-fee#.UE5-
nY5ZGQI

Ensemble Theatre of Chattanooga
Short Attention Span Theatre Festival
Contact Person: Garry Posey
(Artistic Director)
garryposey@gmail.com
www.ensembletheatreofchattanooga.
com

Fell's Point Corner Theatre 10 x 10
Festival
Contact Person: Richard Dean Stover
(rick@fpct.org)
Website of theatre: www.fpct.org

Fine Arts Association
Annual One Act Festival-Hot from
the Oven Smorgasbord
ahedger@fineartsassociation.org

Firehouse Center for the Arts, New-
buryport MA
New Works Festival
Kimm Wilkinson, Director
www.firehouse.org
Limited to New England playwrights

Fire Rose Productions
www.fireroseproductions.com
kazmatura@gmail.com

Flush Ink Productions
Asphalt Jungle Shorts Festival
www.flushink.net/AJS.html

The Fringe of Marin Festival
Contact Person: Annette Lust
email: jeanlust@aol.com

Fury Theatre
katie@furytheare.org

Fusion Theatre Co.
http://www.fusionabq.org
info@fusionabq.org

Future Ten
info@futuretenant.org

Gallery Players
Annual Black Box Festival
info@galleryplayers.com

Gaslight Theatre
www.gaslight-theatre.org
gaslighttheatre@gmail.com

GI60
Steve Ansell
screammedia@yahoo.com

Generic Theatre Co.
www.generictheatre.org
contact@generictheatre.org

The Gift Theater
TEN Festival
Contact: Michael Patrick Thornton
www.thegifttheatre.org

Good Works Theatre Festival
Good Acting Studio
www.goodactingstudio.com

The Greenhouse Ensemble
Ten-Minute Play Soiree
www.greenhouseensemble.com
Half Moon Theatre
www.halfmoontheatre.org

Heartland Theatre Company
Themed 10-Minute Play Festival
Every Year
Contact: Mike Dobbins
(Artistic Director)
boxoffice@heartlandtheatre.org
www.heartlandtheatre.org

Hella Fresh Fish
freshfish2submit@gmail.com

Hobo Junction Productions
Hobo Robo Festival
Spenser Davis, Literary Manager
hobojunctionsubmissions@gmail.com
www.hobojunctionproductions.com

The Hovey Players, Waltham MA
Hovey Summer Shorts
www.hoveyplayers.com

Illustrious Theatre Co.
www.illustrioustheatre.org
illustrioustheatre@gmail.com

Image Theatre
Naughty Shorts
jbisantz@comcast.net

Independent Actors Theatre
(Columbia, MO)
Short Women's Play Festival
Emily Rollie, Artistic Director
e.rollie@iatheatre.org
www.iatheatre.org

Island Theatre 10-minute Play Festival
www.islandtheatre.org

Kings Theatre
www.kingstheatre.ca

Lake Shore Players
www.lakeshoreplayers.com
Joan Elwell
office@lakeshoreplayers.com

La Petite Morgue (Fresh Blood)
Kellie Powell at
Lapetitemorgue@gmail.com
www.lapetitemorgue.blogspot.com

Lebanon Community Theatre
Playwriting Contest
Plays must be at least 10 minutes and

no longer than 20 minutes.
www.lct.cc/PlayWriteContest.htm

Lee Street Theatre, Salisbury, NC
(themed)
Original 10-Minute Play Festival
Justin Dionne, managing artistic
director
info@leestreet.org
www.leestreet.org

Little Fish Theatre Co.
www.litlefishtheatre.org

Live Girls Theatre
submissions@lgtheater.org

Little Fish Theatre
Pick of the Vine Festival
holly@littlefishtheatre.org
www.littlefishtheatre.org/wp/partici-
pate/submit-a-script/

LiveWire Chicago VisionFest
livewirechicago@gmail.com
Artistic Director: Joel Ewing
joel.b.ewing@gmail.com
I think they do an annual festival of
10 minute plays with a specific theme

Lourdes University Drama Society
One Act Play Festival, Sylvania, Ohio
Keith Ramsdell, Drama Society
Advisor
dramasociety@lourdes.edu
www.lourdes.edu/dramasociety.aspx

Luna Theater
Contact: Greg Campbell
Email: lunatheater@gmail.com
Website: www.lunatheater.org

Madlab Theatre
Theatre Roulette
Andy Batt (andy@madlab.net)
www.madlab.net/MadLab/Home.
html

Magnolia Arts Center, Greenville, NC
Ten Minute Play Contest
info@magnoliaartscenter.com
www.magnoliaartscenter.com
Fee charged

Manhattan Repertory Theatre, New
York, NY
Ken Wolf
manhattanrep@yahoo.com
www.manhattanrep.com

McLean Drama Co.
www.mcleandramacompany.org
Rachel Bail (rachbail@yahoo.com)

Miami 1-Acts Festival (two sessions
– Winter (December) and Summer
(July)
Contact: Steven A. Chambers, Literary Manager (schambers@new-
theatre.org Ricky J. Martinez, Artistic
Director (rjmartinez@new-theatre.org)
Website of theatre: www.new-theatre.org
Submission Requirements No more
than 10-15 pages in length; subject is
not specific, though plays can reflect
life in South Florida and the tropics
and the rich culture therein. Area
playwrights are encouraged to submit,
though the festival is open to national
participation. Deadline for the Winter
Session is October 15 of each year;
deadline for the Summer Session is
May 1 of each year.

Milburn Stone One Act Festival
www.milburnstone.org

Mildred's Umbrella
Museum of Dysfunction Festival
www.mildredsumbrella.com
e-mail: info@mildredsumbrella.com

Mill 6 Collaborative
John Edward O'Brien, Artistic Director
mill6theatre@gmail.com

Monkeyman Productions
The Simian Showcase
submissions@monkeymanproduc-
tions.com.
www.monkeymanproductions.com

Nantucket Short Play Competition
Jim Patrick
www.nantucketshortplayfestival.com
nantucketshortplay@comcast.net

Napa Valley Players
8 x 10: A Festival of 10 Minute Plays
www.napavalleyplayhouse.org

Newburgh Free Academy
tsandler@necsd.net

New American Theatre
www.newamericantheatre.com
Play Submissions: JoeBays44@
earthlink.net

New Urban Theatre Laboratory
5 & Dime
Jackie Davis, Artistic Director:
jackie.newurbantheatrelab@gmail.com

New Voices Original Short Play
Festival
Kurtis Donnelly (kurtis@gvtheatre.org)

NFA New Play Festival
Newburgh Free Academy
201 Fullerton Ave, Newburgh, NY
12550
Terry Sandler (terrysandle@hotmail.com)
(may not accept electronic submissions)

North Park Playwright Festival
New short plays (no more than 15
pages, less is fine)
Submissions via mail to:
North Park Vaudeville and Candy
Shoppe
2031 El Cajon Blvd.
San Diego, CA 92104

Attn: Summer Golden,
Artistic Director.
www.northparkvaudeville.com

Northport One-Act Play Festival
Jo Ann Katz (joannkatz@gmail.com)
www.northportarts.org

NYC Playwrights
Play of the Month Project
http://nycp.blogspot.com/p/play-of-
month.html

Northwest 10 Festival of 10-Minute
Plays
Sponsored by Oregon Contemporary
Theatre
www.octheatre.org/nw10-festival
Email: NW10Festival@gmail.com

Nylon Fusion
nylonsubmissions@gmail.com
www.nylonfusioncollective.org

Old Brick Theatre (Scranton, PA)
Diva Productions

Open Tent Theatre Co.
Ourglass 24 Hour Play Festival
opententtheater@gmail.com

Over Our Head Players, Racine WI
www.overourheadplayers.org/oohp15

Pan Theater, Oakland, CA
Anything Can Happen Festival
David Alger,
pantheater@comcast.net
http://www.facebook.com/sanfran-
ciscoimprov

Pandora Theatre, Houston, Texas
Vox Feminina
Melissa Mumper, Artistic Director
pandoratheatre@sbcglobal.net
Paw Paw Players One Act Festival
www.ppvp.org/oneacts.htm

Pegasus Theater Company (in Sonoma County, north of San Francisco)
Tapas Short Plays Festival
www.pegasustheater.com/html/submissions.html
Lois Pearlman lois5@sonic.net

Philadelphia Theatre Company
PTC@Play New Work Festival
Contact: Jill Harrison
Email: jillian.harrison@gmail.com
Website: www.philadelphiatheatre-company.org

PianoFight Productions, L.A.
ShortLivedLA@gmail.com

Piney Fork Press Theater Play Festival
Johnny Culver, submissions@pineyforkpress.com
www.pineyforkpress.com

Playhouse Creatures
Page to Stage
newplays@playhousecreatures.org

Play on Words Productions
playonwordsproductions@gmail.com
Megan Kosmoski, Producing Artist Director

Playmakers Spokane
Hit& Run
Sandra Hosking
playmakersspokane@gmail.com
www.sandrahosking.webs.com
Playpalooza
Backstage at SPTC (Santa Paula Theatre Co.)
John McKinley, Artistic Director
sptcbackstage@gmail.com

Playwrights' Arena
Flash Theater LA
Contact person: Jon Lawrence Rivera
email: jonlawrencerivera@gmail.com
Website: www.playwrightsarena.org

Playwrights' Round Table,
Orlando, FL
Summer Shorts
Chuck Dent charlesrdent@hotmail.com
www.theprt.com

Playwrights Studio Theater
5210 W. Wisconsin Ave.
Milwaukee, WI 53208
Attn: Michael Neville, Artistic Dir.

Renaissance Guild
www.therenaissanceguild.org/article/aos-xv
actoneseries@therenaissanceguild.org

Renegade Theatre Festival
www.renegadetheatre.org
Ruckus Theatre
Allison Shoemaker
theruckus@theruckustheater.org
www.ruckustheater.org/home/contact.html

Salem Theatre Co.
Moments of Play
New England playwrights only
mop@salemtheatre.com

Salve Regina University
www.salvetheatreplayfestival.submishmash.com/submit

Santa Cruz Actor's Theatre
Eight Tens at Eight
Wilma Chandler, Artistic Director
ronziob@email.com
http://www.sccat.org

Secret Room Theatre
Contact: Alex Dremann
alexdremann@me.com
www.secretroomtheatre.com

Secret Rose Theatre
www.secretrose.com
info@secretrose.com

Secret Theatre (Midsummer Night Festival), Queens, NY.
Odalis Hernandez, odalis.hernandez@gmail.com
www.secrettheatre.com/

She Speaks, Kitchener, Ontario.
Paddy Gillard-Bentley
paddy@skyedragon.com
Women playwrights

Shelterbelt Theatre, Omaha, NB
From Shelterbelt with Love
McClain Smouse, associate-artistic@shelterbelt.org
submissions@shelterbelt.org
www.shelterbelt.org

Shepparton Theatre Arts Group
"Ten in 10" is a performance of 10 plays each running for 10 minutes every year.
Email: info@stagtheatre.com
Website: www.stagtheatre.com

Short+Sweet
Literary Manager, Pete Malicki
Pete@shortandsweet.org
http://www.shortandsweet.org/short-sweet-theatre/submit-script

Silver Spring Stage, Silver Spring, MD
Jacy D'Aiutolo
oneacts2012.ssstage@gmail.com
www.ssstage.org

Sixth Street Theatre
Snowdance 10-Minute Comedy Festival
Rich Smith
Snowdance318@gmail.com

Six Women Play Festival
www.sixwomenplayfestival.com

Source Festival
jenny@culturaldc.org

Southern Repertory Theatre 6 x6
Aimee Hayes
literary@southernrep.com
www.southernrep.com/

Stage Door Productions
Original One-Act Play Festival
www.stagedoorproductions.org

Stage Door Repertory Theatre
www.stagedoorrep.org

Stage Q
www.stageq.com

Stageworks/Hudson
Play by Play Festival
Laura Margolis is the Artistic Director
literary@stageworkshudson.org
www.stageworkshudson.org

Stonington Players
HVPanciera@aol.com

Stratton Summer Shorts
Stratton Players
President: Rachel D'onfro
www.strattonplayers.com
info@strattonplayers.com
Subversive Theatre Collective
Kurt Schneiderman, Artistic Director
www.subversivetheatre.org
info@subversivetheatre.org

Ten Minute Playhouse (Nashville)
Nate Eppler, Curator
newworksnashville@gmail.com
www.tenminuteplayhouse.com

Ten Minute Play Workshop
www.tenminuteplayworkshop.com

Ten Tuckey Festival
doug@thebardstown.com
The Theatre Lab
733 8th St., NW
Washington, DC 20001

https://www.theatrelab.org/
Contact: Buzz Mauro (buzz@the-atrelab.org, 202-824-0449)

Theatre Odyssey
Sarasota, Florida
Tom Aposporos Vice President
www.theatreodyssey.org

Theatre One Productions
theatreoneproductions@yahoo.com

Theatre Out, Santa Ana CA
David Carnevale
david@theatreout.com LGBT plays

Theatre Oxford 10 Minute Play Contest
http://www.theatreoxford.com
Alice Walker
10minuteplays@gmail.com

Theatre Roulette Play Festival
Madlab Theatre Co.
andyb@mablab.net

Theatre Three
www.theatrethree.com
Jeffrey Sanzel
jeffrey@theatrethree.com

Theatre Westminster
Ten Minute New (And Nearly New) Play Festival
ATTN: Terry Dana Jachimiak II
jachimtd@westminster.edu

Those Women Productions
www.thosewomenproductions.com

TouchMe Philly Productions
www.touchmephilly.wordpress.com
touchmephilly@gmail.com

Towne Street Theatre Ten-Minute Play Festival
info@townestreet.org

Underground Railway Theatre
www.undergroundrailwaytheatre.org
Debra Wise, Artistic Director
(debra@undergroundrailwaytheatre.org)

Unrenovated Play Festival
unrenovatedplayfest@gmail.com

Vivarium Theatre Co.
www.vivariumtheatre.com

Walking Fish Theatre
freshfish2submit@gmail.com

Weathervane Playhouse
8 X 10 Theatrefest
info@weathervaneplayhouse.com

Wide Eyed Productions
www.wideeyedproductions.com
playsubmissions@wideeyedproduc-tions.com

Wild Claw Theatre:
Death Scribe 10 Minute Radio Horror Festival
www.wildclawtheatre.com/index.html
literary@wildclawtheatre.com
Winston-Salem Writers
Annual 10 Minute Play Contest
www.wswriters.org
info@wswriters.org

Write Act
www.writeactrep.org
John Lant (j316tlc@pacbell.net)